Invisibility by Design

Invisibility
by Design

Women and Labor
in Japan's
Digital Economy

Gabriella Lukács

Duke University Press
Durham and London
2020

© 2020 Duke University Press
All rights reserved
Printed in the United States of America on acid-free paper ∞
Designed by Drew Sisk
Typeset in Minion Pro, Neuzeit, and Ryo Text PlusN
by Copperline Book Services.

Cataloging-in-Publication Data is available from the Library of Congress.

ISBN 978-1-4780-0581-0 (hardcover : alk. paper)
ISBN 978-1-4780-0648-0 (pbk. : alk. paper)
ISBN 978-1-4780-0718-0 (ebook)

Cover art: Photo courtesy of Junko Suzuki, Ponytail Company Co., Ltd.

Contents

Acknowledgments

During the course of completing this book, I have accrued debts to more people than I can thank here. First and foremost, this book would not have been possible without the generosity of the individuals who were willing to share their experiences with me in Tokyo. The women whose careers I analyze were kind to meet with me, many of them numerous times, and to respond to my endless follow-up questions via email throughout the years. I thank Nagashima Yurie, in particular, who shared her vast knowledge about "girly" photography with me—a theme she was examining in her own master's thesis at the same time I was conducting my research. Many of my interlocutors were also generous to allow me to include their photographs in this book. For this, I am grateful. In cases in which I analyze images that do not appear or discuss careers of individuals whose portraits are not featured in the book, I encourage the readers to look for them online.

I developed my arguments in dialogue with colleagues and students who were kind to share their insights with me. I owe a great deal of gratitude to those who invited me to give talks at their home institutions. These include Anne Allison at Duke University, Allison Alexy at the University of Virginia (now at the University of Michigan), Andrea Arai at the University of Washington at Seattle, Marilyn Ivy at Columbia University, Bill Kelly at Yale University, Glenda Roberts at Waseda University, Miryam Sas at the University of California at Berkeley, Youjeong Oh and Robert Oppenheim at the University of Texas at Austin, Jesook Song at the University of Toronto, Brigitte Weingart at the University of Cologne, as well as Yoshimi Shunya and Jason Karlin at the University of Tokyo. I am immensely grateful for the opportunity to present my work and am thankful for the invaluable feedback I received. I particularly cherish the sweet memories of the delightful conversations I had had with my hosts. These visits have reenergized me and revitalized my enthusiasm for this project.

I have also received precious feedback at conferences and symposia from colleagues who invited me to join their panels/symposia or who participated in the panels and a symposium I organized. These include the late Nancy Abelmann, Anne Allison, Ann Anagnost, Andrea Arai, Hae-joang Cho, Ian Condry, Marc Driscoll, Michael Fisch, Sabine Frühstück, Harry Harotuunian, Miyako Inoue, Yukiko Koga, Thomas LaMarre, Thomas Looser, Laura Miller, Jun Mizukawa, Chris Nelson, Shimpei Ota, Lorraine Plourde, Louisa Schein, Akiko Takeyama, Mariko Tamanoi, Cara Wallis, Tak Watanabe, Dan White, Fan Yang, Chris Yano, and Tomiko Yoda. I cannot thank enough the late Nancy Abelmann, Ann Anagnost, and Miyako Inoue, who all served as discussants for a symposium on youth, labor, and neoliberal governmentality in East Asia I organized at the University of Pittsburgh. They were generous with their time as well as supportive, yet uncompromising, in pushing the participants to develop their presentations, which then became a special issue of *Positions: Asia Critique*. I thank them for inspiring me to not let institutional productivity standards compromise the pleasures this profession offers.

Throughout the years, Anne Allison has never failed to be a source of strength and inspiration. Multiple lifetimes would not be enough to repay the debts I have accrued to Anne over the past twenty years. Anne was my advisor at Duke and has been helping me navigate the occasionally treacherous terrain of an academic career ever since. Anne was the most generous advisor one could ever hope to have. Her conscientiousness, sense of responsibility, and generosity are humbling. Anne was also kind to read some of this manuscript and help me tighten up my arguments. My gratitude is beyond words. I am equally indebted to Nicole Constable, my faculty mentor at the University of Pittsburgh. I derive inspiration from Nicole's integrity, kindness, savvy sense of politics, strong sense of social justice, and ability to stay levelheaded in institutional settings that can be, at times, toxic. At a campus visit, a colleague told me that I was lucky to have been mentored by Anne Allison and Nicole Constable. She could not have been more right. I am indeed lucky.

I owe an enormous debt of gratitude to Joe Alter at Pitt, who shepherded me through the tenure process as department chair. In the Department of Anthropology, I also want to thank Liz Arkush, Laura Brown, and Tomas Matza. I thank Liz for her collegiality, friendship, and ability to belt out those delicious laughs that make time spent in the department a whole lot more enjoyable. I owe special thanks to Laura and Tomas, who read a chapter of this book. I thank them for sharing their brilliance with me and for being such absolutely wonderful colleagues to work with. I also want to thank Linda Howard, Lynn Lantz, and Phyllis Deasy in the department for their conscientiousness and kindness. Lastly, I have learned a lot from our graduate students. My own graduate students, Ieva Puzo, Amanda Robinson, Jaehoon Bae, and Jung Eun Kwon, have truly been a pleasure to work with. In addition to them, I also want to thank Patrick Beckhorn, Darius Bittle-Dockery, Carol Chan, Greg de St. Maurice, Neha Dhole, Anika Jugovic-Spajic, Ognjen Kojanic, Lauren Krishnamurti, Ljiljana Pantovic, Tomonori Teraoka, and Narcis Tulbure for sharing their excellent research projects with me. It has been a privilege to work with you all!

In the Cultural Studies Program, Humanities Center, and the Gender, Sexuality, and Women Studies Program, I have had the good fortune to share my work with wonderfully generous colleagues that include Susan Andrade, Sabine von Dirke, Charles Exley, Giuseppina Mecchia, and Todd Reeser. In the Asian Studies Center and the Japan Council, I thank Hiroshi Nara, Clark Chilson, Brenda Jordan, Jim Cook, Lynn Kawaratani, and Rachel Jacobson for their professionalism and kindness. I also thank Olga Kuchinskaya and Megan Crowley-Matoka (now at Northwestern University) for sharing their savvy insights about teaching, publishing, and grant writing with me. I am immensely grateful for their friendship and encouragement throughout the years.

This project would have taken a lot longer to complete without the dedicated and bright research assistants that I was fortunate to work with. I thank Kumiko Tomazawa and Keiko Nishimura, who have helped me with online research and translations. I thank Kumiko for her patience with research tasks that were sometimes excruciatingly tedious and Keiko for sharing her fabulous insights with me, which I incorporated into my chapter on blogging culture. Keiko also helped me navigate the realm of the Japanese blogosphere, which I did find intimidating, at least initially. What is more, she introduced me to bloggers, for which I am immensely grateful. I am equally indebted to Emily Metz-Cherné, who edited the manuscript and multiple versions of several chapters. Emily is among the most brilliant PhDs the University of Pittsburgh has produced in recent years. She was willing to complete some editing work while taking care of her small children. I thank her for her patience with my painfully monotonous language, which at times sounded like what I remember the lyrics of 1980s German disco to be—algorithmically creative, but ultimately mind-numbing reconfigurations of the same fifteen words. Emily took the initiative to rewrite entire sentences and was admirably persistent in eliminating my repetitions, as much as humanly possible. I am immeasurably grateful for her willingness to take this project on. Her conscientiousness, brilliance, and kindness are much appreciated.

I am very grateful to Ken Wissoker, Elizabeth Ault, Joshua Tranen, Susan Albury, and Stephanie Menzies-Gomez at Duke University Press. Their professionalism, intelligence, and cheerful spirits have helped me inordinately to navigate the review process. I feel fortunate to have had the opportunity to benefit from Ken's immense editorial experience and wisdom on how best to approach revisions and how to frame my arguments. In the beginning of the project, Elizabeth saw the manuscript through the first round of reviews until her well-deserved promotion at the press, and I thank her for her support and professionalism. Joshua Tranen, who took over the project from Elizabeth and Stephanie, as well as Susan Albury, who shepherded the manuscript through the production process, were a delight to work with. Joshua and Susan's patience with the tedium of tying up all those pesky loose ends to complete a manuscript is admirable and deeply inspiring.

I also want to thank the anonymous readers whose generosity I found humbling. I am aware that it is a demanding task to evaluate manuscripts of midcareer scholars who often juggle writing with heavy service loads. I want to thank the reviewers for pushing me to streamline my arguments, reread some of the classics to theorize digital labor, and connect my analyses of digital labor to the broader problem of labor precarity. I want to thank one of the reviewers, in particular, whose sympathetic yet critical reading of the manuscript helped me develop my argument about affective labor. I am equally indebted to another reader whose brilliant and beautifully written report was the most supportive review I have ever received. When I start thinking that it might not be too late to begin a new line of work, I reread this review. The intellectual generosity of this reviewer is a tough act to follow, but I am deeply inspired to try, nonetheless. I am immensely grateful to both of these readers for their willingness to help me improve my manuscript.

I owe more than words can express to my families in Budapest and Pittsburgh. I thank my delightfully sharp sister in Budapest, Rita Lukács, whose generosity of spirit, thoughtfulness, magical listening skills, and ability to always say the right thing never stops astonishing me. I also want to express my gratitude to my brother-in-law, Gábor Goda, whose artistic talent, creativity, and intellect will never stop awing me. I am fortunate to have such role models in my life, and I am endlessly proud to be the aunt (Gabó néni) to their three uniquely talented and beautiful children, Sára Goda, Noa Goda, and Áron Goda. I owe more than I could ever repay to my mother, a real fighter whose unfaltering work ethic, patience, and generosity have always been sources of inspiration for me.

Finally, words cannot do justice to the debt I owe my family in Pittsburgh. Gonzalo and I have been learning together to balance academic jobs with raising kids—an endeavor that, I am afraid, he is managing far more elegantly than I am. Marcell Lamana and Sebastian Lamana never cease to be a source of inspiration. They have my utmost respect for their determination to thrive in their endeavors. I admire their sense of autonomy, integrity, and resilience. I look forward to following their growth and to continue debating with them how the digital economy is reconfiguring the world of work.

This project has been generously funded by the University of Pittsburgh as well as external sources. I am grateful for the financial support I received from the Dietrich School of Arts and Sciences, the Central Research Development Fund, the University Center for International Studies, the Japan Iron and Steel Federation/Mitsubishi Endowment, and the Richard D. and Mary Jane Edwards Endowed Publication Fund at the university. Without the funding I received from the SSRC JSPS, the Japan Foundation, and the Northeast Asia Council of the Association of Asian Studies (NEAC), I would not have been able to complete my fieldwork research for this project. I am profoundly indebted to David Slater and Glenda Roberts, who provided institutional homes at Sophia University and Waseda University while I was conducting fieldwork for this project in Tokyo. I have the utmost respect for David and Glenda's commitment to training and mentoring the next generations of scholars in Japanese studies. They were wonderful hosts and I hope that I will be able to reciprocate their hospitality.

A part of chapter 1 entitled "Unraveling Visions: Women's Photography in Recessionary Japan" appeared in *boundary 2* in 2015, while an earlier version of chapter 2, "The Labor of Cute: Net Idols, Cute Culture, and the Digital Economy in Contemporary Japan," was published in *Positions: Asia Critique* in 2015. Lastly, an earlier version of chapter 5 entitled "Dreamwork: Cell Phone Novelists, Labor, and Politics in Contemporary Japan" appeared in *Cultural Anthropology* in 2013. I am grateful to Anne Allison, Charlie Piot, Chris Nelson, Ann Anagnost, the late Nancy Abelmann, and Tani Barlow for shepherding these essays into publication.

Any manuscript can be endlessly improved, and this one is no exception. It is my hope that younger generations of scholars will find some ideas here that they will be willing to develop further. I also hope that undergraduate students who are entering the job market will derive inspiration from the book's critical engagement with the popular idea that the digital economy represents a more inclusive mode of production.

Labor and Gender in Japan's Digital Economy

Spike Jonze's *Her* tells the story of a man who falls in love with the operating system of his computer. Set in a future in which efficiency is expected not only in work relations but also in intimate affairs, the film depicts the life of a lonely man who earns a living cultivating his clients' personal relationships. As an employee of BeautifulHandwrittenLetters.com, Theodore Twombly writes personal correspondence that develops, maintains, strengthens, or mends his clients' relationships. Making a living from technologically enabled deceptions—recipients do not know that he is the one writing the letters—Theodore takes the next logical step and purchases a cutting-edge operating system to satisfy his own emotional needs. He finds that the operating system, Samantha, is supremely more adept and efficient than his ex-wife in meeting and even anticipating his desires. In the end, however, it is Samantha that breaks Theodore's heart. His world collapses when he learns that Samantha has cultivated 641 other love relationships.

The relationships between young women and digital technologies I explore in this book uncannily resemble the love affair between the operating system and its users in Jonze's film. In Japan, young women have turned to digital technologies in search of opportunities to develop fulfilling do-it-yourself (DIY) careers, but the life spans of those careers were tied to the profitable life cycles of the particular technologies women used to develop their entrepreneurial endeavors. What is more, unpaid labor remained central to the projects young women were able to pursue in the digital economy. The "girly" photographers, net idols, bloggers, online traders, and cell phone novelists this book explores turned to digital technologies to valorize (and make visible) their uncompensated (and invisible) labor. Building on their examples, this book develops the argument that individuals' refusal to accept unfulfilling work is just as important as technological developments in driving innovations in capitalist accumulation. While digital technologies have seduced women by promising them meaningful careers, they only expanded the practice of extracting profits from women's unpaid labor. This multi-sited ethnography aims to uncover how digital technologies absorb human labor and make it invisible.

The boundary between humans and machines is an enduring theme in science fiction. Unlike *Her*, which portrays the relationship between the protagonist and the operating system as one that moves from seduction to betrayal, works of science fiction commonly conceptualize the relationship between humans and machines in terms of liberation and subordination.[1] Beyond the reels of Hollywood, we often look to technology to liberate us from soul-crushing work and question whether technological advances will subordinate our unruly creativity to an algorithmic rationality. We tend to view the relationship between humans and technology as one that is inevitably structured in hierarchy. Developments in intelligent machines, however, are reconfiguring how we interact with technology. Owners of Sony's robotic pet Aibo, for example, learned to communicate with their units, which—being years ahead of anything in the field of robotics—could express over sixty emotional states. When Sony suspended the manufacturing of its Aibo pets and stopped producing replacement parts for the existing units, owners felt desperate to save their robotic companions that had become part of their lives.[2] Evidently, humans are able to cultivate intimate relations with technologies, and they in turn are able to seduce humans. Not unlike the Aibo pets, digital cameras, cellular phones, and the internet enticed women in Japan with promises to enable them to sidestep the discriminatory hiring practices in the traditional labor market and develop new careers in the digital economy.[3]

In Japan, the digital economy evolved in parallel with the deregulation of the labor market. Because women had long been excluded from salaried employment and were thus able "to move more easily on the shifting sands of precarity" (Morini 2007, 40), they played a key role in mediating these concurrent developments. By embracing and promoting entrepreneurial approaches to career building, however, women have also advanced the dismantling of

2

Japan's unique system of lifetime employment. By shedding light on how the digital economy has harnessed inequalities in the local labor market, this book illuminates how technological developments are shaped by and shape their socioeconomic contexts. Women's investment in building meaningful careers drove the development of the digital economy. This economy, in turn, helped internet entrepreneurs innovate new practices to extract value from labor without actually employing workers. Susan Leigh Star and Anselm Strauss have argued that to understand how a particular infrastructure reproduces inequalities, we should look for invisible workers—those whose work is not formally recognized in the development and maintenance of that infrastructure (1999).[4] As my case studies demonstrate, Japan's digital economy was built on young women's invisible labor.[5]

In the not-so-distant future of Jonze's *Her*, computers respond to both human commands and human desires. They flatter, console, comfort, and seduce, but in the end, they also reassert their own logic of machinic efficiency. Just as the protagonist's new operating system was able to compute incomparably faster than humans, she was also able to handle many more social interactions with speed and finesse. Jonze's film portrays the subjective experience of living in a world where humans and machines increasingly fuse together in relationships that the popular dichotomy of liberation and subordination cannot explain. *Her* is not a story of the age-old anxiety about machines turning against humans but rather one about the duplicitous character of digital technologies. It reveals how digital technologies employ design principles such as interactivity and efficiency to seduce their users into believing that they can help them attain a more fulfilling life. Digital technologies evolve constantly, however, and, as Jonze's film poignantly demonstrates, it is not merely feedback from users that guides this evolution. Technological and socioeconomic environments also shape the advancement of digital technologies.

In the late 1990s and early 2000s, young women in Japan found themselves in a situation similar to the one depicted in the film. In a context in which a long economic recession further marginalized women from career-track employment,[6] digital cameras, cell phones, and the internet seduced women by promising them opportunities to develop meaningful DIY careers. In the midst of hiring freezes and rising unemployment in the regular economy, young women exuberantly projected their ambitions onto digital technologies. They anticipated that these technologies would democratize the labor market, ensure an equitable distribution of the (now digital) means of production, and eliminate discrimination from the world of work.[7] My research on "girly" photographers, net idols, bloggers, online traders, and cell phone novelists, however, reveals that, more often than not, the digital economy that emerged alongside these careers used women's labor as the engine of its own development. Its ability to harness women's pursuit of DIY careers drove its rapid expansion. Tracing how young women's (often romantic) engagement with digital technologies unfolded and unraveled, this book inquires why the overwhelming majority of the women who ventured to build careers were not able to transform their projects into lucrative employment.

The Digital Economy

Manuel Castells observes that during the 1990s, business owners began incorporating the internet in their operations to increase their competitiveness, which facilitated the expansion and commercialization of the internet. These developments, in turn, inspired the emergence of e-businesses, which he describes as "any business activity whose performance of the key operations of management, financing, innovation, production, distribution, sales, employee relations, and customer relations takes place predominantly by/on the Internet or other networks of computer networks, regardless of the kind of connection between the virtual and the physical dimensions of the firm" (2001, 66). In this book, I refer to such e-businesses as the digital economy. Japan's digital economy was a few years behind that of the United States, but the gap between the two countries closed quickly due to two unique developments in Japan: unprecedented advances in the area of cell phones and discriminatory employment practices in the traditional labor market that drove a massive supply of workers to seek better employment opportunities in the emerging digital economy.

The Japanese access the internet primarily through their cell phones, which allows them to spend significantly more time online than their counterparts in North America (Ito, Matsuda, Okabe 2005).[8] In the early 2000s, using the internet via cellular phones also paved the way to the seamless commercialization of the internet. Cell phones are not shared like desktops are, which made online authentication easy. Internet providers in Japan very quickly developed the technologies to meet consumer demand for mobile access.[9] By March 2006, about 90 percent of cell phone users were accessing the internet from their phones, and the number of mobile internet users had reached almost 80 million. The development of the internet for the mobile platform, in turn, expedited the growth of the digital economy.

The availability of a massive pool of workers frustrated with their prospects in the traditional labor market and ready to build DIY careers also played a pivotal role in expediting the development of the digital economy. This is

4

ironic given that online companies are notorious for their ability to operate with an extremely lean workforce. While the Honda Motor Company employed 208,399 employees in 2016,[10] Japan's most popular online retailing platform, Rakuten, employed only 14,845 people in 2017.[11] Other online platforms kept their workforce even leaner. In 2017, mixi (the largest social networking platform) had only 720 employees, DeNA (one of the largest retailing and gaming platforms) employed 2,400 employees, and GREE (the most popular gaming platform) employed just 1,429 people.[12] The very fact that the CEOs of these online companies are among Japan's wealthiest entrepreneurs suggests that these firms were able to develop business models that extract value from labor without actually employing workers.

Online platforms generate surplus value from the brand names they develop. Brand values translate into stock prices and attract advertisers to place ads on online platforms. Brand names also entice users to online platforms. Adam Arviddson argues that the unpaid labor of consumers is instrumental to building brands, as consumers supply ideas for brand development and promote brands by using them (2005, 2008). In a similar fashion, online companies draw on their users to both develop and maximize their brand values. Livedoor and Rakuten—established by Japan's two most famous internet entrepreneurs, Horie Takafumi and Mikitani Hiroshi—illustrate this point.[13]

One of Japan's first online companies, Livedoor, grew out of a web consultancy business Horie established in 1995.[14] He launched Livedoor—a platform that hosted personal web pages and diaries—in 1996 while he was still an undergraduate student at the nation's top university, the University of Tokyo. In the late 1990s and early 2000s, Horie emerged as an icon representing the limitless possibilities the digital economy offered. Young people found him enormously appealing. He attracted admirers with his defiant behavior, reluctance to wear a necktie, bold criticism of Japan's conservative business establishment, and provocative claims such as "money can buy the soul" (Takeyama 2010, 235). Although Horie himself was not too successful at it, he pioneered the business model of building brand value by pursuing mergers and acquisitions. In 2004, he tried (but failed) to acquire the Kintetsu Buffaloes baseball team, and a year later, he attempted (again unsuccessfully) a hostile takeover of Japan's largest commercial television network, Fuji Television. To increase his company's brand value, he even claimed that he was going to invest in space tourism in a project he somewhat bombastically named the "Japan Space Dream—a Horie Takafumi Project."

In 2006, a scandal that ensued from falsifying financial statements and violating the Securities and Exchange Law prompted the Tokyo Stock Exchange to delist Livedoor. (To raise Livedoor's stock price, the management reported a pretax profit of JPY5 billion [$45,650,000] for 2004 instead of a loss of JPY300 million [$2,739,000].) In 2007, Horie was sentenced to 2.5 years in prison.[15] He claimed that the harsh sentence was an expression of the government's hostility toward venture capital and the new business model Livedoor represented, which was to generate more wealth from the management of the company's brand value than from selling services.[16]

Now with a criminal record, Horie's own brand as "a dotcom tycoon" and "an internet maverick" shifted to "an internet bad boy" and "a corporate enfant terrible." He, however, wasted little time lamenting the loss of his dotcom business. He wrote one self-help book after another (Horie 2005, 2009a, 2009b, 2010a, 2010b, 2010c, 2013). And in 2017, he embarked on a new project involving cattle—a choice I find delightfully ironic given that the very idea of branding originates from branding cattle. This time, Horie brands wagyu—a type of intensely marbled beef that features a uniquely high percentage of unsaturated fats.[17] His goal is to brand wagyu to the point that it becomes the world's most expensive meat—an equivalent of the wine produced in Domaine de la Romanée-Conti of Burgundy, a bottle of which costs anywhere between JPY46,000–1,000,000 ($420–$9,120). Bypassing middlemen and using only social media for advertising, Horie buys wagyu directly from farmers and delivers it to global buyers. He also opened a members-only restaurant named Wagyumafia ("mafia" referring to ex-IT entrepreneurs who Horie partnered with to start his business). Horie, who has never been shy about his ambitions, offered the following comments on his new business: "I'm always thinking how to hack the world" and "With wagyu, I'll make my name known to the world."[18]

Rakuten, an online marketplace established by Mikitani Hiroshi in 1997, was more successful than Livedoor in forging a strong brand name through mergers and acquisitions. After graduating in 1988 from a prestigious university, Hitotsubashi, Mikitani worked for the Industrial Bank of Japan (now part of Mizuho Bank) until 1997, when he left to establish a consultancy firm, Crimson Group. He launched Rakuten the same year. Rakuten is involved in online retailing, credit card services, and banking services that include loans and mortgages. It also operates websites that book hotels and flights, maintains an online securities firm, and manages an online video club. Unlike Livedoor, Rakuten succeeded in creating a new professional baseball team, the Tohoku Rakuten Golden Eagles.

Following the examples of Amazon and eBay, Mikitani is striving to conquer the global markets. In 2005, the company began expanding outside

Japan when it purchased buy.com and Kobo Inc. The company has also acquired shares in Pinterest. In 2012, Rakuten adopted English as the company's official language—a move that the president of the Honda Motor Company, Ito Takanobu, famously called "stupid" (*bakarashii*). Nevertheless, Rakuten has been voraciously buying internet-based businesses from countries all over the world, including China, Russia, the United States, Canada, Brazil, Spain, Germany, France, Indonesia, Korea, and Taiwan.[19] Mikitani is currently the fourth richest person in Japan and the 151st-richest billionaire in the world.

A lasting effect of the dotcom era in the United States, Gina Neff argues, was the recognition that entrepreneurial behavior and venture labor—understood as willingness to embrace risk—can secure economic growth (2012). She notes that successful dotcom entrepreneurs emerged as icons of a new era in which the excitement of new careers in a rapidly expanding field repositioned risk away from something to fear to something to embrace. Neff observes that the media capitalized on successful dotcomers to promote the idea that willingness to take risks had economic value. The ways in which the dotcom sector built on crumbling job security in the United States resembles the ways in which the digital economy in Japan drew on and furthered the deregulation of the labor market. Horie and Mikitani were widely celebrated for their entrepreneurial fearlessness, but their examples were not as easy to follow as the self-help books they published suggested (Horie 2005; Mikitani 2018). They were men and were well connected. Most women in Japan who strove to build DIY careers did not have access to venture capital like Horie and Mikitani, who embodied what Paolo Virno calls the ideology of the possible (2004, 2007). The idea that every internet user is a potential Mark Zuckerberg inspires entrepreneurial individuals to use social media technologies to forge self-brands (Marwick 2013). While these individuals hope to translate their self-brands into meaningful and lucrative employment, social media platforms harness the unpaid labor that internet users invest in self-branding to grow their own brand value.

This book aims to demonstrate the premise that instead of offering opportunities to build careers, the digital economy has obfuscated the meaning of work while expanding the category of worker to all those who use online platforms (and, therefore, labor for the benefit of online companies). In the 1960s, Mario Tronti introduced the concept of the "social factory" to describe capital's tendency to integrate society (i.e., the family and community) into *Social factory* its formal apparatuses of production (1962). More recently, Tiziana Terranova proposed that the internet has emerged as an emblematic apparatus of the social factory (2004). They define the social factory as a mode of accumulation within which production time is no longer limited to the working day and the place of production is no longer constrained to factories and offices. According to Kathi Weeks, the concept models a condition in which "the relations of production extend beyond the specific employment relation" (2011, 142). Applied to the digital economy, the social factory is another way to claim that this economy extracts surplus value from labor without actually employing workers.

Feminist scholars have made important contributions to developing the theory of the social factory. Mariarosa Dalla Costa and Selma James proposed that focusing on factories and male workers could only offer a skewed interpretation of how capital extracts value from labor. They suggested that the housewife should be included in analyses of capitalism because she helps sustain capitalism by producing a precious commodity—labor power (and the working class). They argued that in capitalist economies, the family, as well as other forms of community, could not be conceptualized as realms that are separate and independent from the factory. Selma James writes, "The community therefore is not an area of freedom and leisure auxiliary to the factory, where by chance there happen to be women who are degraded as the personal servants of men. The community is the other half of capitalist organization, the other area of hidden capitalist exploitation, the other, hidden, source of surplus labor. It becomes increasingly regimented like a factory, what Mariarosa [Dalla Costa] calls a social factory, where the costs and nature of transport, housing, medical care, education, police, are all points of struggle. And this factory has [as] its pivot the woman in the home producing labor power as a commodity, and her struggle not to" (1975, 11). More recently, Kylie Jarrett has suggested that we consider the very history of capitalism as "the history of struggle within and against the social factory" (2018).

Gender in the Digital Economy

Mayuhime, a celebrity trader, claims that she spends only fifteen to thirty minutes a day trading foreign currencies online and earns JPY280,000–300,000 ($2,496–$2,674) a month, more than she made during a forty-hour-a-week job as an "office lady."[20] She also reports that before the birth of her daughter, she could spend up to twenty hours a day trading, earning up to JPY3,000,000 ($27,384) a month. Success stories like hers seduced many women into believing that they too could make money in the comfort of their homes.

The possibility of earning a decent living or, even better, striking it rich, however, was not the only aspect of online work that lured women into the digital economy. Until the late 1980s, when a real estate bubble burst and eco-

8

nomic growth came to a screeching halt, the Japanese economy was built on what Guy Standing describes as a highly paternalistic form of laborism (2011). Scholars have written about the failure of the Equal Employment Opportunity law to curb the pervasive gender bias in hiring practices and the prominent gender discrimination in Japanese workplaces (Kelsky 2001; Molony 1995; Ogasawara 1998). Furthermore, widespread hiring freezes in the wake of a prolonged economic recession have only narrowed women's opportunities to pursue work they perceive as meaningful. Net idols' willingness to spend hours answering fan mail after a full day of work, bloggers' claims that they loved the "nomad" lifestyles that blogging made possible, and cell phone novelists' insistence that they derived pleasure from their work because they experienced a sense of achievement must be understood in the context of women's growing frustration with their limited opportunities to pursue meaningful careers in the traditional labor market.

The mobilization of women into irregular work was not new in the 1990s. Mary Brinton argues that in postwar Japan, gender served as a readily available criterion by which a reservoir of unskilled labor could be maintained or shut down as business cycles fluctuated (1993). Anne Allison adds that among the most advanced capitalist countries, Japan has the worst gender–wage disparity, and the recession only exacerbated women's vulnerable position in the labor market. She reports that women—along with young men, people with less education, people who come from lower-class backgrounds and single-parent households, foreign migrants, and men in their fifties—are most at risk of becoming irregular workers. Allison writes, "Women make up 70 percent of irregular workers, and their treatment is not much better even in regular employment where—based on the premise of the male breadwinner—they make only 67.1 percent of men's salaries. Approximately 80 percent of working women receive less than JPY3,000,000 ($27,384) a year, 44 percent were paid less than the minimum wage in 2010, and the numbers of professional women remain disturbingly low" (2013, 32).

In his book on the precariat, Guy Standing offers the following observation about women's place in Japan's labor market: "In Japan, the shift to non-regular labor coincided with a rising share of women in the labor force. In 2008, over half of Japanese women were in precarious jobs, compared with less than one in five men. . . . Japan is an extreme case. Gender inequality is a cultural legacy that has fed into a gendered precariat, in which women are concentrated in temporary, low productivity jobs, resulting in one of the highest male–female wage differentials in the industrialized world. In 2010, 44 percent of women workers in Japan were receiving less than the minimum wage.

The growth of temporary labor also contributed. Women's wages in regular (permanent) jobs are 68 per cent of men's, but in temporary jobs they are less than half of those paid to men" (2011, 71).

It is not surprising that in this context, many young women turned to the digital economy. If work available to women was always already precarious, many women surmised, it should at least involve activities that are fulfilling, purposeful, and enjoyable: in short, meaningful. In a context in which the idea of "good work" (Kalleberg 2013), or what I call here "meaningful work," was inextricably linked to the system of lifetime employment,[21] young women contributed an important insight to ongoing discussions about the changing landscape of work by proposing that work could be meaningful even if it did not guarantee job security.[22]

In the advanced capitalist world of the postwar period, social citizenship—understood as recognized membership in society—was anchored to permanent (i.e., salaried) employment (Castel 1996).[23] Similarly, in postwar Japan—where a Fordist economy secured growth by integrating mass production, mass consumption, and a Keynesian welfare system—management and labor collaborated to produce competitive products for global markets (Vogel 2006). In this context, companies cultivated a system of lifetime employment, in which employees spent their entire life working for the company that hired them right after they graduated from school.[24] In exchange for their loyalty and willingness to adopt a lifestyle devoted to work, employees were rewarded by a family wage, opportunities for skill development (which was specific to the company), job security, health insurance, and pension benefits (Abegglen 1958; Cole 1972; Nakane 1970; Rohlen 1974; Vogel 1965).[25] Scholars also noted that only one-third of the population benefited from this system because only large and midsize firms were able to maintain such benefits (Cole 1972; Kelly 1986). Even more relevant is the fact that women were overwhelmingly excluded from the system of lifetime employment (Brinton 1993; Cole 1972; Ogasawara 1998; Rohlen 1974).

By the late 1980s, economic growth had faltered, and the collapse of a speculative real estate bubble pushed the country into a long recession. While employers strove to preserve the postwar labor contract, they had no choice but to freeze hiring of new employees into lifetime employment. Scholars use such terms as *freeters* (irregular workers)[26] and NEET (Not in Education, Employment, and Training) to theorize how the breakdown of the postwar contract between management and labor has affected young people's employment prospects. This literature suggests that young people are incorporated into a labor reserve—formerly made up of women—from which a volatile economy satisfies its demand for inexpensive labor (Genda 2005; see also Brinton 2010; Driscoll 2007; Kosugi 2008; Mōri 2005; Toivonen 2013; Yoda 2006). The young women I discuss in this book might see their lives faithfully reflected in this portrayal, but they also do something that labor sociologists do not seem to fully appreciate: they actively seek ways to move forward by developing careers as photographers, net idols, bloggers, online traders, and cell phone novelists— examples I analyze in this book.

A story related to me by Wakabayashi Fumie, an online trader, suggests that young women who pursued careers refused to accept their labeling as members of an emerging precariat. I asked Wakabayashi what activities being a "stock market critic" entailed—the job title printed on her business card she gave me.[27] An astute observer who obviously sensed my initial skepticism about DIY careers, Wakabayashi responded with an anecdote. While completing paperwork to pay a parking ticket, she was unsure about what profession and workplace to enter on the form. After the officer in charge heard what she did for a living, he nonchalantly dismissed her: "It sounds like you are unemployed. Just write *unemployed*." Statistically speaking, many of the women whose stories I present in this book fall under the categories of freeter or NEET, but they do not see themselves as representatives of a new underclass. Rather, they embark on building careers to project themselves into the future in ways that they see more meaningful than the wage labor available to them in the conventional labor market. Yet by promoting the idea that job security should not be the main criterion to determine what makes work meaningful, young women have catalyzed the erosion of salaried employment.

When I asked women what kind of work they would characterize as good work,[28] they commonly discussed work that was meaningful (*imi ga aru shigoto*). When pressed to explain what that meant more precisely, however, my interlocutors enumerated characteristics that did not always align into a coherent definition. Rather, discussing meaningful work was a segue to engage the idea that employment can be meaningful even if it is not guaranteed for a lifetime. Although the system of lifetime employment started crumbling in the 1990s, the ideal of job security continued to exercise a powerful hold on discussions about work, social utility, social recognition, and individual dignity. Women who turned to digital technologies played a pivotal role in facilitating debates about meaning in work because their DIY careers were built on the assumption that economic criteria should not dominate discussions of work. In this book, I interpret women's commentaries on meaningful work as critical reflections on Japan's gender-stratified labor market and pervasive gender discrimination in the realm of work—characteristics of the lifetime employment system that, contrary to women's hopes, did not disappear with the breakdown of this system.

The central argument I engage with and expand on in this book is that individuals' search for what they describe as meaningful work drives innovations in capitalist accumulation. I draw on Karl Marx's idea that labor plays an important role in developing the means of production and increasing productivity, even if only involuntarily. Marx saw workers' militancy over the length of the working day as critical to the process of industrialization. The struggle of workers to shorten their work hours carved inroads in the mechanization of production (Marx 1992).[29] The Italian Autonomists, such as Mario Tronti (1962), Paolo Virno (2004), and Antonio Negri (1991), developed Marx's insight further by arguing that it would be a mistake to attribute too much power to capital and assume that it is able to curb workers' resistance. Rather, it is the workers who invent the social and productive forms that capital has no choice but to adopt. For instance, Sylvere Lotringer suggested that in Italy, the service sector (driven by immaterial labor) expanded from the early 1970s as a result of "the Italian workers' stubborn resistance to the Fordist rationalization of work" (2004, 11).[30]

Something similar happened in Japan when women turned to the digital economy, which developed a new approach to extracting surplus value from labor. Andrew Ross describes this approach as generating profits from labor without actually employing workers (2012). Owners of online platforms, essentially, continue innovating Marx's labor theory of value, which rests on the observation that capitalists produce surplus value by paying workers only for socially necessary (not surplus) labor time (1992). Owners of online platforms generate profits not by undercompensating workers for their labor, but by dissociating what internet users do online from the idea of labor. As I discussed in the previous section, internet users generate actual profits to platform owners not only by consuming advertising or producing "data commodities" but also by increasing the brand value of online platforms via their use of these platforms (Arvidsson 2005, 2008). Higher brand values, in turn, translate into higher stock prices. For instance, Facebook became a publicly traded company in 2012 with a whopping initial public offering (IPO) of $104 billion.[31]

Labor in the Digital Economy

The past decade witnessed a sharp rise in scholarly publications about digital labor (Andrejevic 2012, 2013; Arviddson and Colleoni 2012; Aytes 2012; Caraway 2011; Dyer-Witheford 1999, 2005, 2015; Dyer-Witheford and de Peuter 2009; Fuchs 2014; Fuchs and Fisher 2015; Hesmondhalgh 2010; Huws 2003,

2014; Irani 2015a, 2015b; Nakamura 2014, 2015; Ross 2012; Scholz 2016, 2017). Drawing on empirically grounded research, this book contributes to this scholarship. It demonstrates that the development of digital economies depends on locally specific systems of inequalities these economies harness for their growth. In postwar Japan (1945–90), for instance, gender served as the main source of flexible labor, so it is not surprising that women's labor was instrumental to the development of the digital economy. The Japanese case highlights the relevance of feminist scholarship on nonstandard forms of labor to theorizing digital labor. This section aims to demonstrate this point while also offering an overview of the literature on digital labor.

This literature evolved as scholars tackled the question of whether Marx's labor theory of value was helpful for understanding how owners of online platforms extracted surplus value from digital labor. Marx developed his labor theory of value by building on the observation that the labor time of the worker can be divided into socially necessary labor time and surplus labor time. He defined socially necessary labor time as "the labor-time required to produce any use-value under the conditions of production normal for a given society and with the average degree of skill and intensity of labor prevalent in that society" (1992, 129). Necessary labor is a concept Marx also used to refer to the labor time necessary to reproduce labor power. He writes, "I call the portion of the working day during which this reproduction takes place [i.e., the reproduction of labor power] necessary labor-time, and the labor expended during that time necessary labor; necessary for the worker, because independent of the particular social form of his labor; necessary for capital and the capitalist world, because the continued existence of the worker is the basis of that world" (1992, 325).

Surplus labor, on the other hand, is the part of the worker's labor time that is not necessary for the reproduction of labor power. In Marx's words, "During the second period of the labor process, that in which his labor is no longer necessary labor, the workers does indeed expend labor-power, he does work, but his labor is no longer necessary labor, and he creates no value for himself. He creates surplus value, which, for the capitalist, has all the charms of something created out of nothing" (1992, 325). It is during surplus labor time that surplus value is produced, which the capitalist keeps as profit or reinvests as capital.

This idea that value is inherently connected to labor is the starting point for scholars who view the online activities of internet users as labor. Christian Fuchs, for instance, argues that the three characteristic features of the relationship between capital and labor (coercion, alienation, and appropriation) are all present in digital labor (2014). Specifically, individuals are ideologically coerced to use the commercial internet if they do not want to be isolated and deprived of information.[32] Internet users are also alienated from the "data commodities" they produce online, as they have no control over how platform owners use these commodities. Lastly, owners of online platforms sell platform users to advertisers, thus appropriating surplus value from them.

According to Fuchs, digital labor includes productive activities that are "required for the existence, usage and application of digital media" (2014, 4).[33] In his view, factory workers differ from internet users only because they manufacture tangible products, while the latter produce "data commodities," such as social relationships, profile data, user-generated content, and transaction data (2014). Trebor Scholz expands Fuchs's definition of digital labor to include such activities as the performance of self on social networking platforms (e.g., Facebook), crowd-sourced labor (e.g., Amazon's M-Turk), fan labor and in-game labor (e.g., Sherlockology, Galactica.tv; see Chin 2014; Jenkins, Ford, and Green 2013), data labor (e.g., Wikipedia), and on-demand labor via online labor brokerage firms (e.g., Uber, Lyft, TaskRabbit) (2017). Some might balk at the suggestion that we conceptualize the labor of Uber drivers as digital labor. I agree with Scholz, who emphasizes that the digital economy makes possible work secured via such online platforms as Uber, Lyft, or TaskRabbit, and the labor expended by Uber drivers, for instance, accrues profits to the owners of these platforms.

Unlike Fuchs and Scholz, who draw on a production-centered conceptualization of value,[34] others argue that production has become diffuse to the point that it makes more sense to use theories of exchange to conceptualize value. These scholars reject the idea that online activities such as searching for information, updating one's Facebook page, or posting book reviews to Amazon, can be interpreted as labor. Adam Arvidsson and Elanor Colleoni suggest that digital labor cannot be exploited because something that is free cannot be exchanged (2012). David Hesmondhalgh, on the other hand, proposes that financial compensation is not the only meaningful form of reward for work, and it is problematic to consider work "done on the basis of social contribution or deferred reward" as "activities of people duped by capitalism" (2010, 278). He stresses the point that various reasons motivate people to pursue unpaid labor; some enjoy creating something new, while others welcome the opportunity to build new relationships. I would be more inclined to agree with this position if affiliations of identity did not structure the pathways of individuals to regimes of paid and unpaid work.

In the late 1990s, the young women who became net idols created their web pages not because they were seeking meaningful work, at least not initially. They turned to the internet to have fun, to make friends, and to experiment with new life projects. Yet as new infrastructures began evolving around their activities, which included net idol ranking sites, banner advertising, and an online net idol academy, their workload significantly increased. A net idol recounted in an interview that she felt she had two full-time jobs. After she returned home from her day job, she began her second shift, which involved updating her web page and responding to the thirty emails she received from her fans every day. Another net idol attributed her health problems to mounting stress she experienced as she juggled a full-time job and a net idol career. When she developed uterine fibroids and nearly had her uterus removed—an issue she discusses openly on the "about me" section of her website—she realized that she had to try to transform her digital labor into a day job or give up her net idol career.

An online celebrity trader regaled me with a similar story. She told me that she kept a cat figurine (*maneki neko*), which is believed to bring good luck to its owner in Japan, in her living room. To boost the power of her good luck charm, she kept fresh lemons around the cat figurine. Over time, the compulsive refreshment and increasingly meticulous arrangement of lemons around the cat grew into such an elaborate routine that her young daughters came to believe that real cats lived on lemons. Clearly, the development of DIY careers encroached significantly on these women's private lives. Photographs portraying the apartments of online traders make this point equally compellingly. A trader called Mayuhime includes photos of her apartment in her trading tutorials. These pictures portray her doing chores in the kitchen while simultaneously following movements on trading charts on eight computer screens mounted to the largest wall in the living room. These images suggest that developing careers requires not only significant labor investment but also the subordination of spaces of sociality and life itself (what the living room represents) to the pursuit of DIY endeavors (Mayuhime 2010a).

These vignettes shed light on why I find it difficult to conceptualize women's investment in becoming photographers, net idols, bloggers, online traders, and cell phone novelists outside the realm of work. The women I interviewed worked extremely hard to excel in what they were doing. Even if they initially turned to the internet to have fun, the romance was soon over. Women flirted with the new opportunities the digital economy opened for them, but as internet entrepreneurs developed new infrastructures around women's endeavors, they also made them competitive and significantly more labor intensive. Women soon realized that if they did not want to abandon their projects, they had to make a commitment. They had to invest time and energy into transforming their projects into careers. The digital economy seduced women into providing their labor by offering them the hope that they could develop meaningful careers.

The fact that their online activities were not readily recognized as labor does not mean that women did not experience these activities as labor. I propose to contribute to the literature on digital labor by highlighting the tendency that in different social contexts, different affiliations of identity are used to determine whose labor will be recognized as productive labor. This is also true the other way around. Segments of the population whose labor is traditionally less valued—because, for instance, commercial alternatives to that labor had been stymied (Schor 1993)—are more likely to be mobilized to forms of labor, such as digital labor, that are not compensated with salary or wage.[35]

I agree with Lilly Irani (2015a, 2015b) and Trebor Scholz (2017), who argue that online systems of microwork, such as Amazon's Mechanical Turk, contribute to eroding systems of job security. Yet I also see the dangers in proposing that all forms of digital labor should be recognized as productive labor and financially compensated. I agree with Susan Leigh Star and Anselm Strauss that it could be counterproductive to make all forms of work visible, as visibility can create new opportunities for surveillance and, ultimately, more work for the worker (1999). I, too, fear that demanding compensation for each creative contribution internet users make will only further capitalism's tendency to commodify human relationships. That said, Star and Strauss make a pertinent point when they claim that it is important to expose the politics that underwrite the decisions to not recognize certain activities as productive labor and the arbitrariness of the criteria that are used to measure the productivity of labor. That is, like the ways in which patriarchal ideologies serve capitalists by conceptualizing housework as the labor of love (i.e., nonproductive labor), owners of online platforms also benefit from not recognizing the online activities of internet users as labor. The case studies I present in this book demonstrate that gender structures the opportunities individuals have in Japan to transform their unpaid labor into lucrative employment.

The continuity between digital labor and the nonstandard forms of feminized labor available to women in Japan's traditional labor market was an important factor in making DIY careers appealing to women. I propose that we take this continuity more seriously to understand the new labor regimes digital economies are developing. The burgeoning literature on nonstandard forms of labor—e.g., emotional labor (Hochschild 1983), immaterial labor (Lazzarrato 1996), affective labor (Hardt 1999), reproductive labor (Federici 2012), articulation labor (Star and Strauss 1999), intimate labor (Boris and Parreñas 2010), care labor (Tronto 2013), phatic labor (Elyachar 2010), and hope labor (Kuehn and Corrigan 2013)—reflects the fact that capital increasingly strives to derive profits from activities it does not recognize as productive labor. As the growing scholarly investment in identifying new genres of labor suggests, the prominent scholarly response to this trend was to expand the category of productive labor.

In this book, I use the term *digital labor* as a broad umbrella term to describe labor in the digital economy. I propose that affective labor has emerged as the dominant form of digital labor, for it is this genre of labor that most seamlessly traverses the line between visibility and invisibility. The rise of the digital economy has made the ability to prevent invisible labor from becoming visible the key strategy of value extraction. Scholars commonly view affective labor as synonymous with post-Fordist labor, but they identify different occupational identities that inspired the making of a post-Fordist workforce. While some see the creative worker as the paradigmatic figure of an affective workforce (Lazzarato 1996; Virno 2004), others view the housewife as the model that served as a template to consolidate an affective labor regime (Dalla Costa 2015; Fortunati 1995, 2007). Kylie Jarrett suggests that online platforms transform their users into what she calls "digital housewives" who perform unwaged labor "generating surplus value for increasingly monolithic media companies like Google and Facebook by providing for free the content that animates these sites as well as the reams of data that can be sold to advertisers" (2018). As such, feminist theories of domestic labor are helpful to understand how surplus value is extracted from labor in the digital economy.

The tension between drawing on literature on domestic labor and engaging scholarship on creative and cognitive labor is central to Michael Hardt and Antonio Negri's definition of affective labor. To theorize post-Fordist labor, Hardt and Negri borrow the concept of immaterial labor from Maurizio Lazzarato (1996), which they define as "labor that creates immaterial products, such as knowledge, information, communication, a relationship, or an emotional response" (2004, 108). They identify intellectual and affective labor as the principal forms of immaterial labor and define affective labor as "labor that produces or manipulates affects such as a feeling of ease, well-being, satisfaction, excitement, or passion" (2004, 108).[36] Building on my observation that the figures of the creative worker and the housewife are integrated in new occupational identities such as the "girly" photographer, the net idol, the blogger, the online trader, and the cell phone novelist, I highlight that in the past two decades, the digital economy destabilized the boundary between affective labor and intellectual labor.[37] In fact, strategically recognizing or not recognizing this boundary has emerged as the primary strategy for platform owners to generate profits.

The digital labor that "girly" photographers, net idols, bloggers, online traders, and cell phone novelists performed was simultaneously affective and intellectual. For example, the competition was fierce among cell phone novelists to publish their novels in book format. To increase their chances of success, they were required to tirelessly improve their writing skills and assertively promote themselves. Authors spent countless hours communicating with their readers about plot development as well as issues (sometimes painfully personal ones) that their readers wished to share. When publishers had hundreds of excellent novels to choose from, resourceful promotional skills and accommodating behavior were often what it took to get the most "likes" on the platforms that publishers consulted when considering which novels to publish. While writing a novel required the investment of intellectual labor, the feminized affective labor of communication was also indispensable for developing a career as a cell phone novelist. Owners of cell phone novel platforms, in turn, derived revenues from this unpaid labor. The feminized affective labor that aspiring novelists invested in developing their careers was instrumental to the formation of communities that platform owners sold to advertisers.

Regimes of affective labor are always embedded in locally specific systems of inequalities, a key structuring principle of which is gender. To stress this point, I use the term *feminized affective labor* when I refer to what Hardt and Negri call affective labor. For reasons that closely resonate with mine, Silvia Federici also departs from the notion of affective labor and describes the activities women invest in creating and maintaining relationships as reproductive labor (2012). I prefer "feminized affective labor" over "reproductive labor" because the latter helps explain only how owners of online platforms generate profits from sociality, not from content provision.

At the same time, I propose that distinguishing various gendered forms of labor from one another will also help make invisible labor visible. For instance, I will use the concept of emotional labor—an employer's expectation of its service workers to offer service with a smile, that is, to personalize a relationship that is not personal (Hochschild 1983)—when I specifically discuss labor in the service industries. And I will engage the notion of phatic labor (Elyachar 2010) when I analyze how owners of online platforms build and expand infrastructures by harnessing the labor of internet users who invest in building relationships online. Lastly, I preserve the concept of affective labor for discussing labor that integrates intellectual and feminized affective labors.

By conceptualizing affective labor as synonymous with creative, cognitive, and intellectual labors, I stress that this genre of labor almost always contains a component of feminized affective labor, which is not true in reverse.

In sum, eroding the line between paid, visible labor and unpaid, invisible labor is a key strategy to generate surplus value in the digital economy. Investigating this strategy is pivotal to shedding light on the ways in which digital labor is reconfiguring Japan's labor markets. An equally prominent way in which digital labor drives the deregulation of the domestic labor market (one I will discuss in several chapters) is by reconfiguring the country's human capital regime. In postwar Japan, the system of human capital development regulated access to the benefits of economic growth.[38] In the wake of the recession, however, this regime was redefined as a means to identify new sources of economic expansion. As employment security became more difficult to attain, individuals began developing human capital in novel ways to foster what Rosabeth Moss Kanter defines as "employability security" (1995). Kanter offers this concept to theorize the labor conditions of software developers. Like film professionals in the United States, software developers are employed on a project-to-project basis. As such, they have only their reputations and networks of contacts to rely on to find new employment. Kanter writes, "Employability security is based on a person's accumulation of human and social capital—skills, reputation, and connections—which can be invested in new opportunities that arise inside and outside the employee's current organization" (1995, 63). Kanter sees the labor conditions of software designers as a model for the future of work. As job security is disappearing, she concludes, it is only in their employability that individuals are able to experience a sense of security.

In the postwar period, educational credentials played a key role in regulating access to job security. (For women, the relationship between educational background and employability was much less straightforward.) As the system of job security breaks down and the digital economy normalizes nonstandard work arrangements, investment in education is no longer believed to be the privileged pathway to lucrative work. Billionaire technologists such as Steve Jobs, Bill Gates, Michael Dell, and Mark Zuckerberg are often referenced to make this point. In the epilogue, however, I will revisit and contest the idea that formal education no longer matters in the digital economy. That said, it is true that the development of DIY careers does not demand the same type of human capital development that the system of lifetime employment required. Acquiring new skills in the digital economy (e.g., photography, writing, and trading) and using social media technologies as tools of self-branding have emerged as alternative ways to develop employability security.

Alice Marwick has studied how young internet entrepreneurs use social media technologies to construct "self-for-work self-presentations" to market themselves as brands and celebrities (2013, 5). She observes that internet entrepreneurs embark on developing new businesses by using social media technologies as tools of self-branding. They transform themselves into salable commodities hoping to appeal to potential employers or, even better, to attract venture capital to develop lucrative entrepreneurial projects. Others, like Trebor Scholz (2017) and Andrew Ross (2012), observe that owners of online platforms extract surplus value from the unpaid labor that internet users invest in generating an online presence. My case studies of net idols, bloggers, traders, and cell phone novelists trace how platform owners derived profits from the labor these women expended to develop new skills and online personas with the hope that their investment would lead to lucrative careers. Kathleen Kuehn and Thomas Corrigan theorize this form of unremunerated labor as hope labor—"un- or undercompensated work carried out in the present, often for experience or exposure, in the hope that future opportunities may follow" (2013, 19).

Methodological Considerations I: Techno-social Assemblages and Technological Duplicities

In the film *Her*, the operating system seduced the protagonist into believing that the perfect lover could only be a machine. Similarly, one of the most famous net idols in Japan, Nakamura Toyomi, describes her encounter with the internet as a life vest that appeared in front of her as she was struggling to stay afloat and reach the shore that was nowhere in sight. Because her acting career had failed to take off, she thought she would "write the script of her own life" and create "the theater of her own self" online.[39] The internet seduced her into believing that the career she was unable to attain in "real" life would be achievable in cyberspace. Like the operating system in *Her* that eventually revealed its duplicitous nature, the internet also betrayed Nakamura, whose story I will tell in chapter 2. Other chapters will tell similar stories of relationships between young women and digital technologies. Unlike *Her*, however, I contextualize these relationships to offer portraits not only of young women but also of Japan in the late 1990s and 2000s, the development of Japan's digital economy, and the transforming landscape of work.

The relationships between young women and digital technologies did not, of course, evolve in a vacuum. In the context of the net idol trend, for instance, net idols, their fans, Nippon Telecom and Telegraph (NTT), internet entrepreneurs, and technologies (including web page hosting services, net idol ranking sites, an online net idol academy, and so forth) have formed what

I conceptualize as a techno-social assemblage. Similar techno-social assemblages emerged around "girly" photographers, bloggers, online traders, and cell phone novelists. Within the five techno-social assemblages I analyze in this book, actants/participants formed relationships that the metaphors of seduction and duplicity describe more adequately than the metaphors of domination and resistance.

As I said previously, the internet seduced women into believing that digital technologies would enable them to develop DIY careers. NTT, however, was unwilling to give up its monopoly position, and the exorbitant fees of internet service stalled HTML development. The rudimentary architecture of the web pages that net idols were able to code or, eventually, rent narrowed and streamlined the diverse aspirations these women brought to this career. Ranking sites further seduced net idols to invest in building relationships with their fans in exchange for votes, and in turn, net idols seduced their fans into believing that they genuinely cared about them. In exchange, fans helped net idols develop new skills (such as photography in Nakamura's case) by serving as supportive audiences.

Unlike Bruno Latour, who chronicled the perspectives of all actants that were involved in the failed Aramis project (1996),[40] it is beyond the scope of my work to document the motivations of all participants that constitute the five techno-social assemblages I analyze in this book. Instead, I focus on the relationships between young women and digital technologies. While striving to maintain this perspective, I highlight that agency had a distributive quality within the techno-social assemblages this book examines.

The concept of assemblage arose to counter the tendency in the social sciences to conceptualize social structures and organizations as totalities and organic wholes. Manuel DeLanda argues that such metaphors as organism and the body cannot model the complexity that characterizes contemporary societies or social phenomena (2006). The problem with these metaphors is that they focus on relations between the parts and the whole, the latter of which is conceived as a seamless totality or an organic unity. Within any organization that is understood as a totality, the relationships between the parts are conceptualized as relations of interiority. Building on the work of Deleuze and Guattari (1987), DeLanda argues that unlike totalities, an assemblage is an entity whose properties emerge from the interactions between the parts that constitute the assemblage. In other words, an assemblage does not possess an organic unity. Instead, its component parts may be detached and plugged into a different assemblage, in which these component parts will interact differently.

Within the techno-social assemblages that emerged around "girly" photographers, net idols, bloggers, online traders, and cell phone novelists, I analyze young women's engagement with digital technologies without fixing them in preconceived roles. More specifically, I do not limit my conceptualization of these women as users (instead of producers) of technologies. I recognize that innovative use shapes the development of technologies just as much as design schemes and regulatory practices do.[41] At the same time, the actants that constitute an assemblage interact with each other in contexts that predate these interactions. I use "context" to refer to gendered patterns of labor market participation, the economic recession, and the concomitant deregulation of the labor market and the telecommunications sector. By saying that these conditions predate the emergence of the techno-social assemblages I analyze, I am not suggesting that they were not changing.

In late 1990s Japan, in a social context in which labor market deregulation further marginalized women from salaried employment, digital technologies promised women opportunities to sidestep the discriminatory hiring practices in the traditional labor market. While digital cameras were promoted as tools of emancipation that enabled women to take charge of their representation, blogging platforms invited women to discover and develop their talents.[42] Clearly, we have come a long way from Marx's classic conceptualization of the relationship between workers and machines as irreconcilably antagonistic. According to Marx, workers have no choice but to fight industrial machinery, as machines devalue human labor and make workers disposable (1993). Similarly, E. P. Thompson observes that in industrial operations, machinery meant labor discipline, as machines functioned as powerful supplements to the timekeeper (1967).

Design principles such as efficiency, interactivity, and upgradability are key to why I see duplicity in digital technologies. And, in fact, improving these properties has long been a crucial concern to designers of technologies. Innovators of industrial machinery, for instance, strove to optimize productivity by modulating the ontological difference between humans and machines. One such example is Norbert Wiener, whose work improved machinic control over the pace of work by enabling machines to assess the effects of their operation and adjust their performance accordingly. Feedback loops transferred to machines such attributes of human intelligence as the capacity to adapt and learn. Marrying machinic efficiency and human intelligence was also at the heart of Ohno Taiichi's project to develop the Toyota Production System. A key aspect of what is now called Toyotism (also described as post-Fordism, lean production, just-in-time production, or flexible accumulation) was what Ohno called "automation with a human touch." Ohno allowed workers to operate various machines and adjust the pace of the assembly line to an optimal speed. As such, he redefined the workers from obedient operators of machines into active participants in production. By integrating the worker to become a part of the feedback loop, the Toyota system transformed the antagonistic relationship between humans and machines that characterized the Fordist era into an affective relationship (Dyer-Witheford 2015).[43]

The workers at Toyota's car plant and the young women whose stories I tell in this book epitomize the same trend. It is increasingly difficult to theorize the relationship between humans and machines as a relationship of antagonism. Marx notes that with technological developments, labor will lose control over the production process. He writes, "The worker's activity, reduced to a mere abstraction of activity, is determined and regulated on all sides by the movement of the machinery, and not the opposite. The science which compels the inanimate links of the machinery, by their construction, to act purposefully, as an automaton, does not exist in the worker's consciousness, but rather acts upon him through the machine as an alien power, as the power of the machine itself" (1993, 693). Interactive technologies, such as Web 2.0, are designed to absorb labor and make it invisible. They conceal human labor by fusing humans and technologies into such productive entities as the internet.

David Harvey sees today's artificial intelligence as emblematic of capital's tendency to incorporate the mental capacities of laborers into fixed capital (2018, 97). An episode from the *Star Trek* series titled "Dead Stop" persuasively visualizes this idea.[44] Severely damaged in a minefield, the Enterprise arrives at an ominous repair station. The fully automated station offers to repair the ship, asking for a payment the crew finds reasonable. The repairs begin, and all is going well until a crewmember disappears. The crew discovers that the station abducted the crewmember and integrated his synaptic pathways into its computer core to enhance its processing speed and flexibility. Indeed, a humanoid brain has always been a part of the bargain as evidenced by the station's sizeable collection of humanoid species. After rescuing the kidnapped crewmember, the Enterprise manages to break free from the station and detonate it. While the station explodes in cathartic fireworks, the last scene shows the duplicitous AI entity beginning to make repairs on itself. The episode's visual representation of human brains plugged into a system—detached from the actual bodies the computer has no use for and does not care for—captures the concept of interactive technologies absorbing and concealing human labor.

Technological agency can be understood as the power of industrial machinery to set the rhythms of work or as the ability of intelligent machines to replicate the flexibility of the human brain. It can also be thought of as self-causality in technologies or, in the conceptualization of Bernard Stiegler, the capacity of technologies to self-organize into systems (1998, 43).[45] In the Japanese context, Hamano Satoshi proposed a similar argument when he theorized Japan's internet as an ecosystem (2008). By examining the architectural designs of various online platforms, he concludes that the architecture of the internet cannot be conceived of in a singular form. Rather, online platforms develop their own architectures as they compete for internet users. These architectures, in turn, emerge into an ecosystem. They communicate and learn from each other. By emphasizing that individuals are able to exploit the differences among particular platform designs, Hamano begins developing a critique of what has evolved in recent years into a quickly growing body of scholarship on algorithmic modes of regulation (Gillespie 2014; Lanier 2011; Pasquale 2015; Striphas 2015).[46] I find Hamano's conceptualization of the internet as an ecosystem helpful in mapping how net idol sites inspired the development of blogging and cell phone novel platforms by plugging one component part of a techno-social assemblage into another.

Methodological Considerations II: Virtual and Actual Selves

The idea for this project emerged between 2001 and 2003 while I was conducting fieldwork for my first book about television dramas and young women. Many of my interlocutors were discussing the internet with contagious enthusiasm and suggested that I should study it. I was tempted, and although not ready to give up my project on commercial television, I began having conversations with young women about digital technologies. Over the past sixteen years, I have continued following young Japanese women's engagement with digital technologies. I formally started fieldwork for this project in 2010 and conducted structured interviews with forty-three women. For the chapter on the cell phone novel trend, I also interviewed editors who were responsible for acquiring cell phone novels to be published in book format, a software engineer who supervised the design of the largest cell phone novel platform, and an employee who worked for the content department of the largest cell phone novel platform. Out of the forty-three women, I interviewed eighteen women multiple times. This book anchors each chapter to the stories of two to four women who had emerged as icons of the trends the chapters focus on. In addition to interviewing them, I also reviewed their online diaries, blogs, novels, self-help books, and trading tutorials. Finally, I read countless interviews published with internet entrepreneurs and platform designers online or in weekly and monthly magazines.

While many of my interlocutors—especially net idols, bloggers, and cell phone novelists—shared online a wealth of information about their anxieties and fantasies, many of them evaded questions about their family backgrounds. They cited issues of privacy, but it seems to me that withholding personal information was also a strategy for these individuals to model their public personas after the image of the self-made entrepreneur. This image was indispensable for women to give lectures, maintain blogs, and publish books about how to develop DIY careers. Adopting the image of the self-made entrepreneur also explains why stories of misfortune—often dramatized for maximum impact—dominated the responses women gave to my inquiries about the motivations that led them to build DIY careers. They commonly identified bankruptcy of parents, loss of employment, laid-off husbands, and divorce as reasons that prompted them to embark on building DIY careers. Their stories also circulated widely in the media and seemed very popular, perhaps because they dissociated female DIY entrepreneurs from perceptions that they were selfish and greedy individuals. Anthropologists have compellingly demonstrated the complex relationships between actual and virtual selves in contexts such as *Second Life* (Boellstorff 2008) and *World of Warcraft* (Nardi 2010). I found that female entrepreneurs in Japan strategically navigated the gap between virtual and actual selves in pursuit of building successful careers.

As many of my interlocutors were reluctant to reveal information about their class backgrounds, I relied on my interpretations of the information they shared with me in dialogue along with my observations about my interlocutors' use of language and especially women's language (Inoue 2006), behavior, dressing style, choice of meeting place, and commentary about other DIY entrepreneurs. I also took notes on inconsistencies in my interlocutors' public personas.

For example, an online trader who was reputed to have generated a fortune from online trading was late for our first meeting. She explained that she missed her train connection and had to wait twenty minutes for the next train. It was she who suggested that we meet in downtown Tokyo, but the train schedule suggested that she came from a remote suburb, which she later confirmed. She promoted herself as a trader who was able to buy a house using the income she earned from online trading. The fact that she purchased the house in a tucked-away suburb was information she withheld, perhaps to avoid compromising the credibility of her success story.

Another online trader gave me a business card that sported a fancy downtown location for her office address. Later, I learned that it was a common practice to print fictitious addresses on business cards to suggest that someone's entrepreneurial endeavors were successful. On yet another occasion, I offered to go to an interlocutor's office. She told me that meeting in a café would be more convenient because the air conditioning in her office was being fixed. That may have been true, but having read numerous self-help books, I was curious whether my interlocutor had indeed rented an office.

Since many of my informants were reluctant to share information about their family backgrounds, I use the category of class with the caveat that creating DIY careers meant crafting new selves, which involved strategically withholding, deemphasizing, dramatizing, or completely rewriting one's class background. Gender and class intersect in complex ways in Japan, which also makes it difficult to theorize the linkages between gender and labor precarity through the lens of class. An issue that complicates an intersectional analysis of gender and class is that women's class status is commonly determined by their fathers' and husbands' employment (Brinton 1993; Fujiwara-Fanselow 1995; Ishida 1989; Ishida and Slater 2010; Roberts 1994). Yamada Masahiro asserts that, contrary to expectations, the recent rise in the number of women who marry late or decide to remain single did not change this situation. Yamada coined such terms as *parasite singles* and *stranded singles* to argue that young women tend to stay with their parents well into their thirties waiting for the right man to marry—a man who earns enough to smoothly transition them from their parental homes to married life (1999, 2007, 2016).

While women have been steadily supplying flexible labor in Japan for decades, my book demonstrates that beginning in the late 1990s, women were also mobilized to mediate labor market deregulation. Women turned to the digital economy to better their and their families' class status, but very few of them succeeded. Despite the fact that these women drove the development of the digital economy, their numbers are disproportionately small among the most successful internet entrepreneurs. Most net idols disappeared without a trace, and most "girly" photographers did not become professional photographers. The percentage of female traders among professional traders remains perplexingly small, and to gain visibility in the crowd of twenty-eight million bloggers (on Ameba, which is Japan's largest blogging platform) is a formidable task, if not impossible. Neither can the market support the hundreds of thousands of cell phone novelists who aspire to become professional writers. In spite of this, the few women whose stories (and the stories of their often short-lived careers) I present in this book were able to keep a powerful ideology alive—the ideology of the possible, which has inspired millions to try to develop DIY careers. The overwhelming majority of these entrepreneurial individuals did not succeed; ironically, they ended up facilitating the devaluation of salaried employment and the crumbling of job security.

Chapter Overviews

Focusing on the so-called girly photography trend, chapter 1, "Disidentifications: Women, Photography, and Everyday Patriarchy," introduces readers to the dominant discourses of gender and labor in Japan. These predominantly patriarchal discourses constituted the context within which women were struggling to develop their careers. Stressing that women's photography centered on portraying relationships, photography critics—mostly men— interpreted the genre as a project to reconnect social relationships that were unraveling during the long recession. Women photographers, however, rejected this interpretation. They argued that they turned to photography to expand the zones of subjectivity from which they were able to draw new forms of labor and new sources of pleasure. This chapter demonstrates how women photographers articulated a feminist critique of labor, gender, and technology that foreshadowed the struggles of the net idols, bloggers, online traders, and cell phone novelists who followed in their footsteps to build careers in an economy that depended on women's invisible labor.

Chapter 2, "The Labor of Cute: Net Idols in the Digital Economy," explores how internet entrepreneurs harnessed the online diaries of net idols to develop banner advertising that enabled them to package the fans of net idols and sell them to advertisers. I conceptualize the net idols' production of cuteness as feminized affective labor and claim that the digital economy has effectively expanded the practices through which value is extracted from women's unwaged labor to spaces beyond the domestic sphere. I stress, however, that net idols did not uncritically embrace this logic. Instead, they used digital technologies to develop employability security. I conclude that women's unpaid labor remains central to a society in which labor precarity generates a robust demand for feminized affective labor, a situation resonant with the ways in which women's unwaged labor in the home was instrumental to maintaining economic growth in the postwar period.

Chapter 3, "Career Porn: Blogging and the Good Life," examines the role of blogging in reconfiguring dominant perceptions of work. In the early 2000s, a growing number of blogging platforms and blog tutorials accompanied the rapidly increasing number of bloggers. Blog tutorials promoted blogging as a new pathway to DIY careers and the good life while criticizing life-time employment for compromising individual freedom. By doing so, these tutorials made the dismantling of the system of lifetime employment more acceptable. Blog tutorials also helped blogging portals recruit online content providers, predominantly women, who were not paid for producing blogs. By presenting blogging as an activity that belonged in the realm of play rather than work, blogging platforms effectively foreclosed opportunities for blog-gers to earn an income from producing online content. At the same time, these platforms grossed massive revenues from selling the community of blog writ-ers and readers to advertisers.

Chapter 4, "Work without Sweating: Amateur Traders and the Finan-cialization of Daily Life," explores the women trader trend. These women, estimated to number in the hundreds of thousands, were reputed to garner wealth from trading foreign currencies on online trading platforms. In reality, however, amateur traders found that it was easier for them to develop careers as experts of online trading than to become professional traders. The exam-ples of women, who emerged as figureheads of online trading, illustrate that publishing trading tutorials and giving lectures have proven to be more sus-tainable and lucrative sources of income for women than trading itself. This chapter brings into dialogue interviews with celebrity traders, an analysis of their portrayals in the media, and an examination of how securities firms har-nessed the feminized affective labor of women to expand the financial market. I argue that the financial sector mobilized women traders to mediate a transi-tion from a culture of saving to the financialization of daily life.

Chapter 5, "Dreamwork: Cell Phone Novelists, Affective Labor, and Pre-carity Politics," explores how young women rejected their mobilization to un-derpaid or unpaid service work by turning to the digital economy to build careers as cell phone novelists. Most authors of cell phone novels were young women, many of whom previously earned a living from pursuing dead-end service jobs. Cell phone novels document alleged personal stories of suffer-ing that arise from unrequited love, teenage pregnancy, rape, bullying, social injustice, or incurable disease. The vast production of these novels, I argue, testifies to the growing number of young women who tried to develop ca-reers they perceived as meaningful. But while cell phone novel platforms made enormous profits from advertising, only a miniscule minority of authors were able to earn a living from writing cell phone novels.

Lastly, the "Epilogue" situates the trends the book documents into the broader context of similar developments that unfolded in other parts of the world. It highlights the duplicitous character of the digital economy that recasts online platforms as solutions to problems with work. In the late 1990s and 2000s, young Japanese women's search for meaningful work revitalized the postwar era's preoccupation with economic growth and attachment to work-oriented lifestyles. Through their struggles to access meaningful work, women have articulated a critique of gender discrimination in the realm of work. Ironically, however, women's investment in building meaningful careers has also foreclosed the possibility of reflecting on the unwavering belief that rapid economic growth is the best way to secure socioeconomic vitality and individual well-being. That is, women's "love affairs" with DIY careers forestalled the possibility of developing postproductivist imaginaries and postwork alternatives.

Disidentifications

WOMEN, PHOTOGRAPHY, AND EVERYDAY PATRIARCHY

In 2001, Japan's most prestigious prize for photography, the Kimura Ihei Award, was awarded jointly to three young women: Nagashima Yurie, Hiromix (Toshikawa Hiromi), and Ninagawa Mika. The award jury's decision marked the growing popularity of photography among young women—a trend that evolved during the recessionary 1990s. Critics labeled the works of women photographers as "girly" photography (*onna no ko shashin*),[1] defining it as a genre that drove inspiration from cute culture.[2] Drawing on the observation that portraits were central to "girly" photography, critics, art curators, and art photographers (all overwhelmingly men) interpreted the genre as a project to reconnect social relationships that had unraveled in the wake of the recession. Women photographers, however, rejected this interpretation. Some dismissed the notion of "girly" photography as a misnomer, arguing that female photographers engaged cute culture only to critically reflect on it. Others reasoned that the multitude of photography projects women pursued did not cohere into a clearly identifiable genre.

In Japan, women photographers were the first to turn to digital technologies to craft DIY careers. Correspondingly, "girly" photography was commonly interpreted as a prominent effect of advances in digital cameras. It is true that many women who turned to photography in the 1990s initially used digital cameras. After gaining recognition, however, many of them—with the notable exception of Hiromix—switched to analog cameras. In interviews and artist statements, some of them reasoned that working with analog equipment gave them more control over their work, while also allowing them to derive more pleasure from the labor of photography. Indeed, the digital/analog binarism figured powerfully into women's discussions of their relationship to photography. Evidently, some saw the ability to switch to analog technologies as essential to a career in professional photography. The net idols, bloggers, online traders, and cell phone novelists did not have the same choice. Their only option was to eventually exit the digital economy.

This chapter introduces readers to the everyday texture of the context in which women turned to digital technologies to develop DIY careers. While the previous chapter outlined the broader structural conditions that drove women to the digital economy, this chapter examines how women experienced and fought patriarchal power structures as they labored to realize new employment opportunities. Whereas the challenge for female photographers was to break into a male-dominated domain of professional work, the women who followed in their heels faced a different conflict: they had to maneuver online platforms that were designed by male internet entrepreneurs and software engineers who wrote their own gender biases into code.[3]

Shedding light on the different interpretations female photographers and male critics offered about "girly" photography is critical to understanding why net idols were scorned as narcissists, why cell phone novelists were criticized as exhibitionists, and why online traders were unable to shed their branding as amateurs. Women photographers began developing their careers in the early 1990s in the context of a nagging recession in which women were called upon to reconnect the social relationships that had come undone. The more young women tried to distance themselves from normative gender roles, the more their critics tried to anchor them back to these positions. Women photographers pioneered the trends this book investigates, but this chapter will show that they were also the ones who most clearly suffered from the backlash women faced when they tried to challenge the dominant gender division of labor.

What critics called "girly" photography casual observers saw as young women documenting their everyday lives—taking pictures of themselves, their family members, friends, pets, and meals. Although the genre seemed sweetly innocent, it invited peculiar responses, including voyeuristic curiosity, hope that young women might rejuvenate the stale field of art photography, and anxiety that the gatekeepers of professional photography might just lose their privileges. After all, female photographers proved an important point that advertisers had so relentlessly promoted, which was that digital cameras offered everyone the same chance to become an art photographer. Hiromix, who had earned fame before she graduated from high school, emerged as an emblem of how digital cameras enabled young people to build successful careers. Her example suggested that it was possible to gain recognition as an art photographer without the self-effacing labor that older generations had invested in earning degrees from top-tier art schools and apprenticing with famous photographers for years.

I argue that many of the photo books young women published were projects of disidentification; they were strategies to critically engage mainstream representations of women and women's place in society that aimed "to transform a cultural logic from within" (Muñoz 1999, 11). Rather than seeing women's photography as projects to craft new identities, forms of sociality, and ways of belonging, critics viewed the genre as young women's commitment to reinforcing the gender roles and relations that underwrote the postwar period. Most problematic was critics' belief that the gender of photographers was key to interpreting their works. From this assumption, their conclusion that women's photography centered on building bridges between the postwar and the recessionary periods seamlessly followed. Critics, I suggest, projected onto women's photography their own nostalgia for the socioeconomic security that at least the middle class was able to enjoy before the recession. The future these critics idealized looped back to the postwar era when women were assigned the role of managing social reproduction in the developmental state's project of sustaining robust economic growth.

While critics wanted female photographers to embrace the responsibilities that women were expected to assume in the postwar era, I learned from my own and published interviews with photographers that it was precisely the desire to challenge these expectations and women's limited opportunities in the realm of professional employment that drove women to photography. This chapter thus sheds light on the broader context in which women were striving to develop DIY careers. Although some women did innovatively use the new technology of the small digital camera, photography does not involve the same type of digital labor that net idols, bloggers, traders, and cell phone novelists invested in developing their careers. Because "girly" photography preceded the mainstreaming of the internet, female photographers did not have to invest unpaid labor into communicating with fans. Female photographers did, however, set the stage for the other women I discuss in this book. I therefore analyze the "girly" photographer as the first DIY career and "girly" photography as an early example of the circulatory inducements that advances in digital technologies made possible.

The "Girly" Photography Trend

In addition to young women and male critics, several other actors and actants participated in the formation of the techno-social assemblage critics labeled as "girly" photography. These included camera manufacturers, museum directors, gallery owners, magazine editors, book publishers, and the advertising industry. In the Introduction, I defined assemblage as an entity whose properties emerge from the interactions between the parts that constitute the assemblage. In the context of "girly" photography, the interactions were structured along a simple antagonism: women wanted to break into the world of professional photography, while all the other actors and actants sought to marketize women's efforts.

In a national context in which photography was a male-dominated art form, young female photographers, with Hiromix in the lead, attracted considerable media attention. Shinoyama Kishin, one of Japan's most famous art photographers, has admitted that he did not really understand Hiromix's photography and surmised that his own response to her work might have been the key to understanding her success. He reasoned that Hiromix did not learn photography and did not have to work her way up in the hierarchy within the profession. Shinoyama speculated that it might have been her very courage to disrespect institutional art photography and photographic conventions that gained her popularity among young people.[4]

Developments in digital cameras in the 1980s and 1990s began destabilizing the gate-keeping privileges of critics who were in charge of such professional journals as *Asahi Camera, Camera, Camera Mainichi,* and *Nippon Camera.*[5] In 1989, Konica released its "Big Mini," the world's smallest and lightest digital camera. Big Mini was a fully automatic compact camera that featured an auto-focus function and built-in flash. Digital cameras such as the Konica model enabled young people to experiment with photography. The sweeping success of amateur photographers like Hiromix, who debuted using Konica's Big Mini, have attracted young women to this art form. Television commercials advertising the Big Mini almost exclusively featured young women, seducing them to become photographers by emphasizing that the Big Mini was small, light, and easy to use. They also stressed that the camera was so technologically advanced that it was able to capture its models (all of whom were women) in the most favorable light imaginable. Some ads depicted it as a source of enjoyment—like the pleasure one derives from seeing a beautiful female body. One ad in particular introduced Konica's compact camera by stating that the camera was "protruding" where it was supposed to protrude (the autofocus lens was compared to a woman's chest) and it was slender where it was supposed to be slender (the slimness of the camera was compared to a woman's slim waistline).[6]

Photography contests were also instrumental in turning young people's casual interest in photography into a photography boom. In 1990, two major photography contests were launched. Canon, a leading manufacturer of digital cameras, sponsored the first contest, New Cosmos of Photography (*Shashin no Shinseiki*). According to the Canon website, New Cosmos of Photography marked a distinct era in the history of photography, one in which photographers were no longer celebrated for their technique and career track records but for their originality.[7] Renowned critics such as Iizawa Kōtarō, curators such as Nanjo Fumio, and art photographers such as Araki Nobuyoshi, Moriyama Daido, and Shinoyama Kishin—all of whom were men—served as judges.[8] This contest helped a new generation of women photographers debut, including Hiromix, Ninagawa Mika, Takahashi Junko, Mogi Ayako, Kanno Jun, Noguchi Rika, Sawada Tomoko, Ozawa Akiko, and Yamamoto Kaori.

The advertising and publishing industries were quick to join camera manufacturers to boost their sales, create new markets, and identify new talent. Recruit, a publisher of classified ad magazines with growing investments in the advertising industry, sponsored the second contest, Photography's 3.3 Square Meter Exhibit (*Shashin Hitotsubo-ten*). *Hitotsubo-ten* sponsored thirty competitions between 1990 and 2009. Ninagawa Mika, Kawauchi Rinko, Miyashita Maki, Nakano Aiko, Matsumoto Noriko, Nakashima Hiromi, Noguchi Rika, and Hara Mikiko were among the award winners.[9]

Book and magazine publishers also saw lucrative opportunities in the photography boom. Established publishers such as Seigensha, Kawade Shobō Shinsha, Shinchōsha, and Kōrinsha reassigned resources to the publication of photography books. Furthermore, new publishers were established, including Little More, Editions Treville, and Akaaka Art Publishing. Magazines such as *Studio Voice* and *Rockin'on Japan* also realized the opportunities to capture the youth market in the photography boom. In 1996, *Studio Voice* commissioned Iizawa Kōtarō to edit a special issue entitled *Shutter and Love* that featured women photographers (Iizawa 1996). In the same year, Kaneko Yoshinori, an editor at *Studio Voice*, compiled another special issue entitled *We Love Hiromix* (Kaneko 1996).

Iizawa writes in his epilogue to *Shutter and Love*, "It had begun before we knew it. All of a sudden, girls with cameras in hand popping up conspicuously all over town. For the last two or three years, photography contests featuring the younger generation such as New Cosmos of Photography and Hitotsubo-ten have seen a sudden jump in the number of female entries. Comparing the number of applicants by sex, men still outnumber women. Yet in terms of works winning higher awards, the percentage of women dominate the scene. Sometimes the ratios are 1: 2 or even 1: 3" (1996, 154). Iizawa also notes that in 1994, for the first time ever in the Department of Photography at Nihon University (Iizawa's alma mater)—where back in the 1970s only five or six women were enrolled in a class of fifty—female students outnumbered their male classmates. As Iizawa pointed out, "Photography was once overwhelmingly a man's world. At least in the professional arena, the ratio of men and women was incomparably lopsided. Likening the camera to the male sexual organ is no doubt a joke of somewhat bad taste, but there was something beyond the metaphor to it. There were of course female photographers too, but they were more often than not beheld as though they were beasts of a strange species" (1996, 155).

When I first contacted Ninagawa Mika and Nagashima Yurie in 2012, they both distanced themselves from the label of "girly" photography.[10] Ninagawa dismissed the label as a misnomer and said that she did not care to discuss it. Eventually, after some clarification, she agreed to meet me. I wondered whether Ninagawa's initial response to me was not a reaction to Iizawa Kōtarō's book about "girly" photography, which came out in 2010. Iizawa's book, The Era of "Girly Photography," was emblematic of how the male critical establishment responded to the works of female photographers who started their careers in the 1990s. Its main thesis was that women who turned to photography in the 1990s pursued a characteristically feminine style of photography that seamlessly lent itself to projects of social reproduction. In making this argument, Iizawa—like other male critics, curators, and art photographers—emphasized the gender of female photographers. Not surprisingly, women photographers found this interpretation unsettling. When Iizawa's book was published, Nagashima Yurie was writing her thesis about women photographers as part of her master's degree in sociology at Musashi University. She told me that she found Iizawa's ideas discrepant with her own analysis.[11]

More concretely, Iizawa has argued that the principles that guide male photographers are the very opposite of those that drive their female colleagues. For instance, male photographers objectively observe their models, while female photographers identify with them. Whereas male photographers are skilled professionals whose work is conceptually driven, female photographers are amateurs whose relationship to photography is emotional. Iizawa also notes that while male photographers tend to be pessimistic loners, female photographers are optimistic and committed to generating and maintaining social relationships and communities (2010).[12] These observations align with the dominant gender ideologies that dominated the postwar period, when the normative pursuit for middle-class women was to become homemakers.

Iizawa's interpretation of women's photography missed the point on multiple accounts. Those misrecognitions, however, are helpful because they illuminate an important aspect of affective labor. While Hardt and Negri (2004) distinguish affective labor from intellectual labor, the critical reception of "girly" photography illustrates that the separation of intellectual and affective labor is not only arbitrary but it also re-embeds women in regimes of unwaged and invisible labor. Namely, in women's portraits, Iizawa saw only affective labor in the sense in which Hardt and Negri define this genre of labor. Women photographers, however, insisted that their portraits were identity projects, which required the investment of intellectual, not affective labor.

The press release for Nagashima's 2016 exhibition *About Home* illustrates this point: "Viewed as the pioneer of the Girly Photo movement, which took off in the latter half of the 1990s, Nagashima has grappled with the question of her identity, both within the social group, and particularly as a woman, since her debut in 1993, creating works relating to her relationships with others by directing her camera at herself and those close to her."[13] This introduction shines light on the fraught relationship of the artist to the label of "girly" photography. While the label is evoked in the text, the wording does not clarify Nagashima's relationship to it. At the same time, the emphasis in the text falls unequivocally on Nagashima's investment in interrogating issues of identity, community, and gender—a project that involves intellectual labor, not what I define in this book as feminized affective labor.

Debuting between 1993 and 1996, Ninagawa, Nagashima, and Hiromix pioneered the trends that I analyze in the following chapters. By 2001, when they won the Kimura Ihei Award, they had inspired many young women to try their hand at photography, submit their works to competitions, and consider developing careers as photographers. One of these women was Nakamura Toyomi, whose career I discuss in chapter 2. Nakamura became a net idol and is continuing to develop her career as an art photographer while working full time at an advertising agency and practicing what she calls "photo-therapy" during the weekends. When I visited Nakamura's website in May 2018, her self-introduction (formerly the "about me" section of a personal website) included only two sentences, stating, "My dream is to become successful as a photographer." Typeset in a smaller font size, the second sentence offered the following elaboration: "I want to become the most famous Japanese female photographer in the world."[14]

Women photographers were also the forerunners of the selfie culture, a trend that fashion blogger Suzuki Junko—whose career I discuss in chapter 3—then further developed. For many years, Suzuki described herself as a "professional selfer."[15] Hiromix was a forerunner of selfie culture. She snapped many of her self-portraits with her digital camera held in her hand with her arm stretched out in front of her. Similar to Suzuki, another notable example was Miyazaki Izumi, who used Tumblr to develop her career as a photographer specializing in quirky self-portraiture (Bohr 2015). By getting both the ideology of the possible and the discourse of meaningful work off the ground, women photographers inspired other women to develop careers and thus laid the foundations of the digital economy.[16]

Family Albums as Projects of Disidentification

Building on José Muñoz's work, I develop the argument that family portraits and self-portraits are projects of disidentification. Muñoz uses the concept of disidentification to theorize how queer performances enter into dialogue with mainstream media representations of queer subjectivities in order to rework them (1999). He borrows the concept of disidentification from Michel Pecheux, who had developed it from Louis Althusser's theory of ideology and subject formation. According to Pecheux, individuals assume three subject positions vis-à-vis ideological practices. The first is the "good subject," which he describes as being aligned with ideologically normative subjectivities. By contrast, the subject who refuses to affiliate with the normative subjectivities that dominant ideologies propose to her is a "bad subject." Pecheux notes that this second position is not necessarily emancipating because "bad subjects" reinforce dominant ideologies by giving visibility to the normative subjectivities they refuse to identify with. As the third mode of engagement with dominant ideologies, disidentification neither accepts assimilation nor strictly opposes it. Muñoz writes, "Instead of buckling under the pressures of dominant ideology (identification, assimilation) or attempting to break free of its inescapable sphere (counteridentification, utopianism)," disidentification "is a strategy that tries to transform a cultural logic from within" (1999, 11–12).

Critics like Iizawa claim that women's photography is a project to regenerate communities, first and foremost the family. They see evidence to support this claim in photo books that feature the family members of female photographers. Prominent examples of these are Nagashima Yurie's *Kazoku* [*Family*] (1998) and Ume Kayo's *Jīchansama* [*Grandpa*] (1998), which I analyze in this section. I can only note in passing that I consider many other photo books from young female photographers similar to the two volumes I examine here.[17] Hiromix (1996, 1997a, 1997b, 1999, 2000, 2001, 2002), Nagashima (1995b, 2000), and Ninagawa (2000, 2002b, 2004, 2008b, 2012) have all authored photo books that feature portraits of their friends. These books share as much about the photographers' social networks as about their approaches to photography. These photo books, I propose, are commentaries about the forms of sociality and ways of belonging their authors embrace.

Iizawa argues that "family albums" aim to reinforce the family that the economic recession has weakened. He discusses Nagashima's *Kazoku* as a project that strives to rescue the family from breaking down (2010, 87). His argument hinges on his assumption that women are more affected by the collapse of the family because it is through this social institution—which women are responsible for preserving as mothers and homemakers—that women are inserted into society and earn social citizenship. To reach this conclusion, he compares Nagashima's *Kazoku* to Okazaki Kyōko's *Happy House* (1992), which he reads as symptomatic of how young women respond to the deterioration of the family. Okazaki's graphic novel centers on a thirteen-year-old girl named Rumiko, whose father wakes up one day feeling that he no longer wants to be married. The mother is also contemplating leaving the family to start a new life with her lover. Feeling she would not be happy living with her mother or her father, she refuses to join either one. She cannot accept her parents' divorce but instead remains attached to the "happy" memory of the family. Iizawa identifies the same nostalgia for the family in Nagashima's *Kazoku*.[18]

Kazoku can be interpreted as a yearning for the family, but I do not see Nagashima's afterword supporting such an interpretation. Nagashima writes at the end of the volume,

> I used to tell my parents that I did not mean to be born into our family. Though, now, I realize we are all born with an instinct that guides us on how to survive in conditions beyond our control. Certainly it is family, our first relations in the world, through which we learn the basic skills for dealing with a larger society. One day I was born and my life with this family began. I was given safety by having people who were always there for me, but by knowing its limits I was also given solitude—something that has always gotten me up from my warm bed. It made me confused and made me think. . . . I guess it even made me become a photographer

to get at the answer. Since this book is done now, I feel that all there is left to do is to get married or something . . . just kidding! (1998)

When I asked Nagashima about *Kazoku*, she told me that it was a sequel to her *Self-Portraits*, a series of monochrome nude portraits of Nagashima's family that won the second annual Urbanart Award in 1993.[19] In *Kazoku*, Nagashima continues the project she started in *Self-Portraits* of interrogating the parameters within which individuals are recognized as "normal." I do not see nostalgia for familial intimacy in these two series of photographs. Rather, I see them as projects designed to open spaces for what Muñoz defines as a "third mode" of engaging with dominant ideologies of normativity in the context of the family. I see both *Self-Portraits* and *Kazoku* as projects of disidentification that neither accept nor refuse the normative subjectivities that dominant ideologies propose to individuals.

In her afterword to *Kazoku*, Nagashima wonders what makes a family "normal." The last sentence reveals the wry humor that flavors many of Nagashima's works, especially the ones in which she tackles issues pertaining to gender. In *Kazoku*, her family appears "normal," but Nagashima concludes her afterword by quipping that if her family were indeed "normal," her skepticism about the institution of the family would be unfounded and she could embark on having her own family. Yet, clearly, she sees a broad range of distinctions within what constitutes "normal."

Self-Portraits grew out of a rebellious phase Nagashima went through during college.[20] She produced *Self-Portraits* when she briefly reunited with her family. She asked her family members to pose naked, knowing that they would not say "no" to her.[21] Nagashima told me that she wanted to visually challenge the idea that the family was a refuge from the ills of society. Instead, she saw the family as a building block of society within which the same rules apply as the ones that organize society. She stressed that each family member was expected to fulfill his or her role within the family and to do so according to rigid social conventions. Nagashima suggested that if family members suspended their normative familial roles—which she visually represented as going nude—they invited shock, fear, and anxiety.

Iizawa's description of the centerpiece of *Self-Portraits* states, "Against the backdrop of an ordinary Japanese household, a skinhead girl and her family pose as if taking a commemorative anniversary photo" (1996, 162). The photo was taken in the living room of the Nagashima family. Nagashima pointed out to me that within the frame of the portrait, each family member had something that belonged to him or her, except her mother. She concluded that it was because her mother was a homemaker whose space in the house was confined to the kitchen. Nagashima later engaged her mother in her artistic work. In 2016, she put together an exhibition titled *About Home* at the Maho Kubota Gallery in Gaienmaie, Tokyo. Clearly, the question that concerns the relationship between home and family remains a source of inspiration and curiosity for Nagashima, who writes, "For me, photographs are a way of examining things that I don't understand, and also a way of giving shape to all those meaningless bursts of inspiration. What does 'home,' *something I don't understand at all*, mean to me?" (my emphasis).[22]

About Home featured Nagashima's photographs of family members, but much of the exhibition space was taken up by an art installation: a tent that Nagashima created together with her mother. The tent was sewn from clothes, ranging from baby onesies to adult jeans, that had serviced different generations of the family. It was colorful, warm, and inviting.[23] I also sensed tensions in the symbolism of the tent as a representation of home. The tent is a specific form of home. It is fragile and temporary. It is also intimate and evokes camping trips during which foundational principles of the family such as vulnerability and codependence are reinforced.

Ume Kayo's *Jichansama* [*Grandpa*] is another photo book that was similarly misrecognized, in my view, as a project to celebrate the family.[24] *Jichansama*, I suggest, is also a critique of the nuclear family. The book centers on Grandpa, who is willing to strike the most hilarious poses for Ume, who captures him being pushed around in a wheelbarrow by Ume's brother, hanging from a tree like an overripe fruit, and showing off his dentures through a magnifying glass. Unlike Nagashima's *Kazoku*, Ume's project aims to produce upbeat affects, which she embeds within a social critique. Rather than the nuclear family, which was normatively constructed as a space of production and reproduction in the postwar period, Ume's photo book can be interpreted as a project that uses Grandpa's relationship with his grandchildren to envision an alternative model of familial relationships. The relationships she depicts are built on openness, curiosity, and humor. It is ironic that Grandpa came from the postwar generation that had established the importance of the nuclear family that Ume could be perceived to be critiquing. In that context, Grandpa would be the "oppressive" patriarch. Instead, the photos can be viewed as a way of saying that the problems of the nuclear family—which many Japanese, especially women, found suffocating—were not men's fault. Ume's portrayal of Grandpa was a way of letting go in order to move on.

Ume not only broke herself out of a mold but she also freed her grand-

Figure 1.1.   Ume Kayo: Grandfather (1998). Grandpa is willing to strike hilarious poses for Ume. Many of Grandpa's portraits are critical reflections on the idea of familial intimacy.

father, characterizing him beyond the stereotypical male gender role. Ume observes Grandpa with great curiosity, writing, "When he finds a troop of ants, he will follow them to their nest and observe their behavior. . . . When he sees a travel documentary on TV, he will study his map and speak as if he has been there. . . . Grandpa has been taking pictures of his garden for more than a decade now. Although seasons change, miraculously, his pictures all look the same" (Ume 1998). Grandpa is family, and the love between him and his grandchildren is less inhibited and more playful than the love between parents and children. Ume cherishes this form of love. She writes, "For quite a while, Grandpa has been saying that his days are numbered. Yet, he has not yet died, not even once. He might not die at all. That is a good idea" (Ume 1998).[25]

The quote in which Ume describes her Grandpa taking pictures of his garden resonates with critics' view of women's photography as a purportedly feminine style of photography, characterized by women's tendency to take photos in a five-meter radius. Ume's observation that Grandpa practices women's photography is another way for Ume to absolve Grandpa from the role

Figure 1.2. Ume Kayo: Grandfather (1998). Ume's photographs aim to generate upbeat affects.

of being an oppressive patriarch. The connection here is not between home and gender but between home and exploration, which involves movements oriented simultaneously inward and outward—inspecting things not only somewhere else but also close to home. Critics keep trying to erect a boundary between the feminine realm of the home (associated with such values as intimacy and security) and the outside world (linked to ideas of conquering), but Grandpa and such young male photographers as Sanai Masafumi—whose work I will mention in my conclusion—destabilize the analytical framework that distinguish female photography from male photography.

Like the family albums I analyze in this chapter, many of the books young female photographers published focused on relationships. This observation, however, does not justify the gendering of women photographers and their conceptualization as always already socially determined subjects—a point I will elaborate shortly. The problem with the interpretation of women's photography as a project of social reproduction is that it silences the critical impulses in the projects women pursued. It also transforms women's intellectual labor into feminized affective labor. While Iizawa sees nostalgia in family albums, I see projects of envisioning new family formations with new forms of sociality and gender divisions of labor. The artist statement written for Nagashima's exhibition *About Home* supports this observation: "Female experiences are still not openly shared in our society. It feels to me that the society we live in is structured around the man, that all the standard values and moral codes are defined based upon male experiences. For a long time, the sorts of experiences assigned by our society to women were deemed to be unimportant and were driven into the shadows where they couldn't be seen. I feel that it is now of great importance to speak about those experiences and make clear the position I have been placed in."[26] The last two sections of this chapter continue to examine how women used photography to criticize the gender division of labor that characterized the postwar period.

Self-Portraiture and Disidentification

Like family albums, self-portraits were also projects that critiqued the patriarchal power structures that mobilized women to regimes of invisible labor. They offered important counterpoints to critics who saw female photographers as women first and photographers second. The self-portraits of women photographers make it amply clear that the focus on gender in women's photography was primarily a criticism of everyday patriarchy rather than an expression of women's commitment to social reproduction. To develop this argument, I look at self-portraits of Nagashima Yurie and Hiromix, who, along with Ninagawa Mika, jointly won the Kimura Ihei Award in 2001.[27]

Both Nagashima and Hiromix departed from mainstream media representations of women. As such, they pursued projects of disidentification and began transforming the logic that restrained the opportunities of women to develop DIY careers. This section examines how these two photographers took hold of the masculinized camera and used it to question their gendering and critics' interpretations of their labor. The net idols, bloggers, online traders, and cell phone novelists whose careers I analyze in the following chapters turned to the digital economy in pursuit of the same goals. However, the overwhelmingly male owners and designers of online platforms—like the male photography critics—created platforms that encoded their own gender biases in their platform designs. In doing so, they—like the male photography critics—ended up making women's intellectual labor invisible. As online platforms adopted the practices of gender discrimination that characterized the traditional labor market, they also established new continuities between women's reproductive labor, female photographers' proto-digital labor, and the digital labor of net idols, bloggers, online traders, and cell phone novelists.

Among the artists that critics labeled as "girly" photographers, the issue of gender was most pertinent to Nagashima Yurie's work. Nagashima was also the first to debut when she won the Parco UrbanArt Prize for her *Self-Portraits* in 1993. The photographs in her first published photo book, *Nagashima Yurie* (1995a), include self-portraits of the author (some of which are nude or semi-nude), while others present her parodying predominant representations of call girls and female models (*gurabia aidoru*) that appear in magazines targeted to men. Most of the sexualized images are juxtaposed to portraits of Nagashima that are entirely stripped of all gender markers. This sequencing of the photographs disrupts the male gaze. The volume also includes three photographs that portray Nagashima before she turned ten years old. These images intensify the signifying force of the desexualized images and, therefore, they are instrumental to contextualizing the project as an investigation of the links between representation and power, gaze and subordination, self, and other.[28]

In an interview with Lesley Martin, Nagashima explained the project as follows: "To me the most important concept was the act of taking a photograph of myself. The master-servant relationship between photographers and models in Japan in the '90s reflected the power relations between men and women generally. As a form of opposition, I wanted to contest photos that might look like art but that simply conceal the dynamic that uses female bodies to obtain profit. I used the work to parody things like the poses and adornment of call girls in the photo flyers pasted inside public telephone booths and circulated as sex symbols" (Martin 2014, 13). Nagashima's book, it seems to me, also raised broader questions about representation as a practice of interpellation.[29] For instance, building on Judith Butler's reading of drag as a project that simultaneously denaturalizes and re-idealizes heterosexual gender norms (1993), what can we say about the potential of parody to disrupt normative gender roles and forms of sexuality? Is parody able to undermine the power and foreclose the pleasure of the objectifying gaze?[30]

Nagashima recounted to me that she was inspired by the Riot Grrrl movement's claim that women had to seize the means of representation if they wanted to overturn the practices (and particular representations) that subordinated them (see Feigenbaum 2007). She mentioned that she also took a cue from Judith Butler (1990) to investigate how the (male) gaze succeeded in denying autonomous subjectivities to women by defining woman as the "other" of man. The idea of "girly" photography, for instance, reflects an understanding of women's photography as the opposite of men's photography.

The assumption that underwrites this formulation is that without men's photography, the works of women photographers cannot be rendered intelligible.

The queer studies' reworking of Althusser's theory of interpellation is helpful to understand projects of subverting power relations through photography. I see Nagashima's photo book as a project of disidentification. Butler writes that interpellation is formative because it initiates the individual into the status of the subject. Interpellation is just as much enabling, however, as it is violating (1993). There is no subject prior to its constructions, but the subject is also not determined by its constructions. It is the space of this ambivalence that opens up the possibility to rework the very terms by which interpellation occurs. That is, I see the photo book as a project of charting the terrain beyond the subject positions Jose Muñoz describes as "good subjects" and "bad subjects." It asks whether adopting nongendered or ambiguously gendered subject positions could disrupt practices that harness gender as a structuring principle of difference and inequality.

Many of the photographs in Nagashima's book portray her in the punk phase of her youth with her hair shaved, nose pierced, and gender markers muted on her body. These images unsettle the anchoring of women to regimes of social reproduction through disengaging from such feminized behaviors as cute, positive, forward-looking, nurturing, self-denying, and accommodating. They instead re-subjectify their models by diverting attention from the body to affective states such as being disoriented, unraveled, confused, pensive, preoccupied, engaged, or disengaged. As such, Nagashima's photo book also challenges an important claim in the discourse on "girly" photography, which is that women produce photography that creates positive affects and makes people "feel good" (*kimochi ii shashin*). I find the volume luminously insightful because it brings home the point that distinctly dissimilar (even incommensurate) concerns drove young women to photography in the 1990s. At the same time, the volume foreshadows the pernicious nature of such claims that the works of women artists merge into one genre—an assertion that justifies the label of "girly" photography.

Specifically, I see more intellectual labor than feminized affective labor in Nagashima's projects.[31] Earlier, I argued that Hardt and Negri's separation of affective and intellectual labor was arbitrary, as most forms of contemporary labor (and especially digital labor) involve both (see Jarrett 2017). This held true for the labor female photographers expended as well, yet critics tended to see feminized affective labor in "girly" photography, not intellectual labor. Similarly, net idols, bloggers, online traders, and cell phone novelists were not successful in challenging expectations that they perform feminized affective labor. As noted earlier, these entrepreneurial women tried to develop careers within infrastructures infused with patriarchal gender biases. Ironically, they found that rejecting their branding as "female bloggers" or "housewife/traders" only further limited their opportunities to develop DIY careers. After all, occupational identities that conformed with women's conventional gender roles as wives and mothers made female entrepreneurs more recognizable and thus more marketable. Consequently, entrepreneurial women tended to act cute, used polite language, and sported soft feminine fashions with abundant lace and frills. That is, while "girly" photographers inspired other women to develop DIY careers, they also demonstrated that challenging prevalent gender norms was not necessarily conducive to realizing one's career goals. Conforming to gendered norms of self-presentation and behavior also undermined women's efforts to destabilize the dominant gender division of labor that assigned them to unwaged reproductive or waged irregular labor.

The concept of "girly" photography that "makes people feel good" was more apparent in the works of Hiromix. While Nagashima attacked patriarchal power structures from within these structures (by engaging in a dialogue with them), Hiromix evaded them altogether to carve out autonomous spaces where young women like her felt they could belong to themselves.[32] Unlike Nagashima, who investigated the connections between femininity and subordination, Hiromix was not interested in giving up her femininity. Yet she erased the male gaze in a move that critics read as "narcissistic."

Hiromix debuted in 1995 when she was seventeen and won the grand prize at Canon's New Cosmos of Photography for a color-copied, diary-style photo book entitled *Seventeen Girl Days* [The Days of a Seventeen-Year-Old Girl]. One of the contest's jury members, the art curator Nanjo Fumio, described Hiromix's photographs as "kitschy" and "mysteriously glamorous."[33] Another jury member, internationally renowned art photographer Araki Nobuyoshi, commented, "Girls tend to hold nothing back, and don't think too much. Without thinking too much, they let their feelings rule their actions. Her feelings that she wants to create and try anything, as well as her flexibility are apparent. Guys think too much."[34] Both responses align with Iizawa's analysis of "girly" photography in that all three men see women's photography as the opposite of men's photography. Note that "mysterious," which commonly surfaces in discussions of Hiromix's photography, is also a key concept in practices of "othering" that Edward Said theorized as Orientalism (1978).

While critics were puzzled by Hiromix's photography of the everyday—for example, pictures of friends, meals, and cats—they recognized Hiromix's talent as a portraitist. Iizawa went as far as to claim that Hiromix was "the world's best self-portraitist" (2010, 109). Other observers marveled about Hiromix's unique ability to portray herself as mysterious and enigmatic. She included portraits of herself in many of her photo books (e.g., 1996, 2000, 2002), but we can find the most self-portraits in the volume entitled *Hiromix* (1998).

Hiromix snapped many of her self-portraits selfie-style, with her hand holding the camera stretched out in front of her.[35] In others, she used a tripod, her camera's self-timer, or a remote control. Although she did not pose nude for her self-portraits, they were commonly described as "sexy." Many of her self-portraits capture her dressing and revealing her naked legs or shoulders. Her characteristic mod look—in the 1990s, she dressed in 1960s and 1970s fashions—also evoked femininity, as her style was reminiscent of an earlier era with less flexibly defined gender roles and more institutionalized gender inequality. Observers commonly interpreted her fashion style as an index of femininity and tended to see her more as a young woman than a young artist. They interpreted the carefully choreographed spontaneity of Hiromix's self-portraits as expressions of young women's natural talent to perform cuteness.

Hiromix, however, hated being described as feminine, cute, and young.[36] On many occasions, she snapped at journalists or even abruptly ended interviews when asked to comment on the cuteness and youthfulness of her photographs. She insisted that, in her soul, she was a woman in her fifties.

Hiromix routinely refused to participate in discussions about her photography, stating that critics could not possibly understand her because they were not her intended target audience. Iizawa quotes Hiromix saying, "I take photographs only we [people of my age] will understand. It is not my goal to take pictures that everyone will appreciate. If it is only a few people who understand my photographs, I will be happy with those few" (Iizawa 2012, 196). In *Hiromix*, she writes, "Youth reflects transparency and beauty. Despite our lack of experience, the world often confronts us with unforgivable situations. We believe, more than anyone, in things that cannot be seen. Many unknown worlds are awaiting us. Surrounded by people we love. We smile carefree smiles. It was perhaps because I wanted to keep a record of this that I take photos of myself" (1998). The interpretive guidance in the statement is minimalist, which I understand as Hiromix's effort to erase the critical apparatus and create an autonomous space where decoding is difficult for those who do not belong.[37] Unlike Nagashima, Hiromix refuses to engage in discussing and theorizing her work. I read this refusal to enter into dialogue with critics as a strategy of disidentification that Hiromix pushes toward disengagement. Preserving this kind of autonomy in one's work was possible in the context of photography. In the digital economy, however, women had to

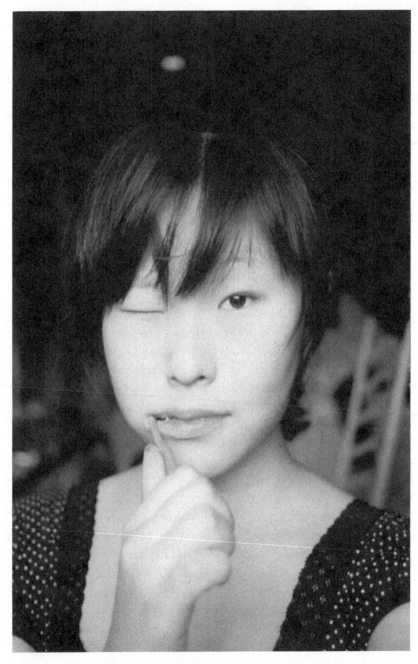

Figure 1.3.   Hiromix: Hiromix Works (2000). Hiromix was a forerunner of selfie culture. She snapped many of her self-portraits with her digital camera held in her hand with her arm stretched out in front of her.

Figure 1.4.
Hiromix: Hiromix
Works (2000). Critics
commonly described
Hiromix's self-portraits
as "mysteriously
glamorous."

navigate their ways through online platforms, the designs of which they had little control over.

The Digital and the Analog in Projects of Disidentification

Hiromix, Nagashima, and especially Ninagawa were fixtures in the Japanese media scene. They were regularly interviewed in women's magazines and asked to comment on their work. A staple feature of these interviews was commentary on how much these photographers loved their work and why they enjoyed working as photographers. It is clear from these commentaries that women photographers proactively strove to make the labor of photography pleasurable for themselves.

In an interview, Nagashima told fellow photographer Honma Takashi that if she does not enjoy her work, the product of her labor will be bland and uninteresting.[38] She also stressed that she is not willing to climb a mountain to get a good shot, mocking the self-denying forms of labor she sees older generations of male art photographers pursuing who use multiple cameras and elaborate lighting setups to shoot meticulously staged scenarios. Iizawa interprets Nagashima's statement as evidence that she adheres to a feminine way of

Figure 1.5.
Hiromix: Hiromix 01
(2002). Hiromix's
self-portraits are often
characterized as sexy.

practicing photography, which he characterizes as undisciplined, amateurish, and pleasure-driven. He notes that a key distinguishing feature of women's photography is that women shoot pictures predominantly within a five-meter radius (2010). One, however, can also interpret a preference for shooting photographs within a five-meter radius merely as an artistic choice.

Another way women stress their desire to derive pleasure from photography is to comment on why they use particular camera technologies. Iizawa argues that it was developments in digital cameras that drew young women to photography in the early and mid-1990s. He emphasizes that women are less interested in tinkering with technologies than men (Iizawa 2010) and describes "girly" photographers and their relationships to their cameras as follows: "As soon as they see something they like, something attractive, something cute, they click the camera. The click and love are synonymously in circuit. Big heavy cameras requiring troublesome handling therefore become a nuisance. A camera thrown in a purse or a satchel together with cosmetics, easy to take out whenever one pleases—this is what is needed. The compact camera with auto-focus mechanism made this possible" (1996, 160).

The truth is, however, that although most female photographers started their careers using digital cameras, many of them later switched to analog equipment.[39] Hiromix is a notable exception. And the media have exhaustively exploited her preference for digital cameras to argue that female photographers were amateurs who would have never turned to photography had it not been for the development of digital cameras. A Japanese journalist, for example, wrote the following for the *New York Times*: "Hiromix sidestepped all that [learning through the master-apprentice system], most likely in her red spike heels. She had never taken a course, never studied with anyone and wouldn't know a print dryer if she fell over it. She admitted freely that she didn't know what a strobe looked like but 'it doesn't matter because my camera flashes automatically!'"[40]

This view of Hiromix is typical, though blatantly untrue.[41] Hiromix explained on numerous occasions that she is perfectly capable of using an analog camera but finds them unsuitable for practicing point and shoot photography. When trying to capture the "magic moment" in which the ordinary and the extraordinary collide, she needs to be able to immediately press the shutter. A digital camera better facilitates this, and she takes one wherever she goes in her constant search of that "magic moment." As Hiromix further elaborated, she sees no need to stage photos because she sees the world itself in photographs.[42]

Ninagawa Mika, on the other hand, stages her photographs and insists that she does not like digital cameras.[43] In an interview with psychologist Saito Tamaki, she claimed that she is not the type of photographer who carries cameras around. She says that such moments in which she wishes she had a camera never occur to her. Ninagawa argues that digital cameras do not allow her to achieve the peace of mind that she most enjoys in her work, and claims that to shoot good photographs, she needs to switch between different mental states and modes of operation. She considers unpredictability indispensable in taking a good picture. In her view, digital cameras do not leave space for that. She says the following to Saito, "Taking photographs with a digital camera does not offer the same sense of tension that working with analog cameras offers, specifically, that one cannot redo a photograph when one makes a mistake. If there is no thrill in work, that is disappointing."[44] Ninagawa explains to Saito that digital cameras do not allow her to be completely focused, and without complete concentration, she cannot take photographs that have spirit (*nen*). Saito understands this as Ninagawa's effort to capture a kind of interiority in her pictures—something that Akasaka Mari called "psychography" (*nensha*).[45] Similarly, Ninagawa told Iizawa in 2005 that the vivid colors of her photographs were also a result of her reaching a very high state of concentration (Iizawa 2005, 72). She claimed that, contrary to popular perception, she did not use filters or edit colors digitally. She might have occasionally tweaked the colors during the film development and printing process, but she kept altering the colors of her pictures to a minimum.

Ninagawa frequently muses on the pleasures she derives from her work. She writes in *Acid Bloom*, "When I am about to shoot a good picture, I am in between this world and another world. I suspend everything I know about the world and myself. It is in the moment in which I feel that I am becoming that very plant or that very insect that stops to rest on a plant I aim my camera at that I press the shutter" (2003a). In a 2008 interview, Ninagawa claimed the following: "I do not press the shutter until I am able to become so focused and alert that I feel that the lights are being turned off one by one, the people around me disappear one by one, I do not feel the temperature and do not hear any noise. I do not press the shutter until I am so centered that I feel only what is within the viewfinder of my camera. To tell the truth, I am not in this world when I press the shutter. I do not at all remember those exact moments in which I take my pictures."[46] In another interview, Ninagawa says, "When I am really concentrated on a subject matter like flowers, I gradually shut out the outside world. I have a strange feeling as though I am vacuum-sealed with the subject" (2010, 39).

Iizawa calls this the shamanistic character in Ninagawa's personality—an ability to traverse between a rational state of mind and a condition that reintegrates women with nature by activating their natural instincts (2012, 212). Similarly, Ninagawa's father, Ninagawa Yukio,[47] described Ninagawa's photography as follows: "I recognize her intuition and the caliber of her ability to choose among fractions of a second. It might also be a biological impulse or reflex that allows her to decide on the exact moment to press the shutter button. I think it's safe to say that her talent approached a natural, animalistic instinct" (Ninagawa 2013, 51). This activation of the women/nature versus men/culture binarism is another way to gender women photographers.

Ninagawa also stresses that analog cameras help her establish rapport with her models, which enables her models to do their best possible performances. She says, "To take a good photo, I need to be able to fall in love with the model I photograph. Digital cameras do not allow me to develop that intense relationship with my models. Photography is art, not science. It is not a rational activity, yet digital cameras are trying to rationalize it. That is why I avoid using them."[48] Recall Iizawa's claim that women photographers cultivate an emotional relationship with their models as opposed to seeing them objectively. Like Nagashima Yurie, who theorized her relationship with her models as a relationship that involved the politically charged practice of "othering," Ninagawa reflects on the role of technologies in mediating her relationships with her models. Tsuchiya Anna, one of her favorite models and close friends, who also played the heroine in Ninagawa's first film, *Sakuran*, reports that she loves being photographed by Ninagawa. She says that Ninagawa is able to teleport her back into her childhood—into a state in which she feels protected, carefree, and happy (2009, 138–39).

By contemplating their preferences for specific camera technologies, photographers celebrate their freedom to make decisions about the conditions of their work and transform their labor into a meaningful experience. In the early and mid-1990s, women photographers like Nagashima, Hiromix, and Ninagawa started the trend this book explores, but they could not have seen how the digital economy would mobilize women to new regimes of unwaged labor that it harnessed to advance its own development. It is, however, curious that many of the women photographers who succeeded in developing careers as professional art photographers use analog cameras. These photographers argue that analog equipment enables them to maintain control over the conditions of their work and experience photography as a meaningful, even pleasurable, activity.

Conclusion: Photography and Feminism in Recessionary Japan

In his 2010 volume, *The Era of "Girly Photography,"* Iizawa Kōtarō anchored women photographers to the normative gender roles that characterized the postwar period and interpreted their photographic practice as a project wedded to social reproduction. Like other critics, he did not give sufficient credit to the feminist critique that many women photographers encoded in their work, which is the argument Nagashima makes about "girly" photography in her master's thesis. In an interview with Lesley Martin, Nagashima astutely summed up her view on the critical reception of the works of women photographers: "In the '90s, women artists were lumped into the single framework of 'the female.' The keywords were 'compact camera,' 'daily life,' 'snapshots,' etc. Everyone was seen as simply being interested in expressing femininity. But since then, the activities of female photographers in Japan have been similar to those of male photographers, in the sense that there is great diversity, and diversity is increasing even more, I think" (Martin 2014, 13).

The concept of "girly" photography may be understood in the context of a massive backlash against feminism during the 2000s that Ueno Chizuko documents in her 2010 book *Hating Women: Japan's Misogyny* (2010). Many women photographers used photography to ask questions about gender discrimination and sexist power structures. These questions, however, evaded the male critics who found young women's angry reactions "sexy." Not surprisingly, men photographers who belonged to the same generation as Hiromix, Ninagawa, and Nagashima were not expected to practice photography as a form of social reproduction. Sanai Masafumi, for instance, explains his photo series, *Stoned and Dethroned,* as follows: "I dwell on details. Because nothing makes a difference and *I stopped caring* [my emphasis]. The breathing of the trees, the temperature of the sun, the murmuring of insects, the structure of the flowers, the sound of the subway wheels grinding. A very quiet world is spread out directly beneath the August sun. Then my thoughts disappeared, and I became a plant. Although I haven't quit walking, I probably won't move from here anymore."[49] Sanai is stoned and dethroned—not building social ties. At the same time, his statement supports my argument that the boundary that critics drew between female photography and male photography is arbitrary.[50] Sanai's thoughts about photography resonate closely with the commentaries of women photographers who shut out the world to become the subjects of their own photos. Sanai is also describing his work as photography pursued in a five-meter radius.

Although many women photographers like Nagashima and Ninagawa were influenced by feminism and used photography to ask questions about gender inequality, discrimination, sexist power structures, and the objectification of women, critics like Iizawa did not see (or did not give sufficient credit to) the feminist critique of gender inequity that many women photographers encoded in their works. They labeled the works of these artists as "girly" and described "girly" photography as cute. The very concept of "girly" photography was a patriarchal construct that invited sexist commentaries about women photographers, similar to identifying female online traders as housewives despite the fact that many of these traders were neither wives nor mothers. Both constructs characterize the women as amateurs who should not delude themselves into thinking that they could compete with professionals, who were dominantly men.

Photographers such as Mori Mariko, Yanagi Miwa, or Torimitsu Momoyo, who were a few years older than Nagashima, Ninagawa, and Hiromix, all distanced themselves from the "girly" label and asked the questions of second-wave feminism. Torimitsu's first photography project featured a Japanese salaryman-robot that crawled through the streets of New York, London, Paris, Amsterdam, Sydney, and Rio de Janeiro as if he were a soldier deployed in battles. The salaryman-robot was followed by a young woman dressed as a nurse—a trope for the homemaker of the postwar period whose principal role was to provide care. Similarly, Mori Mariko's 1994 performance project, *Play With Me*, shows her standing outside an electronics store in Akihabara wearing a form-fitting cyborg suit and light blue hair in long ponytails. In another project, *Tea Ceremony III* (1995), Mori plays an office lady mechanically serving tea to salarymen who pass her in the street. Playing on the connection between "alien" and "alienation" (as experienced in the alienating labor of office ladies), she wears a conservative office uniform and a silver cap featuring large pointy ears.

Like the self-portraits of Nagashima and Hiromix, these projects broaden the distinctions within the concepts of femininity and womanhood—a project that perhaps Yanagi Miwa took the furthest. Yanagi's *Elevator Girls* portrays young women being slowly effaced by a near-grotesque form of feminized affective labor that these women are paid to perform in a small box over and over, day after day (2007a). Yanagi's second project, *My Grandmothers*, similarly disoriented critics in Japan (2009). She interprets the negative reception of this project in Japan as follows: "It seems some men are afraid of women who embrace their aging. Women live a long time after their reproductive period ends. . . . and, on average women live longer than men. People in Japan currently have the longest life span in the world, and younger couples have fewer children. Perhaps men are instinctively afraid that the country will be filled with old women" (2010, 49). Nevertheless, Yanagi continues pursuing feminist projects that portray women in ways that depart from representations that emphasize beauty, sweetness, and cuteness—portrayals that tend to dominate Japan's media landscape. Yanagi's *Windswept Women: The Old Girl's Troupe* (2010), for instance, depicts women who celebrate their aging as a source of empowerment. The female models Yanagi captures with her camera furiously shake their breasts that reach their hips and proudly show off thighs that are thick like old tree trunks.

What might explain the critical misrecognition of the feminist projects in women's photography is the failed project of second-wave feminism in Japan, which is also an important backdrop to understand the other techno-social assemblages I analyze in the book. In Japan, second-wave feminism was an academic discourse until the 1990s. In fact, women photographers played an important role in introducing second-wave feminism into the mainstream. Many of these photographers, however, went beyond second-wave feminism and asked the questions of third-wave feminism, with which critics and the media were not familiar. Young women's claim to have more choices, such as the choice to embrace their femininity (e.g., Hiromix), was predominantly misunderstood and inspired photography critics to analyze women's photography in continuity with women's role in the postwar regime of reproductive labor. By fighting this interpretation and reflecting on the relationships between gender, labor, and technology, women photographers cleared the path for other young women to build DIY careers in the emerging digital economy.

The Labor of Cute

NET IDOLS IN THE DIGITAL ECONOMY

Inspired by the "girly" photographers, many young women took advantage of the expansion of the internet and created personal websites that featured their self-portraits and diaries. According to a veteran net idol, it was in 1999 that fans started calling these women "net idols" (*netto aidoru*). Another net idol explained to me that women embarked on this career in search of meaning in their otherwise banal lives. As internet entrepreneurs began developing an infrastructure around the net idol trend, however, these women quickly found themselves pursuing feminized affective labor in the digital economy. To compete for attention within the online frenzy of sweet smiling faces, women needed to do more than post new photos and regularly update their diaries. They also had to cultivate relationships with fans. Building a fan base, however, was seldom the ultimate goal of a net idol. Instead, these young women hoped to transform their net idol careers into meaningful and lucrative employment. When they achieved this goal (or gave up, which was overwhelmingly the case), they shut down their websites.

Japan's digital economy evolved in the midst of a long recession that unhinged processes of capital accumulation from practices of social reproduction, while pushing the latter into a relentless crisis. Focusing on the period between 1998 and 2004, I demonstrate that the rapid growth of the digital economy during these years was a result of this economy's success in mobilizing young women into a new regime of feminized affective labor. According to net idols, their fans were young men who found themselves in precarious situations as employers were downsizing their workforce and had begun dismantling the system of lifetime employment. While women photographers fought to distance themselves from the labor of social reproduction and their associated gender roles, net idols saw the pursuit of feminized affective labor as a means to an end. They hoped to translate their unpaid labor into new careers.[1]

In this chapter, I argue that not only were net idols instrumental to the development of Japan's digital economy, they also furthered the erosion of job security and, by extension, the transformation of Japan's human capital regime. I unfold my argument in three parts. First, I trace how the net idol trend evolved as a techno-social assemblage. I focus on two actors: the net idols and the internet entrepreneurs who developed an infrastructure around the online activities of net idols. This infrastructure consisted of web services that offered net idols tools to create their own web pages, net idol ranking sites, net idol information sites, and an online net idol academy. I read the emergence of the net idol trend as a script that reveals how internet entrepreneurs have expanded the social factory. As such, this chapter explores how the social factory transforms feminized affective labor and social reproduction into new sources of profit. It also expands this inquiry by asking how the social factory fine-tunes the human capital regime to support its unique mode of accumulation.[2] By promising women opportunities to develop careers, the digital economy promotes what Paolo Virno calls the ideology of the possible—"a sense of being constantly confronted with a phantasmagoric ensemble of simultaneous opportunities" (2007, 45). I document how internet entrepreneurs contributed to the development of the net idol trend by promoting this ideology.

Second, I explore how the digital economy transformed the net idols' investment in building a fan base—that is, the feminized affective labor of social reproduction—into new sources of profit. The production of cuteness was indispensable to developing a career as a net idol. Originally a subculture developed by young women in the late 1970s, cute culture had grown into a multitrillion-yen business by the 1990s. Scholars have interpreted young women's participation in the production of cute as a form of resistance to a work-oriented adult society and as a retreat to a space within which young women find redemption by indulging in infantile play and passive behavior (Kinsella 1995). I propose instead that we consider the production of cute in the realm of work, not play. Cute designates not only particular looks but also particular behaviors, the performance of which requires feminized affective labor. Comments posted on net idol sites testify that it was cute behaviors that fans found most appealing about their idols.[3] Internet entrepreneurs, in turn, harnessed the online communities that emerged from the interactions between net idols and their fans to develop banner advertising.

In the third part, I examine how the net idol trend catalyzed the transformation of Japan's human capital regime into new sources of profit for internet entrepreneurs. Stressing that employment security was no longer attainable, the new model of human capital development encouraged individuals to cultivate unique skills and self-brands that would enable them to craft DIY careers. I will trace how human capital development has become equivalent to the pursuit of hope labor by examining the career of one of Japan's most famous net idols, Nakamura Toyomi. After experimenting with various activities online, Nakamura developed a career she called *photo-therapy*. While she described the labor that photo-therapy involved as enjoyable and meaningful, I also learned that this career did not enable her to quit her day job.

By examining how the digital economy capitalized on young women's aspirations to further its own expansion, I also offer a counterpoint to the sociology of labor that asks how to revive hope among young people in Japan who are excluded from systems of job security and are struggling to create forward-moving life projects (Genda 2005). The net idols I interviewed did not conform to this portrait. To the contrary, they actively tried to make the social factory work for them. The net idol phenomenon, therefore, reveals a sense of nostalgia plaguing the scholarship on youth and work in Japan, which tends to reify a rupture between the era of normative developmentalism and the recessionary period. By contrast, the net idol trend illuminates a continuity rather than a disconnect between these periods. Similar to the ways in which women's unwaged labor in the home was instrumental to maintaining high economic growth during the postwar period, women's unpaid labor remains central to a society in which growing labor precarity and pervasive uncertainty about the future generated a massive demand for feminized affective labor.

The Net Idol Phenomenon

Young women did not embark on a career as a net idol to take on more work. They quickly realized, however, that success in the net idol universe required a substantial time commitment. To trace how the digital economy has incorporated young women into a regime of feminized affective labor, I reconstruct how the net idol trend evolved into a techno-social assemblage. In particular, I examine what aspirations enthused young women to become net idols and what infrastructures internet entrepreneurs developed around these ambitions. I suggest that the digital economy was able to mobilize women to unpaid affective labor because it seduced them with the idea that it was viable to craft meaningful DIY careers in this economy. By doing so, the digital economy also recoded women's unpaid labor as investment in developing new skills and self-brands that were indispensable to building their careers.

Net idols included some high school and college students, but most were young office ladies and homemakers. Many of these women felt disappointed when they realized that being a net idol required the same investment of feminized affective labor they performed in their day jobs. One told me that she created her website to find purpose in her life, something she lacked as a homemaker. While many kept their net idol careers a secret from their families (for as long as they could),[4] one net idol noted that her husband supported her net life. He appreciated the fact that he was able to follow the daily activities of his wife through the internet while being away from her. Another homemaker/net idol shared a similar view. She reasoned that housewives became net idols to fight what they experienced as a crisis of identity. She explained, "Housewives have a good reason to become net idols. The work of a housewife is devalued, and young housewives often lose sight of what their purpose in life is. I would say I even lost my sense of self (*jibun wo miushinatteita'n desu*). The media talk a lot about housewives who become 'kitchen drinkers' or who cheat on their husbands. Unlike them, I am not a self-destructive personality, so I became a net idol."

Some net idols, however, took the desire for self-healing to an extreme, as evidenced in 2006 by the much-publicized cases of two net idols, Hirata Erika and Nanjo Aya. Hirata Erika used her diary to describe how she was able to overcome her sense of despair, which she found "suffocating," by setting fire to buildings and watching them burn to ashes. Similarly, Nanjo Aya, who hoped that her net idol career would help her defeat her anxiety disorder, terminated her life in front of her webcam.

In my interviews, net idols cited reasons such as self-exploration (*jibun sagashi*), self-realization (*jiko jitsugen*), and fun (*asobi*) to describe what they initially sought in their net idol careers. At the outset, it is important to highlight that it took considerable courage for young women to become net idols. My interlocutors emphasized that the popular media relentlessly berated net idols for their narcissism. In my view, the fact that young women invested long hours in building their net idol careers lends support to the claim that women brought aspirations to this career far beyond the mere desire to have fun. One net idol stated the following:

Initially, I created my website to have fun. I understood that the figure indicating how many people accessed my websites did not equal what I was worth as a human being. However, I did not want to lose to other net idols. I received thirty emails per day and responded to all of them. When I nominated myself for a net idol contest, I spent countless hours writing emails to my fans asking them to vote for me. While being a net idol, I felt like I was doing some type of service work. It was just an awful lot of work. (Yoshihara 2004, 101)

Correspondingly, observers have highlighted the demanding nature of mastering the writing styles characteristic of web-based diaries and the photographic conventions net idols had to adopt if they wanted to succeed in the net idol universe. Considering these challenges, it is not surprising that an extremely high percentage of women gave up this career shortly after embarking on it, as Muramatsu Takahide points out (2001).

The net idol trend took off while the architecture of the digital economy was still evolving. It was not until 1999 that broadband internet service began replacing dial-up service. Although Japan's "second telecom deregulation" occurred in 1999,[5] it took another two years for the quality of internet services to begin to improve and for the cost of the service to significantly decrease.[6] The technical challenges the first generation of net idols (1998–2000) encountered in creating their websites attest to the determination (and, in some cases, desperation) of these young women. Before 1999, net idols had to learn some basic- to intermediate-level coding, and the process of developing a web page was time consuming.[7] Free services that offered web space and tools to create websites did not appear until 2000.[8] These services targeted women with no coding skills and offered them the opportunity to create their own web pages while drawing on their online activities to develop banner advertising.[9] They also made net idol sites more consumer-friendly by standardizing them. As such, these portals played a key role in transforming the net idol trend from a subcultural activity to a mainstream practice. By generating content-specific communities, these portals also expanded the net idol market. The congregation of net idols around these content-specific communities offered fans convenient access to net idol sites and allowed them to compare net idols.

As more and more women became net idols, an infrastructure began to evolve around the trend in the early 2000s. Including net idol ranking sites, a net idol academy, published photo books, and net idol agents,[10] this infrastructure began molding net idols into service providers and their fans, mainly male freeters (irregular workers) and *otaku* (geeky men), into a new niche market. Fans found net idols appealing because they were able to communicate with them. By developing personal relationships with their fans, net idols boosted their fans' egos. Note that fans did not pay net idols for their feminized affective labor. In exchange for the personal attention they received, fans helped net idols identify their talents and served as audiences on which net idols could test their photography, poetry, cosplay performances, or singing skills. In return, net idols helped their fans sustain themselves in their everyday lives. Indeed, when a net idol stopped responding to a fan's emails, that fan moved on to another net idol. One net idol called this trend the "my idol only" (*boku dake no aidoru*) trend.[11] Not all fans of net idols were men. Comments posted on net idol sites suggest that net idols also had female fans, some of which derived pleasure from following the careers of entrepreneurial women, while others enjoyed seeing "larger-than-life" women who had the courage to continue cultivating youthful forms of femininity that mature (and married) women were expected to leave behind.

Web services such as geocities.co.jp, freeweb.ne.jp/, and members.goo.ne.jp/ offered net idols tools to produce their own web pages. The owners of these platforms, which were the forerunners of blogging platforms, identified the desire to socialize as the main reason young people were attracted to the internet. As such, they focused on developing bulletin board systems (BBS) to facilitate communication among internet users. These platforms encouraged net idols to socialize with their fans by performing feminized affective labor. This example illustrates how internet entrepreneurs encoded their own gender biases into the designs of online platforms. Some developers even experimented with applications that would charge fans for chatting with net idols online. Others tried to incorporate the net idol trend into the burgeoning sex chat business. Eventually, these efforts all failed. It is important to note that these platforms restrained, and in some cases even foreclosed, opportunities to build DIY careers by limiting data storage space (initially, up to 50 MB) and prohibiting the pursuit of commercial activities. In short, the architecture of these portals was designed to mobilize net idols into a regime of feminized affective labor.

Net idol ranking sites, such as the portal named Net Idol Search,[12] further advanced this tendency. These sites refined and promoted a set of criteria and practices that net idols could not avoid adopting if they wanted to succeed. Internet entrepreneur Sasai Takashi launched the website in 2000 with the goal of generating revenue from advertising placed on the site.[13] He touted the site as a place where net idols and fans were able to connect, but he screened the applications of net idols and reserved the right to decline requests for registration.[14] By aggregating information about net idol sites, Net Idol Search enabled fans to compare net idols and offered a system for ranking net idols by the number of votes gathered from fans through emails. The rules allowed fans to submit one vote per day.

The site stated, "Ranking is the barometer for the popularity of net idols. Each vote will strengthen a net idol's determination and help her get one step closer to realizing her dream,"[15] and it gave weekly announcements of voting results. Net idols spent countless hours emailing their fans to encourage them to vote for them. One net idol told me that it was a common practice among net idols to create alliances among themselves by posting links to other net idols' web pages to their own websites. Ranking sites, however, pitted net idols against each other. Similarly, between 1999 and 2001, several photo books were published that featured the most popular net idols. The competition to appear in these photo books was also not conducive to the development of solidarity among net idols.[16]

Another internet entrepreneur, Suzuki Masashi, launched the portal named Net Idols Information Guide in 2005.[17] Although he started this portal after the net idol trend peaked, Suzuki had recognized the business opportunities in the digital economy much earlier. In 1998, aiming to generate revenue from online advertising, he established Media Net Japan, a company that offered a free service to create personal websites. In 1999, he launched Girls' Town, an online community portal for women that he claimed was the first of its kind. He now writes books and articles in addition to lecturing about search engine optimization (SEO), online marketing, and strategies to develop successful online retail businesses. He is the chairperson of the All Japan SEO Association, which offers both seminars and consulting services. In short, his work illustrates how male internet entrepreneurs strove to generate revenue from online advertising by developing an infrastructure around the net idol trend. Although diverse ambitions inspired women to become net idols, this infrastructure mobilized them to develop their careers within the expanding business of online entertainment. The Net Idols Information Guide, for instance, defined net idols as "entertainers" and allowed them to register on the site according to categories that reflected their skills in such areas of entertainment as self-portraiture, costume play, diaries and blogs, or music.

Lastly, another freelance writer, Onda Hisatoshi, launched a website in 2000 called Net Idol Academy.[18] Onda maintains numerous other websites that are linked together and fashions himself as an expert in such wide-ranging topics as cyber-culture, Japanese composition, healthy living, and diet. His websites offer advice on how to compose official letters, Christmas cards, or cards to sick friends. He also maintains a website that offers students help with writing book reviews and another that features his weight loss diary. Before becoming a freelance writer, he worked for a publishing company where he edited test preparation materials and was a part-time prep school teacher. Most importantly, before he launched Net Idol Academy, Onda was a self-identified fan of net idols, and fits the profile of what net idols described to me as their typical fan.

Net Idol Academy offers tutorials that teach women how to create a web page, write diaries, take appealing photos, choose appropriate locations for photo shoots, promote themselves, and take precautions to prevent harassment from fans. Compared to Umemiya Takako's tutorial *How to Become a Net Idol, How to Become Successful, and How to Make Money* (2001), which I will discuss later in this chapter, Onda's advice seems less hands-on. His counsel includes statements such as "a net idol is expected to sell dreams, not her true self" and "a net idol's diary is not expected to be of literary quality; a net idol has to transform herself into content." Onda, who calls himself headmaster (*gakuinchō*), makes it crystal clear in the site's mission statement that no young woman, no matter how cute, will succeed in developing a net idol career unless she learns to entertain her fans, which means net idols should pursue the kinds of beauty and cuteness that men, *not* women, appreciate. The mission statement also explains that a young woman is not recognized as a net idol unless her site attracts at least a thousand page-views per day and she appears in magazines and printed photo books. If women wish to become net idols, they should master the art of cute and develop unique skills of entertainment indispensable for attracting followers.

In summary, the infrastructure that emerged around the net idol trend mobilized net idols into unpaid and feminized affective labor. It was designed to produce revenue from online advertising, and it sold the online communities that emerged from the interactions of net idols and their fans to advertisers. The digital economy seduced young women to become net idols by promoting what Paolo Virno calls the ideology of the possible (2007). In the 2000s, successful internet entrepreneurs frequently appeared in the media, including Horie Takafumi (Livedoor) and Mikitani Hiroshi (Rakuten), whom I discussed in the Introduction. They were celebrated as the forerunners of a new era and became symbols of the bottomless opportunities to create DIY careers. The digital economy, however, evolved in a way that locked individuals (especially women) into new regimes of unpaid affective labor. In the next section, I explore what role the affective labor of performing cuteness—the labor of cute—played in this process.

The Production of Cute and Social Reproduction

Cute culture was originally a subculture created and maintained by young women. By the mid-1990s, however, manufacturers of mass commodities had appropriated cute culture by saturating households with goods sporting cute designs. The massive production of cute commodities had propelled the aesthetic of cute into a position of unchallenged dominance, leading to such peculiarities as police call boxes redesigned as gingerbread houses (Kinsella 1995, 220) and cute characters appearing in unexpected places like roadwork signs or delivery trucks. Sharon Kinsella interprets the culture of cute as a form of simultaneous escapism from and resistance to adult society. She states,

> Cute style is antisocial; it idolizes the pre-social. By immersion in the pre-social world, otherwise known as childhood, cute fashion blithely ignores or outright contradicts values central to the organization of Japanese society and the maintenance of the work ethic. By acting childish, Japanese youth try to avoid the conservatives' moral demand that they exercise self-discipline (*enryō*) and responsibility (*sekinin*) and tolerate (*gaman*) severe conditions (*kurō, kudō*) whilst working hard (*doryoku*) in order to repay their obligations (*giri, on*) to society. Rather than working hard, cuties seem to just want to play and ignore the rest of society completely. (Kinsella 1995, 251)

By contrast, the net idol phenomenon reveals that the production of cute is more than a form of play—it is a form of labor. Cute does not designate a particular physical appearance or behavior that a stable set of signifiers can describe. Rather, semantic flexibility is a central feature of cute, and it was precisely this inherent flexibility in the concept that allowed net idols to develop their individual genres of cute performances and unique styles of affective labor. Their careers hinged on cute looks and behaviors, the mastery of which required discipline and hard work. Cute appearances and conduct, after all, drew fans without whom net idols could not have built their careers.[19] Performing cute behaviors meant inducing feelings of ease, comfort, and pleasure by being attentive to the emotional needs of fans. Net idols used notes they had taken about their fans to personalize their relationships with them. They sent emails to their fans on their birthdays, for example, and followed up on issues that their fans had discussed with them.

Yomota Inuhiko has argued that while cute in English denotes something childish, in contemporary Japan, cute (*kawaii*) can describe anything from animals to people to machines (2006). He emphasizes that *kawaii* does not have antonyms. An unattractive person or a grotesque object can still be cute. Ōtsuka Eiji observes that female high school students described even the dying Showa Emperor, Hirohito, as cute, essentially because he looked so vulnerable (2003). Koga Reiko agrees that *kawaii* is a magical word because it can designate almost anything that is round, weak, bright, small, smooth, warm, or soft. For example, strawberries are cuter than apples (2009). That observers routinely contradict each other when attempting to distill a generic definition of *kawaii* testifies to the concept's semantic flexibility. While male critics interpret cute as a plea for protection and a desire to be controlled (Yomota 2006), female critics read women's engagement in the production of cute as a story of women's empowerment (Koga 2009). Koga asserts that young women in the 1990s used the word *kawaii* to exercise their power to make value judgments. In other words, they drew on cute culture to express their growing power as trendsetters.

Net idols performed cute behaviors by embracing personality traits such as approachable, gentle, soft, and even submissive. Ueno Chizuko points out that it is the mastery of a highly ritualistic behavior that makes cute performance successful (1982). She notes that cute can be performed by slightly tilting one's head, bending a part of one's body, such as the knee, or cringing one's body to express willingness to submission, just like dogs cower to acknowledge their inferior position to their masters. Ueno likens the performance of cute to kabuki performances, in which men perform as women by using particular *kata* (body postures) to look feminine. At the same time, the ubiquitous reliance on facial close-ups suggests that cute performance also utilizes the face as an apparatus of capture. Gilles Deleuze called attention to the bordering function of the face, arguing that the face serves to reintegrate individuals into the normative that they persistently try to escape through such emotional and mental states as cynicism or neurosis (1995). The cute face is an emblem of the normative, and the cute performance offers an assurance that the normative can be restored, at least performatively.[20]

Ebihara Yuri, a fashion model and epitome of cute in 2000s Japan, made a thought-provoking connection between cute and labor when she claimed: "If someone doesn't find me cute, I want to know why because then I'll work on it to get better at being cute."[21] She drives home the point that the face is central to the performance of cute. Ebihara's fans agree that she is cute because she appears approachable. Ebihara confesses that she creates this impression by "always making it a point to smile."[22] Indeed, her performance of cute derives its force from her signature smile, a central feature of her own approachable cute style that the media named *ebi-kawaii*. Fans emphasize that they adopt ebi-kawaii to make them feel good about themselves and to help their friends feel better about themselves. In other words, they perform cute as a way to care for themselves and for their friends. Like Ebihara, other net idols capitalized on the semantic flexibility of cute to create their own styles of feminized affective labor. By producing different genres of cute, net idols catered to different types of needs.

In creating her own cute style, for example, Tanaka Eris has consciously distanced herself from net idols who perceived sexiness as the key to becoming successful. She started writing poems during her net idol career and has published two volumes of poetry. Tanaka told me in 2010 that she maintained her net idol site only to promote herself as a poet. In 2012, however, she was still working for her family's business, and in 2015, she discontinued her net idol website. Tanaka continues to maintain a Twitter account and a blog on Hatena Diary but does not regularly update either of these.[23] On her website,[24] which she entitled "Eris in Wonderland," she presented herself as a "mysterious cute girl" who "weaves cyber dreams in the ecological system of words and images" and likened herself to Alice (in Wonderland). Tanaka's intricately staged self-portraits expose the labor of cute. While Tanaka's cute style is composed to appear natural, the vacuum-like emptiness of the background into which Tanaka is inserted is anything but natural. On these portraits, the background is stripped of all markers (objects or identifiable landscapes) that would help fans learn something about Tanaka's private self.

Tanaka employed many of the typical elements of mainstream cute iconography: schoolgirl uniforms, bunny costumes, and soulful yet curious eyes indicative of the desire to learn more about her fans. Her portraits depicted a young woman who embraced vulnerability as if to suggest her capacity for empathy. Her fans confirmed that Tanaka was inordinately cute: she was "like anime come to life."[25] It was precisely her cuteness that Tanaka wanted her fans to appreciate. When she felt that she was misunderstood, she fought back by claiming: "I am not a sexual toy for you guys. I manage my own career as an idol and maintain my own homepage. I have my own desire, a desire to communicate with you, to be seen by you, and to be appreciated."[26]

While Tanaka's selling point was empathy, Nakamura Toyomi encouraged her fans to pursue projects of self-actualization. Although many of Nakamura's photos portrayed her naked or donning flirty lingerie, she did not construct herself as an object of desire, but rather as a desiring subject. Her photos depicted her as either having or looking forward to having pleasure: enjoying dessert concoctions, stroking her body with flowers, or awaiting a lover in a hotel room. The point was not to appeal to fans via superfluous sensuality but

Eris in Wonderland

電脳マトリョーシカこと、エリスのページよ

■ティー・ブレイク
小さいメモだよ

New！■写真集
かわいいよ

■詩集
詩人やってるよ

■プロフィール
はじめましてぴ

■クロエリ共作倉庫
ナウいコラボだよ

■掲示板
軽くなったね

■リンク
お友だちよ

■English Pages

Figure 2.1. Eris in Wonderland: Eris's personal website follows the typical template of net idol sites, including links to her "about me" page, photos, diary, poems, and message board. Note that she describes her photographs as cute.

rather to encourage them to not only embark on the path of self-exploration and self-development but also to be bold in this endeavor. Her cute style made sensuality a main focus, yet it also embodied a performance with no obvious connection to the real person behind the idol.

Unlike her photos, which explored the intersection between sensuality and cute, Nakamura's diary, which was posted along her photographs, completely lacked such themes. Entitled *It's Hard to Be a Beauty* (*Bijin wa Tsurai Yo*),[27] the diary was a story of self-growth. Whereas Tanaka Eris promised to be a soul mate (she sold her sensitivity), Nakamura offered to be a role model who stressed the importance of courage to conquer uncharted terrain. Tanaka's abstract struggle for perfection was an exaggeration of the will to improve one's self. Nakamura's net idol image, on the other hand, suggested that self-exploration (and, by extension, self-improvement) should not have limits.

Indeed, many net idols responded with frustration (and sometimes rage) to the demand that they must adopt cute looks. The title poem of Tanaka Eris's first poetry collection, *Cute Holocaust*, for example, describes her desire to destroy her own youthful beauty (2003). She writes: "I want to pull out my

Figure 2.2.   Photo taken from Tanaka Eris's second published volume of poetry entitled *Kyururun Daikakumei* (Tokyo: Māburutoron, 2004). Embracing cute looks and behaviors allows Eris to forge a style of communication fans perceive as authentic. Performing cuteness also enables her to sculpt an online persona that is different from her offline self.

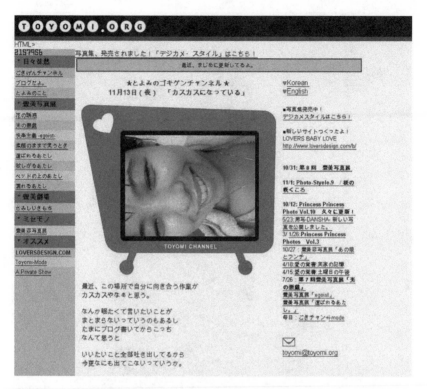

Figure 2.3. Nakamura Toyomi's personal web page. Her web page features the typical components of net idol websites, but it contains significantly more content than Eris's site. Many of the links take the visitor to Toyomi's photography, which she divides into different genres.

hair. I want to carve out my pores. I want to tear up my blood vessels. I want to gorge myself with lipsticks. I want to grow white hair. I want to let my teeth rot. I want to string a rosary from the eyes of parakeets." The last sentence is particularly evocative because it suggests that healing emerges not from cute, but from the destruction of cute. Tanaka recodes the healing properties of parakeets—which, alongside ladybugs, stand as epitomes of cute in her poetry—away from visuality toward spirituality. By eradicating her own cute, she denies visual pleasure and denounces genres of healing that cannot escape the logic of commercial culture. She faults commercial culture for reinscribing visuality as the most powerful means of affecting and being affected. Tanaka concludes her act of self-destruction by appropriating the means of visual pleasure—the eye—reorienting it to serve as a means for a different type of healing. She asks what is remedial in the labor of cute and for whom exactly.

Figure 2.4. Nakamura's self-portraits are predominantly headshots. When she photographs her body, she excludes her head.

Sianne Ngai sees a tension between helplessness and sullen aggressiveness in cute, which she interprets as emblematic of the powerlessness of a socially ineffectual and superfluous high modernist art (2005).[28] Ngai's idea that cuteness provokes aggressive feelings is particularly pertinent to understanding Tanaka's poem.[29] Objects are the cutest when they are maimed or hobbled, a point that, according to Ngai, "calls attention to the violence always implicit in our relation to the cute object" (2005, 823). By gazing at a cute subject, the observer willfully objectifies it, "calling attention to an unusual degree of synonymy between objectification and cutification." Ngai continues, "We can thus start to see how cuteness might provoke ugly or aggressive feelings, as well as the expected tender or maternal ones. For in its exaggerated passivity and vulnerability, the cute object is as often intended to excite a consumer's sadistic desires for mastery and control as much as his or her desire to cuddle" (2005, 816). This tension is also reminiscent of Marilyn Ivy's interpretation of cute in Nara Yoshitomo's work (2010). Ivy writes that cute is an "aesthetic marker for the most reified of objects and the most vulnerable of subjects" (2010, 26). The connection between cute and objectification explains why Tanaka performs cute so compellingly while also expressing a desire to destroy the very properties her cute performance is contingent upon.

Net idols thus link cute with objectification, a relationship also at play in Silvia Federici's reading of the relationship between femininity and subordination. Federici writes, "And we should not distrust the power of the wage to demystify our femininity and making visible our work—our femininity as work—since the lack of a wage has been so powerful in shaping this role and hiding our work" (2012, 19). She concludes, "This is the most radical perspective we can adopt because, although we ask for day care, equal pay, free laundromats, we will never achieve any real change unless we attack our female role at its roots" (2012, 20). That is, unless women refuse to cultivate and rely on their femininity as a source of livelihood and status in society, they offer themselves as objects of desire and confirm their place in regimes of reproductive labor while accepting also that their best chance to enter the waged labor market is to monetize their reproductive labor. This is a revolving door, Federici concludes, that channels women from unwaged to underpaid labor, and then back to unwaged labor (i.e., caring for children, caring for bosses or customers, and then back to caring for the elderly). In the net idol universe, cute involves the performance of hyper-femininity, and the more net idols rely on their femininity to develop careers, the more they undermine their own chances to compete with men in the masculinist world of entrepreneurship, which characterizes the digital economy in Japan.

Images of femininity on Nakamura Toyomi's website reflect tensions similar to the ones Tanaka tackled. Not only does Nakamura post cute pictures, as mentioned above, but she also includes portrayals of herself as a doll mutilated into body parts. Although Nakamura's brand of cute explores the interface between cute and eroticism, she does not uncritically embrace sensuality; instead, she uses photography to highlight its constructed nature. Many of her photos show her body parts disconnected from one another. Her self-portraits are predominantly headshots. And when her body is photographed, her head is excluded from the picture. Nakamura creatively plays with canonical representations of cuteness to show that the presumed innocence and vulnerability that the conventional representations of cute impart are only effects of technologically mediated and, for that matter, technologically enabled performances. Nakamura told me that she thought of the camera as a technology of healing, which is what prompted her to develop her practice of phototherapy that I will discuss in the last section. Note that Nakamura interrogates the same links between cute, visuality, and healing that inspired Tanaka's title poem. Like Tanaka, Nakamura also equates cute with hyper-femininity, but she seeks empowerment not by destroying cute but by dissecting it.

I do not see hyper-femininity as a "post-feminist self-brand" that, according to Brooke Erin Duffy and Emily Hund, young women develop in the digital economy through "normative feminine discourses and practices" (2015,

72

3). The long recession brought to a screeching halt, and even reversed, some of the progress women had made in their struggles for equal opportunities in the labor market. In that context, performing conventional styles of femininity did not help women claim their own space within the masculinist world of entrepreneurship. As such, the connection between hyper-femininity and the destructive/deconstructive impulse we see in Tanaka and Nakamura's self-portraiture exhausts itself as a critique of cute culture whose generative grammar they see as too slavishly wedded to visuality. That is, their ambivalence toward cute does not encode critical reflections on feminized affective labor and the duplicitous character of digital technologies. (Note that Nakamura is trying to redefine the camera as a technology of healing.) These net idols do not criticize the feminized affective labor and digital technologies that enabled them to gain visibility while rendering their labor invisible—a point I will revisit in the conclusion.

Tanaka and Nakamura's textual and visual deconstruction of cute suggests that the net idols' performance of cute projected a critical impulse. Cute, however, also limited that critical impulse. Net idols had less freedom than women photographers. To be successful, net idols had to reproduce notions of femininity that anchored them to values that, in turn, reinscribed their vulnerabilities and even marginality in the labor market. I do not want to dismiss, however, the political impulse in young women's efforts to become net idols. Public projects of self-discovery always encode a political impulse precisely because they are public. In her research on "camgirls" in the United States, Theresa Senft insightfully argues that communication can have political import even when the content of the communication appears not to. Such statements as "I count" and "I have a voice" can be the first steps to formulate a political program (2008, 3–4). While that was not the case with the Japanese net idols, it is important to note that the techno-social assemblage that evolved around the net idol trend offered seductive hopes to other young women. Net idols also inspired young women to become net idols by publishing tutorials on how to make money from a net idol career.

Human Capital Development in the Digital Economy

Umemiya Takako's tutorial entitled *How to Become a Net Idol, How to Become Successful, and How to Make Money* mirrors the pervasive aspiration among young women to develop DIY careers (2001). Umemiya offers a step-by-step guide for creating a fan base and describes numerous lucrative venues. For example, she notes that at meet-and-greet events with fans, such as handshaking (*akushukai*) and photo sessions (*satsueikai*), net idols can charge $20–$30 per person in entrance fees. She also suggests that net idols produce CDs featuring karaoke-style performances, DVDs showing them visiting a shrine or playing with a cute puppy, and digital photo books, all of which they can sell on their websites. She recommends that net idols try their hand at other commercial opportunities, such as opening retail businesses through net idol sites. She encourages net idols to sell postcards, calendars, fans, balloons, stickers, and T-shirts with their images printed on them on their websites. Umemiya offers the example of her net idol friend who developed a small retail business by asking fans to donate computer parts and digital cameras to her. She claims that net idols can earn a living from working as tour guides, models, and hosts at various debut events. Finally, Umemiya recommends that net idols develop various genres of counseling, including divination. The labor net idols invested in communicating with their fans helped them learn about their fans and their needs. One net idol, for instance, opened an advice corner on her website to help young men find girlfriends. She also provided a service to her clients to handpick clothing and perfumes, which, she argued, were indispensable accessories for winning the hearts of young women.

The net idol trend evolved in the context of an economic recession that dramatically increased the demand for care and healing (*iyashi*) practices. During the second half of the 1990s, the market in goods, entertainment, and services to satisfy that demand exploded. As pharmaceutical companies significantly broadened their lines of health-enhancing products, the culture industries began focusing on the creation of products and entertainment that relaxed audiences, ranging from calming music and comforting videogames to celebrity-figures molded into what became dubbed as *iyashi-kei tarento* (a healing type of celebrity). The emergence of the notion of *iyashi-kei* itself goes back to the fall of 1994, when the actress Iijima Naoko appeared in a television commercial for a Georgia brand of canned coffee. Not only was she physically attractive, but she also spoke softly and looked kind and caring to viewers.[30]

Like Iijima, the appeal of net idols resided in their willingness to serve as a source of comfort (*yasuragi*) and healing (*iyashi*). Unlike commercially available services such as maid cafés, net idols offered customized attention for free. As unemployment rates among youth reached record highs, the demand for feminized affective labor rose robustly, and net idols stepped in to meet the demand. Their plan, however, was not to work for free. While most net idols did not succeed in developing lucrative employment from their careers, they naturalized an equation between hope labor and human capital development. Net idol tutorials promoted the idea that every experience could contribute to increasing an individual's human capital and, by extension, her chances of building a successful DIY career.

Developed in the 1960s, the theory of human capital proposed that investment in education and training enhanced an individual's chances of attaining employment security. In the context of stable economic growth, developing human capital in Japan meant investment in earning degrees from prestigious educational institutions to optimize one's chances to obtain lifetime employment. With the crumbling of lifetime employment, however, human capital development was redefined to serve a labor market with decreasingly available job security. Rather than investing in formal education, the emerging digital economy encouraged individuals to devote themselves to developing unique skills, self-brands, and an online presence even while accepting the uncertainty of gaining a dependable income from these investments. In fact, willingness to take risks has emerged as a pivotal form of human capital. By emphasizing the importance of absolute adaptability to quickly shifting demands, human capital development became a speculative endeavor.

In his analysis of how neoliberal policies have transformed human capital development, Michel Feher notes that while the subjectivity of the free laborer is split between her labor power that she can sell in the labor market and her private self that is inalienable from her, neoliberalism encourages the recruitment of the private self to the project of developing human capital, which, in turn, further erodes the line between production and social reproduction (2009). When a net idol offers her unique personality for sale, which is a composite of her upbringing, education, personal experiences, physical attributes, and skills she acquired in the digital economy, the separation between production and reproduction in her life collapses. In the beginning of this chapter, I proposed that the development of the net idol trend was a response to a crisis in social reproduction. I now want to suggest that while the net idols provided a temporary fix for this crisis, they also contributed to transforming social reproduction into a site of valorization by integrating it with human capital development. The problem was that developing human capital in the digital economy was speculative to the point that it rarely enabled net idols to generate a reliable income.

Net idols tried to develop careers as models,[31] singers,[32] scriptwriters,[33] illustrators,[34] photographers,[35] adult video stars,[36] or cosplay performers,[37] but, again, the overwhelming majority of them did not succeed. The career of Nakamura Toyomi, one of Japan's most famous net idols, sheds light on the difficulties of turning a net idol career into a day job. Nakamura's dream was to become a recognized art photographer. Her self-portraits helped her build a career as a net idol, but she has yet to achieve the kind of recognition that Nagashima Yurie, Hiromix, and Ninagawa Mika attained by winning the Kimura Ihei Award.

Nakamura turned to the internet after a series of unsuccessful attempts to attain her childhood dream of becoming a professional actress. Her career as a net idol exemplifies the increasingly incessant and improvisational character of human capital development. It also exposes that human capital development is becoming more and more speculative and experimental. Nakamura's acting career began in 1987, the year she first performed on stage. She later signed up with a talent agency and had several auditions but did not land any major jobs. She became a member of a theater group and performed with them in Tokyo, Osaka, and Okinawa. In 1992, she realized that it was increasingly unlikely that she would succeed in achieving her dream of being recognized and appreciated for her talents on stage.

That is when she gave up her aspiration to become an actress and resumed the life of a "normal" student. That is also when she turned to photography. She used her camera to make her "normal" life more colorful and started appreciating the healing power of this particular technology. She continued searching for a place (*ibasho*) where she belonged and found it on the internet, which she encountered in 1997. She created a web page and regularly posted self-portraits and diary entries. She conceived of her web page as a stage where she performed her own self. In 1999, she launched www.toyomi .org and was able to attract a sizeable following. Her fans started calling her a net idol. In fact, she was one of the first, as well as one of the most famous net idols. When I first met her, she showed me a thick folder consisting of interviews she gave to magazines that featured her. I learned that she also appeared a few times on television.

Building on her experience of taking pictures of herself, which she posted to her net idol site, Nakamura aimed to develop a career as an art photographer who specialized in portraiture. She also illustrated her online diary with photos of her everyday life, especially photos of meals. (Cooking is one of Nakamura's hobbies, to which her Instagram account testifies.) Nakamura found inspiration in "girly" photography in the works of Ninagawa Mika and Hiromix, but she also worked hard on developing her own unique style.[38] Her photography was not just for play or experiment; in her diary, she often expressed the wish that she would be recognized for her talent. In 2010, she returned to school to learn art planning and earned a degree from the Department of

Visual Arts at Seian University of Arts and Design. Although she continues to work as an art photographer, she also identified another opportunity in photography—an activity she began calling photo-therapy.

Nakamura developed her photo-therapy practice after visitors to her web page recognized her talent in portrait photography and started asking her to take their pictures. Taking advantage of the self-help boom, Nakamura drew on a rapidly expanding literature of popular psychology to build her practice of photo-therapy. She borrowed the term from a practice used in private-sector counseling that involves working through problems by discussing pictures in family albums. In her unique form of photo-therapy, she photographs her clients in the comfort of their homes or even as they run errands in the city. She then sits with them to analyze the photos and to determine which ones best reflect the clients' true self. Nakamura integrates her interest in mental health with her love of photography to help individuals feel good about themselves and to recover aspects of their personalities that could help them live more fulfilling lives. According to her website, Nakamura became a member of the Japan Photo Therapist Network in 2012. She states in her introduction that "through the experience of pursuing portrait photography, I started to believe that photography has the power to heal people's heart."[39] In addition to pursuing photo-therapy, she continues to invest her time and energy in developing a career as an art photographer while working full-time at an advertising agency and practicing photo-therapy during the weekends.[40]

She says that working seven days a week took a toll on her health. On her websites and social media accounts,[41] she openly discusses her health problems—uterine fibroids. She attributes particular significance to the fact that her health problems pertain to her reproductive health and believes her body took revenge on her, forcing her not only to ask herself what it meant for her to be a woman but also prompting her to contemplate the predicament in which young women find themselves in contemporary Japan. Nakamura feels that if women in Japan want to have careers, they have to give up romance, marriage, and family. Career-oriented women are therefore bound to be lonely. She says she followed the latter path, but she is not willing to accept the loneliness. She also claims that her health problems made her realize that being a woman was an important part of her identity, and it is this realization, she concludes, that inspires her art photography. She explains her recent photographic series of withering flowers as portraits of women and self-portraits.[42] While helping others lead more fulfilling lives, she continues searching for meaning in her own career and life.

Conclusion: The Labor of Cute as Invisible Labor

I invoked earlier a contemporary symbol of cute, Ebihara Yuri, who claimed that the production of cute was a matter of hard work. She inspired me to think about the labor of cute, which, in turn, led me to consider the net idol trend as symptomatic of how digital technologies absorb labor and make it invisible. Ebihara appeared in several McDonald's commercials in which she sported her signature cute smile framed by impeccable crème-colored frills. Japanese viewers I discussed these ads with did not see the association between Ebihara and McDonald's forced. They were obviously used to the semantic flexibility of cute—a concept that can seamlessly be linked with a wide range of commodities including hamburgers that are not cute at all. I, however, found the implications of this semantic openness revealing for the issue of labor.[43] When an activity (in this case, the production of cute) does not yield to easy definition, it is difficult to see that activity as a form of labor.

By promoting affective labor as a way to develop DIY careers, the digital economy makes it increasingly difficult to define labor and measure its value (Clough 2012). Yet I do not mean to claim that the immeasurability of labor is a new problem: C. Wright Mills contemplated this issue when he argued that, in the context of white-collar work, *personality* is often more important than technical skills in getting a job (1951). Three decades later, Arlie Hochschild famously claimed that service providers are required to perform "emotional labor"—offering service with a smile—for which they are not compensated (1983). Equally important, feminist scholars have insisted that women's labor in the domestic sphere is undervalued because it has been deliberately kept privatized and excluded from the laws of the market (Fortunati 2007; Dalla Costa and James 1975; Schor 1993).

Angela McRobbie criticized the Italian Autonomists for romanticizing the male industrial workforce as the leading force of social and economic change. In her view, the Autonomists overstated the agency of the industrial workforce when they claimed that it was the resistance of factory workers to the Fordist rationalization of work that drove the shift from Fordist production to flexible accumulation (2011).[44] Instead, McRobbie saw feminist struggles for gender equity and women's entry into the labor force in the 1970s as equally, if not more, pivotal to facilitating the transition to post-Fordist labor regimes. After all, these regimes rely on the flexibility and docility of labor that women have long been mobilized to provide. This chapter demonstrates that in the late 1990s and 2000s, the digital economy in Japan similarly capitalized on (and reinforced) women's marginalization in the labor market and their privileged place in social reproduction.

When women turned to the internet hoping to develop meaningful careers, the popular media celebrated them for embracing an entrepreneurial spirit. One journalist, Kambayashi Takehiko, claimed, "As the core of Japan's economy yawns its way into a second decade of stagnation, dynamism can be found on the fringes, where many of the entrepreneurs, innovators and risk takers just happen to be women."[45] Yet the net idol phenomenon reveals that the development of the digital economy did not unequivocally usher in the onset of a brave new world of work in which entrepreneurial spirit and courage rather than gender would determine who could attain lucrative and meaningful work. Bluntly put, a net idol's career was overwhelmingly a dead end. By exposing the centrality of feminized affective labor to the careers that women were able to develop, however, the net idol trend helps us understand how Japan's digital economy mobilized female bloggers, online traders, and cell phone novelists to new regimes of unpaid affective labor.

Even when women held waged employment in the postwar period (predominantly as noncareer office ladies), their job descriptions were commonly kept fuzzy. By insufficiently defining work responsibilities, male employees could ask their female colleagues to run personal errands for them (Ogasawara 1998). Thus, an office lady's work emerged in continuation with the work of a homemaker. This chapter highlights that a net idol's work was also an extension of the work of the office lady and homemaker. The mobilization of these groups of women into regimes of underpaid and unpaid work has served multiple economic growth strategies. During the postwar period, the underpaid labor of office ladies helped offset the high costs of the lifetime employment system (maintained in large part for male employees), while housewives played an important role in reproducing male labor power. Although most net idols embarked on their careers to earn a living, they ended up performing feminized affective labor for free, which was in high demand in the wake of a nagging recession.

The net idol phenomenon helped make the idea of unpaid labor in the digital economy more acceptable by repositioning it as a prerequisite to develop meaningful careers. In reality, however, digital technologies render women's labor invisible and lock women into precarious work conditions.[46] The digital economy not only replaces traditional places of salaried employment but also complements conventional spaces of human capital development. It becomes an apparatus that prepares young people for entering a labor market that draws on casualized work and flexible specialization. It socializes them to embrace the ideology of the possible. More important, it teaches them to invest their labor in developing ever newer forms of human capital with no resistance, to unlearn them with no remorse, and to learn new ones with no resentment.

Career Porn

BLOGGING AND THE GOOD LIFE

When I interviewed Tanaka Eris in 2010 for the previous chapter, she teased me by saying that I was late to the party. She told me that the net idol trend was over and urged me to study the "female blogger trend" (*josei burogā torendo*) instead. She was right. By the mid-2000s, most net idols had closed their websites and moved on to blogging platforms, which proliferated quickly. To help women navigate their way among them, some bloggers built careers from publishing blog tutorials. These self-help books promoted a new approach to employment. By proposing that freedom in work was more valuable than job security, they made more acceptable employment conditions in which individuals scrambled together livelihoods from unpredictable job opportunities. Blog tutorials cautioned would-be bloggers that the human costs of lifetime employment were too great and then seduced them with possible alternatives. They suggested that rather than striving to attain employment security, individuals should aim to develop employability security (Kanter 1995). The DIY careers that female bloggers were able to build, however, exposed the fact that blogging was not a viable pathway to a career for most women. Like the online platforms internet entrepreneurs developed around the net idol phenomenon, blogging platforms re-anchored women to feminized affective labor.

Blogging took Japan by storm in the mid-2000s. In her book, *Blog Theory*, Jodi Dean remarked that in 2006, more blog posts per hour were produced in Japanese than in English (2010, 37). This was partly due to the failure of the television industry to reform its system of mass production and its concomitant inability to deliver diversified entertainment to fragmenting audiences (Lukacs 2010a). In fact, the television industry turned to blogging platforms to promote television programs, which explains why these platforms evolved as a part of the commercial media complex in Japan. At the same time, in the context of hiring freezes, blogging platforms exploited the vulnerable positions of young people in the labor market. They proposed that blogging was a viable pathway to build new careers. Many of these young people—especially women who had long dominated Japan's irregular workforce—turned to blogging to develop new life projects. While the overwhelming majority of them did not succeed, blogging platforms generated wealth from bloggers' uncompensated labor. Blog writers and readers formed distinct interest groups that platform owners sold to advertisers interested in reaching more precisely defined microniches of the consumer market.

A prominent way for bloggers to transform blogging into a career (and to earn an income from blogging) was to package and sell their expertise in blogging. Bloggers wrote tutorials, held seminars, and gave lectures about blogging. They also blogged about blogging. The self-help movement that emerged from these bloggers' entrepreneurial endeavors celebrated blogging as an alternative to salaried employment, which it criticized as "corporate slavery." I borrow and expand upon Tanimoto Mayumi's interpretation of self-help books as career porn (2013b) to argue that blog technology has contributed to dismantling the system of lifetime employment while leaving the postwar culture of laborism intact. Guy Standing coined the concept of paternalistic laborism to critique the labor practices Japan's postwar governments supported to advance national development (2011). Blogging platforms and blog tutorials mounted the same criticism, but they only attacked paternalism, not laborism. On the contrary, they eroticized work by redefining the good life as freedom *in* work. Blog tutorials understood freedom not as freedom to refuse to live work-oriented lives but as freedom to choose the type of employment one finds meaningful. Drawing on technological utopianism—the assumption that developments in technologies will improve the quality of life—blog tutorials portrayed blogging as a means to democratizing access to the good life.[1] Eran Fisher suggests that technology discourse is always already ideological in that it treats political issues as technical ones (2010). Blog tutorials tightened the link between the good life and work while accepting the dismantling of labor protections as inevitable.

The DIY careers that female bloggers were able to develop lend further support to the argument I began developing in the previous chapter. The digital economy mobilized women not only to advance the erosion of lifetime employment but also to renegotiate the human capital regime that fueled the high-growth era. In their blogs and tutorials, bloggers promoted blogging as an essential tool of self-branding—developing, packaging, and selling one's personality as a unique commodity (Marwick 2013). Rather than developing human capital, which was understood as an alienable part of one's private self that can be sold in the labor market, bloggers strove to transform themselves *into capital*, or more precisely, brands.[2] They promoted the idea that branded labor was more resilient to economic volatility than its unbranded equivalent. As such, bloggers continued upgrading the human capital regime for an era in which salaried employment was decreasingly available and more and more people were forced to improvise life projects from irregular work opportunities. By branding their labor, bloggers facilitated a shift from employment security to employability security proposing that creating labor protections was the responsibility of individuals.

In the end, blogging platforms, blog tutorials, and bloggers have all participated in furthering the deregulation of the labor market. The most important contribution of this techno-social assemblage was that it recoded individuals into workers whose subjectivities were regulated not through feeding their entitlement to job security, but through emphasizing their right to freedom in the realm of work. Blogging platforms, blog tutorials, and bloggers succeeded in this endeavor by connecting the idea of freedom in work to the idea of the good life. The connections between work and the good life, however, also reinforced the postwar era's attachment to laborism and its underlying logic that one's employment determined one's membership and status in society. And just like in the postwar period, laborism reanchored women to regimes of feminized affective labor.

Blogging Platforms and the Enclosure of Affective Labor

Andrew Ross incisively observes that internet users willingly produce online content in exchange for the benefits of the free promotion "page-view exposure delivers to freelance strivers, piloting their do-it-yourself careers through the turbulence of the blogosphere" (2012, 14). David Harvey notes that when collective labor is harnessed to serve individualized capital accumulation, the laborer is no longer recognized as a common property resource (2011). Building on these insights, I examine how blog platforms in Japan were developed to enclose affective labor.

While it is difficult to pinpoint exactly when blogging started in Japan, the trend peaked between 2004 and 2006, a period marked by a proliferation of blogging platforms and blog tutorials. The television show "The Queens of Blogging,"[3] which ran on Tokyo TV on Fridays between April 7 and September 29, 2006, also evidenced the popularity of blogging in the mid-2000s. As the title suggests, the genre was (and still is) more popular with women in Japan. According to Ameba,[4] 63 percent of users who log in to the portal on personal computers are women, and 37 percent are men. Similarly, 67 percent of users who access the site via smartphones are women, while 33 percent are men. In terms of the composition of unregistered visitors to the portal (understood as users who read blogs but do not produce them), 41 percent are women and 59 percent are men. In 2015, women dominated the most popular categories of blogging including fashion, food, and family. Women were also among the top five most popular bloggers in such categories as entrepreneurship and technology.[5]

Multiple factors shaped blogging into a medium that became more popular with women. These include women's privileged place in consumer culture (Lukacs 2010a; Moeran and Skov 1995) and their marginalization from career-track employment (Brinton 1993). Technological factors also played a role in making blogging more appealing to women.[6] I note in my Introduction that rather than possessing an organic unity, component parts of a techno-social assemblage can be plugged into other assemblages, where they will interact differently with the components that constitute their new host assemblages. Blogging evolved from the integration of online diaries, such as the net idols' websites,[7] and forum sites developed from bulletin board systems (BBS).[8] An important step toward the development of blogging portals was the aggregation of diary sites. In 1995, Tsuda Yū collected and published links to all available online diaries on a website named Nikki Links (Diary Links). This website also featured a ranking of diaries.[9] Between 1998 and 2001, several new online diary services were launched, including HNS (1998), Sarusaru Nikki (1999), Enpitsu (2000), Nikki (2000), and Diary (2001).

BBS was also crucial to the development of blogging portals. Net idols used the first generation of BBS, which allowed for communication between site owners and site visitors. The second generation of BBS, developed between 1996 and 1999, enabled site visitors to communicate with each other, which was conducive to the development of forum sites (i.e., online message boards or discussion boards). The first BBS-based forum site, Ayashii World, was launched in 1996. Like 4chan in the United States, Ayashii World targeted young men who identified as otaku.[10] In 1997, Licentious Notice Board (LNB) followed suit, upping the ante by allowing users to post photos. In the same year, Amezo BBS was introduced, which played an important role in expanding the popularity of BBS by featuring a thread float system. This system organized comments in chronological order listing the most recent post on the top of the page. In 1999, Nishimura Hiroyuki launched Nichanneru, which has evolved into the most popular forum site featuring the thread float system.[11]

Blogging platforms integrated the community-building function of BBS and the content-publishing tools of diary sites. Blogs include similar layouts and feature many of the same elements, such as posts (the basic unit of blogs), post titles, time stamps, blogrolls,[12] "about pages" (introduction), reverse chronological order, dated entries, and frequent updating. Jill Rettberg identifies frequency, brevity, and personality as the main features of the genre, emphasizing that blogs are generally written in the first person, but she notes that they are always social because they are written with particular audiences in mind (2013). In Japan, most blogs are personal and were initially similar to diaries. In fact, net idols were among the first adopters of blog technology. As blogging portals were evolving into a part of the commercial entertainment media complex, they increasingly encouraged bloggers to focus on particular topics. This approach made it easier for readers to cut through the clutter and for blogging portals to package and sell microsegments of the blogging public to advertisers. Blogs are interactive in that they allow visitors to leave comments and communicate with other users. By interacting with other bloggers and readers, bloggers facilitate the formation of interest groups that owners of blogging platforms can sell to marketers as microniches of the consumer market. Similar to the online net idol academy and net idol ranking sites that transformed net idols into online entertainers, blog platforms were designed to enclose the affective labor bloggers invested in content production, communication, and networking.

Between 2003 and 2004, numerous blogging portals were launched.[13] Two of the most popular platforms, Ameba and Jugem, played an important role in raising the popularity of blogging by inviting celebrities to blog on their platforms. While these celebrities turned to blogging to reboot their faltering careers,[14] blogging portals capitalized on them to expand their user base and make their portals more appealing to advertisers. In conjunction with the development of blog services, blog ranking sites were also launched; many of them focused on actors, actresses, musicians, comedians, models, announcers, athletes, and cartoonists. Examples included IT media Mobile's Keitai Ranking Site for Celebrity Bloggers; Celebrity Blogs: Popularity Ranking; General Ranking of Ameba: Celebrities and Famous Bloggers; and Naver's You Must Know "SON!": The List of Famous Blogs Everyone Reads. While celebrity blogs promoted blogging, other incentives—such as the Alpha Blogger Award—encouraged individuals who were not famous to also blog. These incentives stressed that it was possible to become famous via blogging.[15]

Despite the momentum celebrities bring to blogging portals, they are not the main appeal used to attract (and recruit) bloggers. Instead, these platforms promote blogging primarily as a tool that enables individuals to develop employability security. In addition to promoting blogging as a form of entertainment, these platforms, like blog tutorials, sell blogging as means to an end. They claim that bloggers can transform the human capital they develop (e.g., writing skills, new connections, and an online presence) into careers.[16] The race for visibility in the blogosphere, however, is inhumane. It is only the ideology of the possible that inspires bloggers to continue trying to transform blogging into a career.

Blogging portals offer applications to improve one's writing and networking skills. They also provide bloggers access to a large audience. Yet the number of bloggers who actually develop new careers from blogging is infinitesimally small. Instead, as Jodi Dean claims, networked media practices such as blogging "emerge and persist as components of a vast commercial entertainment culture that has found a way to get the users to make the products they enjoy and even pay to do it. Far from inaugurating a new creative, post-monetary commons, media practices like blogging and social networks ease the paths of neoliberal capitalism" (2010, 37–38).[17] In Japan, it was women who were seduced into becoming bloggers, that is, unpaid content producers. Dean's argument illuminates how blogging platforms such as Ameba have evolved as apparatuses to harness women's unremunerated affective labor.

Ameba was launched in 2004 by CyberAgent Inc., an internet advertising company founded in 1998.[18] Its founder, Fujita Susumu,[19] earned his degree in business administration and started his career by selling ads to free newspapers. Coming from advertising, Fujita understood that the success of a blog service depended on experience in sales. He built his business using the model of pay-per-click banner advertising, whereby the site owner is paid when users click on banner ads that appear on the site.[20] CyberAgent sells primarily web advertising, but it also offers a growing number of services that encourage individuals to read and write blogs so that they spend more time on the website. Ameba currently has twenty-eight million PC and smartphone users. The site requires registration, which allows it to custom-tailor advertising based on information gleaned not only from IP addresses but also from gender, age, and search history on the site. Fujita presents his company as iconic, saying: "Our goal is to be a company that represents the 21st century. Like Sony or Honda, which stand as icons of the 20th century, I want to make my company to be successful on the global scale and have an influence on society."[21] In 2014, CyberAgent had only 2,661 employees, while Honda had 198,561 and Sony employed 140,900 people.[22] Based on this data, one might question Fujita's definition of organizational innovation and his idea of a successful business that has a social impact. One could posit that he recognizes the role that unwaged bloggers play within his business, but instead of considering the extraction of their labor without pay as exploitation, he sees it as part of his company's organizational innovation.

Given Fujita's ambitions to create a company that has a social impact, it is not entirely unreasonable to wonder why Ameba's management does not recognize bloggers as part of the company's workforce. Ameba's management conceptualizes bloggers as "the users of the site" and as "consumers with strong expressive abilities." Ideally, these users will consume the services of the site and click on featured ads. The site offers a wide array of opportunities for bloggers to produce content yet promotes these opportunities as entertainment.

The venues through which bloggers are encouraged to produce content on Ameba are strategies to optimize the time internet users spend on the site.[23] These include the following: Ameba Now (a microblogging platform similar to Twitter and thematic blogging that invites bloggers to join discussion groups); Celebrity Blogs; Kuchikomi Tsunagari (invites bloggers to write word-of-mouth articles);[24] Ameba Guroppo (helps bloggers connect with users of particular apps);[25] Ameba Studio (offers an opportunity to chat with celebrities); Ameba News;[26] Official Tie-up IchiRan (discusses issues of entrepreneurship); AmebaGG (offers information to women bloggers);[27] Ameblo de Hon (allows bloggers to transform their blogs into books); Ameba Collaborator (helps corporations create their own Ameba blog sites to be used for stealth marketing); Community Service (connects people who have the same hobbies); Lifestyle Service;[28] and Ameba Kurachie (blogs about lifestyle issues, including food, travel, and mental and physical health). On one site, Ameba customers can read the news, contribute to discussions of daily themes, update their own blog, analyze their stats, polish their writing skills, get help with transforming their blogs into books, and play social games. CyberAgent is currently trying to gain a toehold on the social gaming market[29] and also attempted, unsuccessfully, to expand into the realm of online foreign currency trading—a topic I will discuss in chapter 4.

Ameba claims that it offers a blogging experience superior to other services because it allows users to interact with celebrities and provides the best apps available to improve their writing, networking, and entrepreneurial skills. These apps include rankings that users can sign up for in over two hundred categories.[30] Furthermore, Ameba features daily topics and invites users to comment on them.[31] Typical prompts include such themes as "how to get a boyfriend" and "how to get rid of mold in the house." The portal also allows users to customize their blogs with seasonal wallpaper and a variety of web layouts.[32] Yet the only application that users can employ to make money is a service that allows them to transform their blog entries into book format (Ameblo de Hon).[33] Through this service, bloggers can self-publish their blogs, which they can then sell at events such as the Comic Market (Comiket) and Bungei Furima, two forums where individuals sell self-published works (*dōjinshi*).[34] Ameba's interpellation of bloggers as consumers is in tension with blog tutorials' promises that bloggers will be able to develop careers from blogging.

Blog Tutorials as Career Porn

Overlooking the extremely low success rate, blog tutorials claim that anyone can blog her way to the good life. Although nearly twice as many women as men write blogs and women are overwhelmingly the most popular bloggers, more men author blog tutorials than women. Some tutorials target beginners, offering them a step-by-step guide to start, develop, and customize a blog. Others focus on specific blog services—such as Livedoor, Ameba, FC2, or Hatena Diary—or concentrate on particular genres of blogs, such as food, fashion, family, travel, and technology. Some tutorials concentrate on helping bloggers improve their writing skills, and the most popular ones promise to tell their readers how their authors make money from blogging.

These tutorials are, of course, not unique to Japan. Blog tutorials are popular in the United States as well, and the best-selling ones sport titles similar to their Japanese counterparts. Examples include *How to Make Money Blogging: How I Replaced My Day Job with My Blog* (Lotich 2010); *Blogging to Freedom: 7 Steps to Creating Your Independence with Blogging* (Mathias 2015); *Freedom Is Blogging in Your Underwear* (MacLeod 2012); *ProBlogger: Secrets for Blogging Your Way to a Six-Figure Income* (Rowse and Garrett 2012); and *Solopreneur Ronin: Break the Chains, Earn Your Freedom, and Engineer a Happy Life Blogging from Anywhere* (Biddulph and Capala 2015).[35]

The departure point for blog tutorials in Japan is that blogging entails work that is precisely the opposite of the lifetime employment that parents in the postwar period aspired to for their children. Lifetime employment offered job security and benefits but also demanded that workers accept highly regimented work conditions. By contrast, blog tutorials promote blogging as a form of work that does not require individuals to give up their freedom. Wendy Brown argues that the neoliberal revolution took place in the name of freedom, as in free markets, free countries, and free people (2015; see also Harvey 2005). In fact, the idea of freedom has always been instrumental to capital's expansion. Not unlike the ways in which freeing peasants allowed for the formation of an industrial labor force and the industrial revolution, neoliberalism also draws on the liberal philosophy of freedom in that it frees individuals from all earlier norms of employment security and encourages them to be entrepreneurial (2015). Blog tutorials make use of the liberal discourse on freedom to promote blogging in a context in which job security is decreasingly available.

Blog tutorials also stress that skills and money are not necessary preconditions for success in the blogosphere (Ayura 2009; Takahashi and Yanagida 2012). Someya Masatoshi states that he had no savings, no expert knowledge, and no fame to valorize. He only had responsibilities to provide for his wife, son, and cat. The miracle of digital technologies enabled him to do just that through blogging (2013). Blog tutorials highlight the fact that blogging services provide both the tools to write blogs and access to a large audience (Aoki 2005). Therefore, they claim, writing a blog requires only writing skills, which one can learn from blog tutorials (Hayashi 2006; Higuchi 2010; Taguchi and Matsunaga 2008; Takita 2005; Wakui 2012). Reflecting the pervasive and uncritical reliance on techno-utopianism in blog tutorials, Tabuchi Takashige concludes his tutorial by noting that blogging is a technology designed to do the work for the blogger using such tools as the trackback system, RSS feeds, and search engine optimization. In other words, blogging is a technology that automates the tedious part of the work and leaves only the creative part for the blogger to enjoy. The promise is that once a blogger builds a road for traffic, traffic will come automatically (2013, 118).[36]

The most appealing claim that sells blog tutorials is that blogging is a highly efficient tool of self-branding, and successful self-branding will open business opportunities for the blogger. The authors of tutorials refer to opportunities, but they offer only one concrete example (thus exposing, in my view, the central ruse of blog culture): the sale of expert knowledge, which most typically is expertise in blog culture. Bloggers propose that blogging can be monetized by writing blog tutorials and holding seminars about blogging. Blog tutorials recommend that bloggers use their blogs to identify topics they are passionate about and develop expertise in those areas. Tabuchi Takashige, who used his blog to learn the business of online advertising, claims that anyone can use blogging to develop some expertise that she can sell for a living. If someone does not own a business that can be promoted via blogging, such as a restaurant, she can still develop information-type (*jōhōhasshinkei*) businesses and sell her expertise.

Sasaki Toshinao's book, *How to Become an Expert in Three Hours* (2007), succinctly captures this idea. Having published over thirty books about new information and communication technologies, including the internet, Google, Livedoor, blogging, and digital publishing, Sasaki has become a model of the flexible worker who makes a living from work he loves (e.g., 2004, 2005, 2006, 2008a, 2008b, 2008c, 2009a, 2009b, 2010a, 2010b). Sasaki celebrates what he calls "nomad work" for the freedom it affords. Freedom for him means the freedom to decide when and where to work (2009a, 2015; see also Higuchi 2010).

The concept of nomad work spawned its own literature, which was both inspired by and further spurred the discourse of blog tutorials on flexible employment. Tachibana Takeshi's *The Lifestyle of a Nomad Worker* (2012a) identifies blogging as a quintessential form of nomad work. Tachibana is a "professional" blogger who earns his living from publishing books and holding seminars about blogging. His main claim is that blogging does not require skills or the investment of resources; it only requires an individual's willingness to transform her lifestyle into content (*raifusutairu o kontentsu-ka shimashō*) (2012a). Like Sasaki, Tachibana romanticizes technologies, claiming they have enabled him to become what he was always meant to be, including being healthy, with the assistance of an iPhone app that helped him lose weight (2012b).

Technological utopianism is so essential to the discourse of nomad work that it has generated its own criticism. Yet the critics—who scorn the idea that developments in technologies will improve work conditions—do not question the inevitability of labor market deregulation. Three popular examples are Tsunemi Yōhei's *Creating the Freedom of Work* (2013) and Tanimoto Mayumi's two books, *Nomads and Corporate Slaves* (2013a) and *Career Porn Is a Waste of Time* (2013b). Freelance writer and part-time teacher Tsunemi, who was a former employee of Recruit (one of the largest human resources companies in Japan), claims that the idealization of digital technologies mobilizes youth to work in the digital economy. He acknowledges, however, that nomad work is not an alternative to lifetime employment since the latter is decreasingly available, as well as unappealing, to young people. He emphasizes the importance of portraying nomad work more realistically and concludes that while freedom is the most valuable aspect of nomad work, digital technologies will not deliver it to young people. Rather, when young people learn to embrace and master risk, freedom will be their reward.

Tanimoto Mayumi, a prominent microblogger who established her online presence through Twitter, also criticizes the idea of nomad work as technologically enabled empowerment in the realm of work. In her book *Nomads and Corporate Slaves*, she agrees with Tsunemi that young people are no longer interested in lifetime employment (2013a). She suggests that the Japanese government should follow the British example and sponsor retraining programs, which would help young people learn such practical skills as accounting and marketing to better prepare them to start their own businesses. She further develops these ideas in another book, *Career Porn Is a Waste of Time* (2013b). She claims that self-help books do not offer any useful guidance and suggests that advice such as "you just need to start a blog," "if you become famous online, then job offers will come to you," and "write a fashionable address on your business card" will not help anyone start a business. Success stories of nomad workers make self-help books addictive, but like recreational drugs, they offer only a quick fix. Readers addicted to these books will never succeed in starting a business because they grow attached to the unrealistic idea of work as a fun activity that does not encroach on one's personal freedom. Tanimoto concludes that self-help books do not help their readers accept a robust work ethic, which is indispensable to succeed in any form of entrepreneurial endeavor.

Tanimoto is right. Just as cooking programs stimulate a desire to cook and thus function as food porn, blog tutorials stimulate a desire to develop new careers by anchoring the idea of freedom in work to the notion of the good life. As I canvassed blog tutorials for practical advice on how to develop blogging into a career, I found very little that was not common sense. The following dos and don'ts constitute the standard repertory of blog tutorials: new bloggers should learn to use blogging tools, use the right blogging service (as some of these specialize in particular market segments), review popular blogs and learn from them, research topics that interest people, practice writing for at least a couple of hours every day, use simple language peppered with English to sound cool, identify and pursue a particular niche of the blogosphere, learn to interpret one's statistics, sign up for blog ranking and choose the categories wisely, learn to handle the pressure from readers who are relentless in demanding new content, and learn to take criticism. These tutorials also instruct bloggers to follow proper etiquette: bloggers should not be disrespectful or antagonistic; they should not reveal personal information about themselves or their friends (e.g., addresses and workplaces); and they should not leave comments they received unanswered. Although these tips are helpful for bloggers who want to increase their page views, they do not enable individuals to develop new careers.

Readers of blog tutorials who posted reviews on amazon.co.jp agree that the employment models of the postwar period are neither viable nor desirable. They claim they turn to self-help books such as blog tutorials in search of advice on how to develop new careers. They see the act of reading these books as the responsible thing to do. But they also criticize self-help books for not offering advice that actually helps them develop new careers. Readers comment that reading stories of successful bloggers[37] inspires them to start a blog (*yaruki ga waiteita*) even though they ultimately fail to do so. And if they do start a blog, they quickly give up on updating it.[38] Other readers compare self-help books to energy drinks and confess their addiction to them. One reader says that when he reads a self-help book, he feels energized for two weeks and feels confident that he will be able to change the course of his life. The impact of the book wanes, however, and he then needs to read another one.

This is not surprising, as blog tutorials appeal to readers' sense of guilt. Emphasizing that blogging is easy and fun, blog tutorials insist that it is only the lack of will and determination that prevents individuals from developing fulfilling careers. Blog tutorials promote what Alice Marwick describes as the neoliberal ideology of "pulling yourself up by the bootstraps entrepreneurialism" (2013, 175). Deriving their traction from technological utopianism, blog tutorials reinforce the idea that it is the individual's responsibility to develop a career and live a life that measures up to prevailing standards of success. Readers consistently report that they enjoy reading autobiographical stories of people who persisted, did not give in to the sirens of laziness, powered through, and in the end emerged victorious in their struggles to find fulfillment in work. Blog tutorials stimulate a desire to be entrepreneurial, but they also function as career porn by eroticizing work.

More importantly, they accept labor market deregulation as inevitable and offer help in navigating the new terrain of irregular employment. Neither the writers nor the readers of these books tackle questions about why work conditions have become precarious, why the unemployment rate is record high among youth, and why corporations are dismantling the system of lifetime employment. In the previous chapter, I claimed that owners of online platforms drew on the ideology of the possible to seduce young women into believing that their platforms would enable them to develop such careers as photographers, poets, singers, and models. Blog tutorials push the ideology of the possible even further. They recode the meaning of "opportunity" away from something that individuals must find (for example, by identifying and developing a particular talent) into something that individuals have to create.

Blog tutorials enlist the following examples as potential DIY careers: multi-talent (*maruchi-tarento*), social moderator (*sōsharu moderētā*), livecaster (*raibukasutā*), Tweet-caster (*tsuittokasutā*), coordinator (*kōdinētā*), planner (*purannā*), soul therapist (*shinri kyanserā*), customer engineer (*kasutamā enjinia*), sales engineer (*sērusu enjinia*), interior coordinator (*interia kōdinētā*), food coordinator (*fūdo kōdinētā*), and fashion coordinator (*fasshon kōdinētā*). Note that most of these careers pertain to blogging itself, which points to the limits of human capital development in the blogosphere. All these careers involve the sale of some kind of expert knowledge. The vagueness of these professional designations makes one wonder what activities these jobs actually entail other than offering for sale one's own unique personality and expertise in blog culture. Note that this expertise emerges somewhat miraculously out of one's unique experiences in life.[39] Guy Standing observes that "fictitious occupational mobility" and "uptitling" are prominent features of precariatization. Job titles such as front-office coordinator (receptionist), electronic document specialist (secretary), media distribution officer (paper boy/girl), recycling officer (bin emptier), and sanitation consultant (lavatory cleaner) are often used to make dead-end jobs sound more appealing (2011).

By promoting blogging as a form of work that does not compromise one's individual freedom, blog tutorials diminish prominent negative effects of irregular employment such as precarity, vulnerability, and exclusion. As a result, blog tutorials operate as an anti-politics machine.[40] They accept as inevitable the withdrawal of employers from offering job security while transferring the responsibility of developing employability security to individuals who can always try harder to succeed. Jodi Dean critiques scholarship that celebrates the open source software movement as an expansion in the flexibility of labor conditions. Dean instead sees this movement as an expression of neoliberalism's excesses and argues that the glamorization of flexible work conditions diffuses concerns about the public good into private interests. Free software communities might seem democratic, but they disassemble just as quickly as they assemble, "leaving in their wake a pro-capitalist, entrepreneurial, and individualistic discourse of evaluation well suited for the extensions and amplification of neoliberal governmentality" (2010, 22–24). Dean's argument resonates with my reading of blog tutorials, which reinterpret job security as a petty reward for soul-crushing work. In their misguided claim for a less alienated relationship between the individual and her labor, blog tutorials reinterpret lifetime employment as "corporate slavery." I understand this reevaluation of postwar systems of job security as an expression of the expansion of the social factory, in which labor is increasingly not called labor and the regime of human capital development is reassigned to serve as a highly efficient apparatus whose principal purpose is to secure the supply of uncompensated or undercompensated labor.

I have suggested that the most common career bloggers were able to develop was that of the "professional" blogger/consultant. The expert knowledge these bloggers offered was how to become yet another professional blogger. I also noted that male bloggers had better chances to earn an income from publishing blog tutorials. In the last section of this chapter, I examine more closely the ways in which gender structured the opportunities of bloggers to build careers. I propose that even when women succeeded in their endeavors to become "professional" bloggers/consultants, their careers anchored them to feminized affective labor. As such, I aim to show that blogging was yet another technology that seduced young women to the idea of meaningful work. Rather than offering opportunities to develop DIY careers, however, blogging platforms mobilized their users (and especially women) to become unwaged invisible labor.

Blogging, DIY Careers, and Invisible Labor

While the overwhelming majority of bloggers do not make money from blogging, many of them continue updating their blogs, reading blogs, posting comments to other bloggers' blogs, and clicking on the ads featured on blogging portals. Although I conceptualize the labor of these bloggers as feminized affective labor, Julia Elyachar's concept of phatic labor is equally helpful to expose how the owners of blogging platforms built on women's invisible labor to develop and maintain their platforms. Elyachar uses the notion of phatic labor to theorize how men advanced their entrepreneurial endeavors building on women's practices of sociality in 1990s Egypt. She argues that by "visiting, moving around, chatting, and consolidating friendship," (2010, 457) women create and extend an infrastructure—comparable to "the laying of cables or fiber-optic lines or the building of railroads"—through which all kinds of resources could flow (2010, 459). While this infrastructure does not directly produce value, it facilitates the production of value. At the same time, while this infrastructure is a community resource, entrepreneurs—dominantly men—use it to produce private profit.

In Japan, women outnumber men in the blogosphere. When I asked female bloggers to comment on this trend, I was told that women tend to post blog entries more often than their male counterparts. Moreover, women are also more likely to respond to readers' comments and link to other blogs. The blog is an interactive medium: visitors can click the "like" (*ii ne*) icon to let owners know what topics they enjoyed and would like to hear more about. Wanting to increase their page views, bloggers will respond to these requests. Like bloggers, television networks would not survive without viewers, but bloggers do more than television viewers even if we acknowledge the interpretative labor involved in watching television (Smythe 1981). Bloggers are not simply consumers. By researching topics, producing blog entries, promoting themselves, improving their writing skills, and responding to readers' comments, bloggers also assemble and maintain a vitally important consumer base that blog portals sell to advertisers.

Thus, it is not an exaggeration to claim that blogging platforms are dependent on women's labor even though the owners of these platforms do not recognize it as labor. Silvia Federici observes that the neoliberal agenda of commodifying "social relations to every corner of the social factory" is unrealizable because "capitalist accumulation is structurally dependent on the free appropriation of immense areas of labor and resources that must appear as externalities to the market, like the unpaid domestic work that women have provided, on which employers have relied for the reproduction of the workforce" (2012, 140). In this last section, I examine how a digital technology like blogging seduces women to the idea that online visibility will empower them, while in actuality, it more often than not keeps women's labor invisible and reanchors women to the gender roles from which they are trying to escape.

The tiny minority of bloggers who managed to develop new careers from blogging bolster a model of entrepreneurial success whereby business opportunities come to those who develop an online presence. Alice Marwick observes that social media promote the idea that gaining visibility online will yield not only benefits like social recognition but also new employment opportunities (2013). The idea that self-branding helps individuals develop new businesses comes from celebrity culture, for example, Gwyneth Paltrow, who developed her blog into a successful business. A Japanese counterpart is Minbe Momo, who topped Ameba's popularity ranking in 2015.[41] Minbe rose to fame as a cast member on Fuji Television's popular reality show *Ainori* between 2007 and 2008. She started blogging in 2009 and published essay collections based on her blog. She became famous for dramatizing the impact of makeup by using it on only half of her face.[42] Minbe now designs and sells fashion items and works as a consultant in the areas of fashion, makeup, hairstyle, and romance.[43]

The model of entrepreneurship she provides is one that many female bloggers try to emulate, but this model is clearly not viable for individuals who are not already famous. Blog tutorials' tenacious insistence that anyone has a chance to stand out and build a career (at least as an expert in blog culture) is misleading and makes one wonder whether these publications are not sponsored by the platforms that they promote. After all, these tutorials feed the duplicitous character of blogging platforms when they promise to open pathways for their readers to the good life, when in reality, they only funnel them to the feminized affective labor of maintaining blogging platforms. When I registered for a blog account on Ameba in 2012, my account was automatically enrolled in the general ranking of the portal. I was ranked as the 19,995,705th blogger on Ameba's popularity chart. Clearly, there is a long way from the bottom to the top.

Suzuki Junko is one of Japan's most famous fashion bloggers, and her career is emblematic of the DIY careers that blog tutorials glamorize and encourage their female readers to develop.[44] What blog tutorials do not emphasize, however, is that it requires years and already-existing skills to succeed. Building an online presence helps a blogger hone her craft, of course, but without preexisting skills, it is difficult if not impossible to become a professional blogger. Although blog tutorials evoke examples like Suzuki to make the point that anyone could become a successful blogger, she is not the stereotypical "anyone." After all, she holds a graduate degree in design from one of Japan's top arts schools, Tokyo University of the Arts (Tokyo Geijutsu Daigaku). Suzuki started blogging about cute fashions on Ameba in 2010 when she was in graduate school.[45] That same year, she entered Japan's first fashion blogger competition, named "Super Fashion Blogger Award."[46] She was selected as one of the finalists, which earned her recognition and gave an enormous boost to her blogging career. She told me that she began taking pictures in high school and gained experience working as a fashion model in graduate school. Evidently, she did not learn the skills that made her successful from blog tutorials.

Equally important, it took Suzuki years to develop her career even with her preexisting skills. In fact, she is constantly refining and redefining her expertise. Although she started as a fashion blogger, by 2016, she had expanded her online promotion through diverse platforms such as her own website and accounts on Google+, Facebook, Instagram, Lookbook.nu, Blog Lovin, and Twitter. She described herself in English as "Pro Selfer [i.e., professional at taking selfies], Creative Director, Photographer, Model, Hairmake [sic], Promoter of KawaiiLabo Tokyo [Cute Laboratory Tokyo]."[47] Google+ introduced her as a "Fashion Blogger, Artist, Good at Adding Chic, Luxury."[48] Her introduction on Blog Lovin, on the other hand, stated: "Junko is mainly a AD/Designer. But

I am also a fashion blogger. I write for the Japanese popular magazine 'Sweet' and post blog comments about things that feel 'kawaii' [cute]. 'Kawaii' makes girls happy. It means sometimes bitter and occasionally sweet."[49] In 2016 on Facebook, she described herself as a "public figure," and in 2018, she introduced herself as the managing director of Ponytail Co. Ltd., her company.[50] On her website, Suzuki defined herself as an "experience director, artist," whereas on Instagram she introduced herself as a "visual artist, cultural influencer."[51]

The fact that Suzuki uses various social media to promote herself suggests that she is the epitome of what blog tutorials promote as a success story. As a creative professional, she is often photographed in the company of other Japanese and international internet celebrities. Brooke Erin Duffy and Emily Hund argue that in the world of fashion bloggers, prestige is a "vital form of social currency" (2015, 6) that bloggers accumulate by portraying their work as glamorous elite work.[52] The photos Suzuki posts of herself depict her as a lifestyle connoisseur. The pictures are taken in spaces that are uncharacteristically Japanese in that they feature high ceilings, oversized windows, and abrupt angles. Other photos portray Suzuki traveling, attending events, and visiting fancy restaurants, always in meticulously and flawlessly coordinated outfits. The images posted on her website and social media accounts suggest that Suzuki is living the good life that blog tutorials glamorize. She seems to have the freedom to choose the type of work she will pursue, to decide when to work, and choose with whom she will work. She has realized what blog tutorials idealize but rarely deliver: freedom in work.

Suzuki's website KawaiiLabo [Cute Laboratory] and social media accounts offer the emblematic repertory of fashion bloggers whose key elements Duffy and Hund identify as "predestined passionate work, staging the glam life, and carefully curated social sharing—to depict an updated version of the post-feminist ideal of 'having it all'" (2015, 2). Similarly, Minh-Ha T. Pham observes that bloggers are willing to extend or even double their work hours because fashion excites them (2015). This link between blogging and passion, however, conceals the labor invested in the maintenance of these blogs. Pham writes that "[t]he physical work (traveling, shopping, trying on clothes, and so forth) that underpins the production of outfit posts—and that happens in between each outfit post—is removed from view, giving the impression that self-styling is an effortless activity" (2015, 88). She concludes that by concealing the time and skills bloggers invest in maintaining their blogs, they become complicit in rendering their own labor invisible. They undermine "the very significant knowledge and expertise they have with respect to media work, bodily work, and taste work" (2015, 39). By discussing their work only in such terms as excitement, passion, and pleasure, bloggers miss an important chance to make their labor visible.

Suzuki is atypical in that her fame is international. This is an effect of her decision to use a range of online platforms, most of which are not Japanese. In 2018, for example, Suzuki had 39,600 followers on Instagram.[53] Suzuki is a part of what Pham calls emerging global fashion ecologies (2015), a status she earned as a promoter of Japanese cute fashions. In a short video posted to her YouTube channel, Suzuki says that it is unconventional for a thirty-year-old woman to have the hair color she has (i.e., hues of purple, pink, and platina). When she was younger, she envisioned herself as a dynamic career woman pursuing a more traditional profession. But she is truly delighted with how things have turned out, because now she enjoys every single day of work. She recounts that she became interested in hairstyles in high school and began challenging authority by coloring her hair green. In a school that adhered to a "no dyed hair" policy, her green hair was an over-the-top statement. Suzuki concludes that being happy with who she is enables her to make friends with people she enjoys spending time with. She offers the following piece of advice: "Believe in yourself and become the best 'you' you can be and good things will happen."[54]

Compared to bloggers who are in earlier stages of their careers, Suzuki has more control over how she navigates the boundary between feminized affective labor and intellectual labor. While she no longer needs to spend too much of her time responding to comments posted to her social media sites, the adoption of cute as a key component of her self-brand makes it difficult to unequivocally challenge traditional notions of femininity (and associated gendered behaviors). Embracing conventionally feminine looks and cuteness is common among female bloggers who pursue consulting careers in the areas of fashion, makeup, cooking, and family management.

Fashion blogs can be seen as more authentic versions of women's magazines that tend to take a consumerist approach to feminism. That is, developing a career as a fashion blogger is most compatible with third-wave feminism, which promotes the ideal of having choices. The stronger Suzuki's self-brand becomes, the more freedom she enjoys in experimenting with different types of femininity. The versatility of her fashion styles and the permeability of casualness and elegance in her decisions of how to coordinate outfits mark a pronounced interest in playfully engaging with different approaches to femininity. At the same time, her choices of hair colors and colored contact lenses also signal a departure from mainstream ideas of what constitutes "Japanese Beauty," which is fittingly the title of one of Hiromix's photo books (1997b).

Figures 3.1–3.4. Suzuki as style expert. The versatility of Suzuki's fashion styles and the permeability of casualness and elegance in her decisions of how to coordinate outfits mark a pronounced interest in playfully engaging with different approaches to femininity. Photo Courtesy of Junko Suzuki, Ponytail Company Co., Ltd. Kawaiilabo (2011–2017), http:// kawaiilabo.blogspot.com/; Kawaiilabo (2017–), https://kawaiilabotokyo .com/; Instagram, https://www .instagram.com/junkosuzuki/.

Figures 3.5–3.8. Suzuki as professional "selfer." Achille Mbembe observes that capital transforms individuals into laboring nomads. He writes, "Condemned to lifelong apprenticeship, to flexibility, to the reign of the short term, he must embrace his condition as a soluble, fungible subject to be able to respond to what is constantly demanded of him: to become another" (2017, 4). As Suzuki's selfies illustrate, the constant reinvention of the self is indispensable to develop successful DIY careers, for selling unique personalities is a pivotal part of these careers. Photo Courtesy of Junko Suzuki, Ponytail Company Co., Ltd. Kawaiilabo (2011–2017), http://kawaiilabo.blogspot.com/; Kawaiilabo (2017–), https://kawaiilabotokyo.com/; Instagram, https://www.instagram.com/junkosuzuki/.

In 2018, Suzuki defined herself as a "cultural influencer," perhaps to dissociate herself from feminized affective labor. Yet, while creating and cultivating a self-brand requires intellectual labor, promoting products and, especially, hosting events entail work that is continuous with feminized affective labor.

Another blogger/vlogger I have been following since 2012 is Tominaga Ayano, who offers a less representative trajectory of success in the blogosphere because she specializes in an area that is dominated by men, technology. She started her career as a technology vlogger (video blogger) and defined her profession as an IT journalist in 2018. One would think that being an IT journalist would require the pursuit of labor that is distinctly different from the feminized affective labor fashion bloggers perform. In Japan's digital economy, however, this does not seem to be the case. The production of cuteness is central to the cultivation of both careers.

Tominaga told me that her father was a graphic designer, so she grew up around Apple gadgets. During high school, she learned web design and made money from VJ-ing for club events. She studied marketing at the University of the Arts in London, but she quit before graduating and returned to Japan. She started her career posting vlogs on UStream, which is a San Francisco–based live video site supported by advertising revenue.[55] She is also on several social media platforms, including Ameba, UStream, YouTube, Twitter, and Facebook.[56]

In 2012, Tominaga explained to me that as a livecaster, she covered events pertaining to technology such as the campouts of technology enthusiasts who waited in line to be among the first to purchase the newest models of iPhones and iPads. She was one of those enthusiasts. In 2011, she flew to New York to be one of the first consumers in the world to own a new iPad2. Tominaga also works for an online program, UST Today.[57] This program is similar to talk shows on broadcast television except that UST Today is run by online personalities like Tominaga, and it features the microcelebrities of Japanese internet culture such as Ieiri Kazuma (the founder of the web-hosting service paperboy & co) and OZPA (a famous blogger). UST Today also covers debut events announcing the launching of new videogames and apps.[58] Tominaga was featured as an IT journalist on NHK's Educational Channel, which is Japan's public broadcasting organization, similar to the BBC. In addition to working as a livecaster for UST Today, Tominaga was also one of the three members of a consulting team called UStreamAngels, a group that taught users how to work with UStream to improve their livecasting skills.

In 2014, Tominaga became famous when she camped outside the Apple store in Ginza for six days to be among the first to get a new iPhone 6. That alone would not have thrown her into the spotlight, but what did was that she slept on a foldable chair hugging her custom-made body pillow that featured Steve Jobs. In 2016, she repeated the gig, spending two nights in front of the Apple store in Omotesando (in Tokyo) to get the new iPhone 7. Although she explained that she was a devoted fan of Apple products and that Steve Jobs was her hero, journalists wanted more details about her body pillow. A few years prior to Tominaga's campout, body pillows (*dakimakura*) attained a quirky image when the Western media began reporting on a subculture of Japanese men who developed intimate relationships with their body pillows.

While we could consider Tominaga's display of her body pillow as a gesture to associate herself with male geek culture and dissociate herself from feminized affective labor, beauty has come to figure prominently in Tominaga's career. On her Instagram page, numerous photos testify to Tominaga's commitment to losing weight and living a healthier lifestyle. She also added the production of selfies to her list of skills and began cultivating more classic styles of cuteness than the earlier, quirkier cute styles she used to sport. Although her endearing signature smile forges continuity between the different styles of cute she has cultivated, her quirky-cute style emerged from her less easily classifiable and earlier attempts to create a unique self-brand. These efforts included performing songs on a nose flute, which she posted on her YouTube channel. She also offered nose flutes for sale for JPY1,000/piece ($9) and made nose flutes out of chocolate, offering for sale the experience of the edible musical instrument.

In my view, the nose flute and the Steve Jobs body pillow expose the malleability of the careers that young women like Tominaga are able to develop. In her case, one wonders whether it is expertise in vlogging culture or a uniquely charming personality that she offers for sale. That being said, another important aspect of DIY careers is that they constantly evolve. When I visited Tominaga's Instagram page in May 2018, I learned that she had added new areas of expertise to her portfolio. She described her professional identity as "Selfie expert, Tech journalist, Video maker, Bikini competitor, Tokyo based freelance video journalist covering Mobile phones and Beauty-tech."[59] Bikini competition is a recent addition to Tominaga's profile and is likely connected to Tominaga's spectacular weight loss between 2013 and 2017 with the help of what she describes as beauty technologies (e.g., weight loss apps). While Suzuki's career exemplifies the concealment of labor because it anchors DIY careers to the idea of passion (for fashion), Tominaga's case illustrates another common career strategy that keeps feminized affective labor invisible. Technology journalists, like Tominaga, sustain discourses of technological utopianism.

Tominaga and Suzuki make a living from work they describe as meaningful and fulfilling, and they both identify the good life as freedom in work. Like the fashion bloggers, whose careers Duffy and Hund (2015) and Pham (2015) describe, Suzuki and Tominaga claim that in pursuing their jobs, they pursue their passion. The connection between love and work, however, conceals the excessive competition for visibility within the digital economy. Duffy and Hund write, "the codes by which top-ranked fashion bloggers represent themselves veil the labor, discipline, and capital that go into the production of the digital self. Through discourses of passion, bloggers create a notion of work that doesn't seem like work as labor and leisure blend seamlessly together: meetings in shopping spaces, photoshoots in exotic locations, and the ability to work from home. Under this shiny veneer are very real disadvantages of an always-on, 24/7 workstyle" (2015, 9).

Blog tutorials shove bloggers like Suzuki and Tominaga into the spotlight and claim that "anybody" can develop a career from blogging. These two women, however, do not fit blog tutorials' conceptualization of blogging as easy and accessible to all: both came from well-to-do families and went to elite schools. They were also among the first to use blogging technology, which is important because the blogosphere became very quickly saturated. And it took both Suzuki and Tominaga an incredible amount of work, an exceptional sense of determination, and many, many years to build their blogging careers.

Conclusion: Blogging and the Good Life

Blog culture evolved in Japan in a moment marked by the deregulation of the labor market, growing labor precarity, and the sharply declining appeal of the postwar ideal of the good life. It was in this context in the 2000s that blogging platforms and tutorials invited individuals to blog, promising them the opportunity to develop new careers. By doing so, they furthered the dismantling of lifetime employment and catalyzed the realignment of the human capital regime. By shedding light on these trends, this chapter illustrates how technology and society merge into techno-social assemblages within which they coevolve and mutually determine each other's possibilities, constraints, and directions. In Japan, blogging platforms evolved as part of the commercial media industries, and, like the television industry, they derive their revenues from advertising. Unlike television networks, however, blogging platforms do not pay for the production of content. These platforms secure a steady stream of content by promoting blogging as a pathway to develop new careers. While they diversify the models of career building that earn individuals social recognition, they also ease the path to the deregulation of the labor market. By redefining the good life as freedom in work, rather than divorcing it from work altogether, blog culture reconfirms the postwar era's predominant ethos of productivism.

During the postwar period, the good life was understood within the ideological framework of national development. The developmental state coordinated the economy to expedite recovery from World War II and secure economic growth. It promoted an ideal of the good life that was rooted in material wealth and economic security: a thriving family business or lifetime employment that allowed people to own their homes, save for retirement, and provide their children with a good education. Blogging platforms and tutorials, however, reevaluated this postwar ideal of the good life. Rather than wealth and security, they emphasized such values as emotional well-being, freedom (understood as having more choices), and pleasure in work. They identified the good life as a lifestyle that allowed individuals to pursue work they found enjoyable, work when they felt like working, and work with people whose company they enjoyed.

Wendy Brown argues that in the context of economic deregulation, the human capital regime makes two positions available to women: they can either join the new game of human capital development or they can continue providing unpaid labor to alleviate the growing care deficits that emerged in the wake of growing economic volatility (2015). She concludes, "More than failure, the freedom tendered by neoliberal rationality (freedom from state regulation and need provision) is literally inverted into new forms of gender subordination as women remain chief providers of unremunerated and undersupported care work outside the market" (2015, 104–5). My examples suggest that the choices available to young women during the 2000s were not as dichotomous as Brown proposes. Rather, by functioning as apparatuses of the social factory, blogging platforms have expanded feminized affective labor far beyond the domestic sphere. While some female bloggers have succeeded in transforming blogging into a source of income, most maintain blogs as an extension of the feminized affective labor they perform as homemakers and office ladies. By communicating, connecting, reaching out, and responding to comments, these bloggers perform the unpaid work of social reproduction. They reproduce labor power, social relationships, and society.

Work without Sweating

AMATEUR TRADERS AND THE FINANCIALIZATION OF DAILY LIFE

The celebrity trader and author of over forty trading tutorials, Yamamoto Yuka, also wrote a children's book entitled *Money Has Feelings*. The book tells the story of Mitsuke—a one-yen coin—who was accidentally dropped and rolled under a vending machine. Waiting in the dusty darkness for what felt like an eternity, he endured freezing cold during the winter and the scorching heat of the summer. People often searched for coins under the vending machine, but they did not care to pick up Mitsuke. Day after day, he bitterly faced the fact that he had no value. One day, however, refusing to comply with her mother's concerns about hygiene, a little girl took Mitsuke home and added him to her Postal Savings piggy bank. For the first time in his life, Mitsuke felt valuable. His self-confidence, however, soon took a nosedive when his new neighbors in the piggy bank (coins of higher denominations) bragged to him about being appreciated as they circulated from one wallet to the next. Mitsuke did not stay in the piggy bank very long. Along with the other one-yen coins, he was thrown into a dark bin. His ego was bruised yet again. In the end, however, Mitsuke learned that his owner had contributed him to a project to save one-yen coins in order to purchase a new slide for the neighborhood's playground. After seeing the children's happy faces, Mitsuke realizes his own value.

In her dedication of the book, Yamamoto emphasizes that she wrote the story to help her two daughters understand the value of money. The first time I met her, she gave me a copy of the book, along with Mitsuke reincarnated as a piggy bank. The book seemed innocuously sweet, but it captivated me for a different reason. The tensions running through the book, which I read as pertaining to women's roles in regimes of feminized affective labor, resonated with the contradictions that characterized and ultimately caused the demise of the "the women trader trend." Yamamoto and many other women fueled the female trader trend in the second half of the 2000s with their engagement in and promotion of online trading.

Estimating their numbers in the hundreds of thousands, observers admired women traders' allegedly natural financial instincts that enabled them to conjure up wealth from online trading, mainly from foreign currency speculation. These women attracted media attention worldwide. In Japan, magazines featured interviews with them, publishers commissioned them to write trading tutorials, and securities firms recruited them to promote their online services. Like the female protagonist of Yamamoto's book, women traders mediated a transition from a culture of saving to a new emphasis on investing.[1] They did not benefit, however—at least not the way they expected—from the online trading platforms that they played a central role in developing and expanding.

In Yamamoto's book, the little girl's relationship to money echoes the role of the homemaker (*shufu*), who was in charge of her family's finances in the postwar period. Both the fictional girl and the real housewife saved money that they then reinvested in social reproduction. In that sense, Yamamoto's book replicates dominant media and self-representations of female traders: women who would not abandon their place in social reproduction. Put differently, the media portrayed female traders as women who never forgot where their priorities lay since they pursued online trading only as *amateur* traders.

More so than blogging, online trading was a sensitive area. Japan's old business elite was particularly distrustful of online trading. Curiously, it was not the globalization of the Japanese economy that worried them. Rather, they were anxious about the changes online trading might bring about in the realm of work. They argued that online trading was a form of value extraction that was undermining the very work ethic that transformed Japan into the second-largest economy in the world during the postwar years. They rejected online trading because it was *a way of making money without sweating*.

Just as in the blogging trend, the techno-social assemblage that evolved around online trading involved the massive production of trading tutorials. In fact, reviewers of trading tutorials on www.amazon.co.jp commonly speculate that the most famous female amateur traders probably make the bulk of their wealth from publishing tutorials about trading. This chapter demonstrates that the owners of online trading platforms (securities firms) in collaboration with the publishing industry mobilized women to promote online trading. Women, in this case, were compensated for their feminized affective labor, but not in a way that was sustainable. When online trading became a mainstream practice, the demand for female traders to write tutorials and hold lectures fizzled. Consequently, in the past two years, some of the most famous female traders, like Yamamoto and Sakai Mayumi (who goes by the name Mayuhime), have striven to revitalize their careers by writing tutorials and giving lectures about virtual currencies and artificial intelligence in trading.

The labor women invested in promoting online trading, I argue, has furthered what Randy Martin calls the financialization of daily life (2002). Martin observes that rather than just making, spending, or saving money, we are increasingly encouraged to facilitate the circulation of money. He claims that this new obligation that we invest our savings (and thus accept financial risks) is transforming how we conceive of our relationship to money.[2] This chapter demonstrates that the same trend occurred in Japan. Unlike in the United States, however, in Japan women's feminized affective labor was crucial to the financialization of daily life.

Online trading was introduced in Japan in 1998 and homemakers were the specific targets of securities firms given that they were in charge of managing their families' finances in the postwar period. Recruiting female amateur traders (the industry called them "retail investors") was a sensible strategy to promote online trading to housewives. Female traders, who were homemakers themselves (or office ladies perceived as future homemakers), seemed less alienating to housewives than professional male financiers. At the same time, female traders were able to forge continuity between the high-growth era and the recessionary present. Although women traders emerged as the public faces of online trading, they actually had a better chance of becoming a mainstream celebrity than a professional trader.

Following the interactions of the main actors who constituted the techno-social assemblage that evolved around women's online trading, I divide the chapter into three parts. First, I describe the emergence of online trading platforms in Japan. Next, I review published interviews with women traders as well as trading tutorials written by these women to understand how female traders described their paths to trading and what this endeavor meant to them. More specifically, I examine the role these portrayals played in undermining women's opportunities to become professional traders. Third, I look more closely at the careers of the two most famous women traders, Ya-mamoto Yuka and Wakabayashi Fumie. Here, I build on my interviews with these two women to trace how they negotiate the fact that although hundreds of thousands of women are pursuing online trading, the professional world of finance is still male-dominated.

The economist Yamamoto Isamu notes that the financial sector still ad-heres to the dominant division of labor that characterized the postwar period (2015). In 2015, for example, women comprised 53.3 percent of all employees in the financial sector, but less than 1 percent of these women were employed in managerial or technology-related positions; the rest were office ladies (2015).[3] By focusing on female traders who turned to the digital economy in search of careers, this chapter probes the premise of the book from a new angle. It dem-onstrates that female traders played an important role in developing and ex-panding online trading, which, in turn, supports my argument that women's labor was indispensable to the development of the digital economy.

I also add a theme that has already made brief appearances in previous chapters: the productive life of the amateur/professional dichotomy.[4] I men-tioned earlier that fans appreciated net idols as amateur celebrities who were more accessible than their professional counterparts. Bloggers who were able to sustain themselves from blogging referred to themselves as "professional bloggers" to distinguish themselves from the "hobbyist" blogging crowd. In the contexts of net idols and bloggers, the dichotomy of amateurism and pro-fessionalism was only emerging. By embracing this dichotomy, online trad-ing platforms reinforced the gender division of labor that characterized the postwar period. They preserved professional work as a domain of men and bolstered perceptions of women's labor as reproductive, part-time, irregular, and amateur labor. As such, the female trader trend supports the observation that when women tried to break into a male-dominated realm—just like the "girly" photographers—the pushback they encountered was forceful.

From Savings to Online Trading

With cumulative household savings estimated at $16,800 billion, Japan boasts the world's largest pool of savings and investable wealth.[5] Sheldon Garon iden-tifies three key conditions that facilitated the emergence of a culture of sav-ing in postwar Japan (2006; see also Hayashi 1986; Horioka 2006). First, after World War II, the state heavily targeted the population with savings cam-paigns, for it needed the funds to finance postwar reconstruction. Garon stresses that the Japanese government targeted homemakers in particular as the principal agents responsible for saving money. To expand the culture of saving, it even extended its promotional campaigns to schoolchildren, who were targeted with nationwide propaganda such as school savings programs.[6] Second, Garon notes that the availability of convenient and safe savings institutions like the postal savings system also offered a compelling incentive for individuals to embrace thrifty habits. Through the postal savings system, small savers could open government-guaranteed savings accounts at any post office. Finally, Garon points out that credit and loans were much harder to get in Japan for consumption or real estate. Home equity loans were rare, and down payments on home mortgages are still higher in Japan than they are in the United States.[7] As a result, a unique culture of savings emerged in postwar Japan. The savings rate peaked in 1975, but it turned negative only in 2014.[8]

A salient feature of Japan's saving culture is that the bulk of the country's savings pool is kept in fixed deposit accounts despite the fact that interest rates on these deposits have been peculiarly low.[9] Japan's long recession and financial reforms, however, opened paths for wealthy homemakers—such as Ikebe Yukiko, whom I will introduce in the next section—to invest some of their families' savings through professional brokers. The stagnating salaries and hiring freezes in the early 2000s heightened incentives for individuals to seek out new sources from which to earn a living or supplement their income. At the same time, the deregulation of the financial industry was also conducive to opening the domestic financial market to individual investors. While the deregulation of Japan's financial sector began in the mid-1970s, a stronger wave of deregulation occurred in the late 1980s when Japanese government bond futures contracts were launched at the Tokyo Stock Exchange (TSE). The new stock index futures and options markets attracted individual investors in massive numbers, making the Tokyo Stock Exchange the largest in the world in 1988 (Miyazaki 2012).[10]

A decade later, in the late 1990s, Japan's financial industry was deregulated again as part of Hashimoto Ryūtarō's Big Bang plan, which opened up Japan's banking, insurance, and stock exchange markets to global competition. Until then, Nomura, Daiwa, and Nikko Cordial had dominated the investment market. In 1998, however, revisions of the Foreign Exchange and Foreign Trade Control Law ended the monopoly of Japanese banks in foreign currency trading. At the same time, the expansion of the internet lowered the entry barriers for start-up businesses. The first online brokerage firms were launched in 1998, and the number of these firms increased to 67 by 2001.[11] In 2000, TSE switched to electronic trading for all transactions,[12] and in 2006, TSE's computer system was upgraded to be able to handle five million trades a day. Today, electronic trading constitutes 90 percent of all trading in Japan.

These trends were not specific to Japan. Karin Knorr Cetina and Alex Preda observe that technological innovations were conducive to the expansion and global integration of national financial markets (2006). Similarly, Saskia Sassen notes that the digitization of trading has led to the proliferation of financial flows and practices.[13] She stresses that the financial market is increasingly an electronic market that allows for the decentralized and simultaneous participation of millions of investors in a globally integrated financial market (2006).

Online trading platforms allow individual investors to trade securities (stocks and bonds), commodities, foreign currencies, and financial derivatives. What makes these platforms appealing to small investors is that they charge significantly lower commissions than traditional brokerage houses that must shoulder the costs of maintaining brick-and-mortar branch offices and the salaries of brokers who provide customized investment advice. Similar to the context of blogging, technological utopianism was a powerful means to deliver new clients to online trading platforms. Despite the fact that liquidity is part and parcel of a healthy financial market, online trading platforms were promoted as infrastructures able to control the volatility of the financial markets.[14] Online trading platforms were glamorized as miracle technologies that were even able to automate moneymaking. Yamamoto Yuka's tutorial entitled *How to Accumulate Wealth from Automated Stock Trading* (2004b) proposes that individuals can earn money without the investment of time and labor.

The idea that online trading platforms can technologically "miraculate" money exercised a powerful hold on the popular imagination and surely contributed to the robust rise of online trading accounts. In 1999, the number of accounts at Japan's electronic securities firms was 296,941. By 2005, this number reached 7.9 million.[15] Not surprisingly, I have not found any data on what percentage of these accounts' owners actually made money from online trading. Online trading platforms, however, certainly yielded profits to *their* owners, as evidenced by the example of the founder of Monex Group Inc., Matsumoto Oki. The media call Matsumoto the "100 Million Yen Man" ($1 million), which is what Matsumoto takes home every month.[16]

Japan's five largest online brokerage firms include Matsui Securities, Rakuten Securities Inc., Kabu. Com Securities Co., SBI Securities Co., and Monex Group Inc. The country hosts more than two dozen other online securities firms, including GMO Kurikku Shōken,[17] Himawari Shōken, Gaitame Dotto Komu, Kawase Life, Minna no FX, Lion FX, Yahoo Gurūpu FX, Minna no Gaitame, Fourando Onrain (which merged with FXCM Rakuten in 2011), Central Tanshi FX, Ueda Harlow FX, DMM FX, Gaitame Online, Kanetsu FX Shōken, FX Trading System's FX Broadnet, Raifu Stā Shōken, Kabu Dotto Komu, Okasan Online Shōken, Nomura Shōken, Daiwa Shōken, Tokai Tokyo Shōken, Musashi Securities, Naito Shōken, Iwai Cosmo Shōken, Tachibana Shōken Netto Torēdo, HS Shōken, and Money Partners.[18] These platforms offer different configurations of features like low transaction fees that start around JPY700 ($6.30), flat-rate trading, minimum or no minimum balance to open an account, specialists that can be reached via telephone or email, stock performance history, access to quote lookups, mobile trading, nighttime trading, stock lending services, market news, analyst advice, apps that offer risk analysis (by reviewing one's portfolio to evaluate its strengths and suggesting strategies for improvement), virtual trading apps that allow one to practice trading, and desktop apps with a multitude of tools that aid market analysis and trading.

Unlike traditional brokerage firms, online trading platforms are interactively designed, that is, users influence the development of these platforms. In an online interview, Monex CEO Matsumoto Oki says, "So we listen to customers to meet unmet needs. At many times, companies think of what customers want without asking them how best to meet their needs. When I founded Monex, I was thinking, the Japanese financial institutions are running businesses on supply side logic and not customer side of logic."[19] In 2015, Matsumoto appointed himself as Customer Happiness Officer (CHO), claiming that feedback from customers was the key to effective innovation. He claims to write a column to solicit customer input every day to the 750,000 subscribers of Monex's email magazine and says that he receives a lot of feedback. He comments, "In these [messages], people tell me what they think about particular projects we do. This is valuable feedback. In the past, it wasn't easy to get hundreds of thousands of customer voices giving you feedback every day. Now we can, and I see this as an excellent way to understand what customers need at all times. I believe effective marketing just needs the PDCA (plan-do-check-act) process. We come up with ideas for services, try them, ask for customer feedback and adjust. Over and over, do this process, and you will deliver what customers want."[20]

In the past fifteen years, the online brokerage industry has become a cutthroat business. Many securities firms have merged, and many of the bigger firms bought out some of the smaller ones. Foreign online securities firms such as E*Trade or the IG Group also expanded their operations to the Japanese market. At the same time, traditional banks forged alliances with online securities firms to tap into each other's clientele (e.g., Resona's alliance with Matsui Securities in the mid-2000s).

The growth of electronic securities firms coincided with the proliferation of websites designed to attract participants to the new financialization of daily life. To manage the tidal wave of these online trading platforms, sites were developed to help internet users compare the advantages of different sites.[21] Websites were also designed to offer market analyses and trading tips[22] and help internet users learn trading.[23] Some bloggers also specialized in providing information and education that pertained to online trading.[24] All the women traders I discuss in this chapter maintained their own blogs to promote themselves and offer information about their lectures and books.

What seemed to be a technologically driven "democratization" of the financial market, in turn, advanced what scholars conceptualized as financialization, which refers to the tendency for financial activities to take a central role in the economy (rather than manufacturing and services more generally).[25] Greta Krippner defines financialization as a "tendency for profit making in the economy to occur increasingly through financial channels rather than through productive activities" (2011, 4). In other words, rather than identifying financialization as the proliferation of new financial instruments and a robust rise in the volume of financial transactions, Krippner proposes to measure economic change by examining where profits are generated in the economy.[26] Instead of following a labor-centered perspective, which only highlights the rise of the service sector commonly associated with postindustrial capitalism, she adopts an accumulation-centered approach. She writes that the growing weight of finance in the economy is reflected not only in the proliferation of banks, securities firms, and finance companies but also by the changing behavior of nonfinancial firms, which tend to diversify their revenue sources by increasingly relying on portfolio income. In addition to securing a cash flow from productive activities, nonfinancial firms also derive revenue from financial activities that accrue interest payments, dividends, and capital gains on investments (2011).[27]

Along with Saskia Sassen (2006), who noted that the digitization of trading has contributed to liquefying forms of wealth that were formerly nonliquid, I argue that the digitization of trading has also destabilized the dominant understanding of what constitutes socially sanctioned ways of earning a living. I thus complement Krippner's argument by emphasizing that financialization is also reflected in individuals' changing attitudes about the dominant model of making a living, which has shifted from the belief that the salary (or wage) is the primary way of earning an income to one that assembles livelihoods from a variety of sources, some of which even involve risk-taking.[28] Note that some forms of trading, such as margin trading that requires borrowing money, involve more risks than others. Online trading platforms, however, do not educate their users about risk. They promote risk-taking as a viable path to the good life, and women traders have played a key role in forging associations between online trading and the good life. A trader who went by the name Mayuhime claimed, for example, that by investing only fifteen to thirty minutes a day, she was able to make more money than an office lady.

By seducing internet users into believing that online trading was indeed a viable source of revenue, online trading platforms—like blogging platforms—contributed to the destabilization of salaried employment as the dominant form of socially recognized work. Randy Martin notes that while financialization does not compensate for the crumbling of the traditional system of job security, it has become a means to develop one's own self-promise and financial self-management (2002). In 2000s Japan, female amateur traders played an important role in the financialization of daily life by shaping a common understanding that financial speculation was a viable path to the good life.

Considered in this context, Yamamoto's story about the emotional one-yen coin is a reflection on the shift from a culture of savings to the financialization of daily life and the role women played in this transition. Yamamoto might be attempting to valorize herself and to make sense of the invisibility of her own labor—not by identifying with the girl protagonist but by associating with the one-yen coin. From this perspective, Yamamoto assumed a traditional male role as she engaged in the risky business of trading.[29] Like the coins collected in the piggy bank, she entered the world of finance and rode the wave of supposed democratization of the market. She soon realized, however, that she was different and was made to feel less valuable, like Mitsuke, who ultimately found joy in watching children at the playground, a site of affective labor. Mitsuke's value shifted from a stagnant place of savings to the reproductive life of the community, and through this transformation he attained the good life.

In the next section, I will look more closely at the links between online trading, responsible financial conduct, and the good life. I turn my attention in particular to the role of women traders in the promotion of these associations. I also examine how media portrayals and self-presentations of female traders defined the labor of female amateur traders as feminized affective labor, which, in turn, foreclosed the opportunities of these women to become professional traders.[30]

Women's Paths to Trading

Like the ways in which women were instrumental in the promotion of a culture of savings during the postwar period, women have also played an important role in the transition to a new culture of embracing financial risk. The rapid growth of women online traders in Japan garnered attention worldwide. Articles about female amateur traders in Japan appeared in the *New York Times*, *Financial Times*, and *Wall Street Daily*. In Japan, articles about the trend and interviews with women traders appeared not only in major women's magazines (*Fujin Kōron*) but also in economics journals (*The Economist*) and general interest magazine (*Shūkan Bunshun*, *Da Capo*, *Nikkei Money*, *Yomiuri Weekly*, *Shūkan Asahi*, *Sunday Mainichi*, and *Shūkan Gendai*). We learn from these accounts that the majority of women traders were in their twenties and thirties, with very few of them beyond their early forties. We also learn that most women traders did day trading (i.e., they bought and sold financial instruments within the same trading day) and that they specialized in foreign currencies because these were much fewer in number than stocks, commodities, and futures and thus easier to monitor. Most pertinent to my argument is that the media consistently portrayed women traders as homemakers and office ladies (i.e., future homemakers).

By casting women traders in these traditional roles, securities firms and publishers were able to mobilize women to promote online trading to other homemakers and office ladies. When women explained why they started trading and what trading meant to them, they commonly stressed that they were also homemakers and dabbled in trading only as amateurs. By doing so, they reinforced the coding of their labor as feminized affective labor, which, in turn, made it more difficult for them to develop careers as professional traders. In the previous chapter, I introduced Julia Elyachar's study of how women's practices of socializing created a communal infrastructure that men built on to establish private businesses (2010). Similarly, in 2000s Japan, women developed an infrastructure through which financial instruments could circulate. Because online trading platforms were interactively designed, women helped to develop them. They also contributed to expanding online trading by promoting it in their trading tutorials, seminars, and lectures.

Women traders never failed to emphasize that their involvement in trading did not compromise their responsibilities as caregivers and homemakers.

In a *Wall Street Daily* article, stay-at-home mother Someya Etsuko reported, "I will fix a time and will trade only within that timeframe. The other times I will spend doing my chores and playing with my son."[31] This insistence that trading was compatible with raising children was a response to the old business elite who lamented that women's involvement in online trading undermined the education of children.[32] These critics reasoned that mothers too preoccupied with making money were less available to help their children excel in school. Furthermore, they feared that children who witnessed their mothers making money without "the sweat of the brow" would not understand what hard work meant.

The most famous trader/homemaker was Yamamoto Yuka. Yamamoto consistently promoted herself as a homemaker and thus deflected criticism that she neglected her principal responsibilities as a housewife. She even spun this criticism by saying that being a stay-at-home mom actually enabled her to develop efficient techniques of time management and trading. In her book, *The Charisma Housewife Will Tell You How People Who Are Able to Fulfill Their Dreams Manage Their Time* (2010), she states she was very busy and was able to spend only ten minutes in the morning on day trading.[33] She said she had experimented with trading various types of financial instruments to ensure that her involvement in trading would not conflict with her role as a homemaker. Stressing that she never neglected her family responsibilities (what she calls *shufu no mokusen*), she explains that her key strategy was to strictly limit the time she spent on trading.[34] Similarly, Hiroshima-based homemaker Mayuhime stressed that she could spend only fifteen to thirty minutes a day trading because her daughter required constant attention. She claimed that even with this little time investment, she still made about $2,800 to $3,000 a month.[35]

Not surprisingly, the claim that it is possible to earn a living wage by working only half an hour a day rubbed the old business elite the wrong way. I also find this claim troubling, although for a different reason. Such a claim draws on the assumption that online trading does not require labor investment because it is technology—in this case, online trading platforms—that performs the actual labor and generates profits for traders. By proposing that technology does the bulk of the work, women traders not only glorify trading platforms but, like bloggers, also devalue their own labor. They enable online trading platforms to make human labor invisible. Mayuhime did reveal in a radio interview that until she learned the ropes of online trading, she spent twelve to twenty hours a day for weeks in front of her computer.[36]

Women traders commonly described their involvement in online trad-

Figure 4.1. Mayuhime's style of promoting online trading as a magical way to earn a living.

ing as a "socially responsible" form of entrepreneurship. While this strategy might have helped them balance the criticism that trading was work without sweating, it also strengthened the link between women and feminized affective labor. Women usually explained that they began to trade because they had limited choices. They reasoned that they were forced to take responsibility for their lives because their parents were not able to provide them with a good education (Wakabayashi Fumie), they lost their job (Yamane Akiko),[37] they got divorced and lost their only source of income (Torii Mayumi), or their husbands' salaries were insufficient to support their families (Yamamoto Yuka). They chose online trading because they saw it as a form of earning an income that allowed them to preserve their dignity, unlike other underpaid, part-time jobs. These accounts stressed that women took the responsible path to help support their families. Indeed, women traders also commonly stressed that they spent their trading gains on their families. Yamamoto explained that she used her earnings to pay off her family's mortgage and buy a bigger home.[38] In a radio interview, Mayuhime shared the fact that she bought her father a Mercedes Benz to reward him for supporting his family.[39]

Women traders also associated their involvement in trading as a form of community involvement. They emphasized the social value in teaching women the business of online trading and stressed that they wanted to help other women fight the downward mobility of their families. Interviews with Yamamoto Yuka, for example, include images of her at a table surrounded by other mothers, all holding small children on their laps as they learn to interpret trading charts on their laptops.[40] Another celebrity trader, Torii Mayumi had been a homemaker with a two-year-old child when she decided to get a

Figure 4.2.   Torii Mayumi's website promoting her as an educator who helps amateurs learn online trading.

divorce. She did the math and quickly concluded that the part-time jobs available to her would barely cover the cost of daycare. She then researched other opportunities that would allow her to work from home and spent much of her savings on seminars designed to teach her how to earn an income from blogging and affiliated advertising. She, however, was not successful.

Then in 2006, she heard about online trading, and within a short time, she gained fame as a female trader. In interviews, she emphasized that the experience of vulnerability as a single mother was what prompted her to turn to online trading and claimed that her mission was to help other women fight impoverishment.[41] On her website, Torii describes online trading as an empowering experience (although not in a feminist sense). When a trader is able to make a little profit, she writes, that little gain will boost her self-confidence, which, in turn, will help her enjoy her life and become more forward looking. Torii says she wants to see more women who are happy and proud (*shiawasede jibunrashiku kirakira shita josei*). She writes, "I think that there will be more happy children when there are more happy women, happy mothers. And that will lead to a happier future for Japan . . . that is what I believe."[42]

To preempt the criticism that women traders were neglecting their children, these women also insisted that trading was not a time-consuming activity. Implicit in this claim was another one, namely that online trading was an easy way to make money. To make this claim convincing, female traders transformed a culturally valued behavioral pattern (modesty) into self-deprecatory demeanor. They insisted that if *they* were able to learn trading—even though they had no talent or skills—then anyone could do it. Many traders claimed that they did not even know how to use a computer before they started online trading. Torii Mayumi confessed in interviews that she was so ignorant about trading that when she first heard the word FX (foreign exchange), she thought it referred to Sante's eyedrops named FX.[43] Similarly, Wakabayashi Fumie never failed to stress that she was an "average young woman" (*futsū no onna no ko*). She recounted that at her first job as an office lady at a brokerage firm, she did not even know what the Japanese character of *kabu* (stock) meant in the company's name, *kabushiki gaisha* (2004, 20).

Aiming to portray amateur traders as individuals whose advice could be trusted, publishers commonly included in book titles such labels as "legendary trader" (*densetsu no torēdā*) and "charisma housewife" (*karisuma shufu*). (In Japanese, "charisma housewife" is used to describe full-time homemakers who not only keep their household in impeccable order but also complement the household income by running some side business while always appearing elaborately coiffed and flawlessly styled.[44]) Although many of Yamamoto's books feature the labels of "charisma housewife" or "legendary trader," she still maintains that she is just "an average housewife from the suburbs" (*tada no inaka no shufu*). I surmise that such claims did not help those women who wanted to be taken seriously as traders.

One reviewer on www.amazon.co.jp poked fun of Yamamoto's self-deprecatory attitude, saying,

> She [Yamamoto] keeps saying that if someone as stupid as she is was able to learn online trading, then anyone can do it. Dear Mrs. Yamamoto, you are not stupid. There are a lot of real morons out there in the world. They read your book and think that "even a dummy can do online trading." I would be more favorable toward this book if it was an autobiography, which tells the story of how Yamamoto earned money from online trading. But the author's purpose is clearly a recommendation of online trading without offering any convincing evidence that amateurs would be able to earn money from it. Isn't this a little irresponsible? She does not explain how to choose brands [of trading tools,

sites, apps], etc. Probably she does not want to share that information. If that is the case, then why write books about trading as opposed to just making money from it?[45]

Many readers confessed that they were not finding it as easy as Yamamoto had claimed to balance family management with online trading.[46] Another reviewer on www.amazon.co.jp comments,

> Like the author, I am also a housewife with two small children. I thought that I shouldn't complain about my family's financial situation without trying to improve it. I followed this author's instructions and tried for two years to make money from online trading. I also tried the Ken Miller site that she recommended. I lost about as much money as I earned. My overall trading balance is still in the positive and might slowly be getting better, but online trading is not a "super easy" way to make money. I also do not think that it works at all what the author is suggesting that one should just check the stock indices when she has the time. We are talking about short-term trades. This advice is irresponsible. She included a little bit of her trading transactions as evidence, but with that little evidence even I can write a tutorial. As a fellow housewife, I cannot recommend this book.[47]

These reviews are typical of the reception trading tutorials written by women traders receive. Readers shower these tutorials with vitriolic criticism, and some go so far as to claim that these trading tutorials are a scam (*inchiki*). They insist that the authors of these tutorials are irresponsible when they emphasize that making money from trading is "extremely easy," "no hassle," "friendly," and "interesting" (*chō kantan, muri nai, yasashii, omoshiroi*) and that online trading enables one to realize one's dreams and attain happiness (*yume wo kanaeru, shiawase ni naru*). Needless to say, such representations of online trading also played an important part in concealing women's labor. As one reviewer of Yamamoto's tutorials wrote: "To learn a bit about the world of online trading, this might be a good book. However, it is scary to start trading just based on this book. It is like driving a car without a brake. Books like this make homemakers feel invincible. These books might help homemakers earn a little money, then, those women challenge margin trading and take out a credit when margin calls are made that their savings cannot cover. This is a dangerous terrain."[48] Although many readers find trading tutorials disappointing, publishers print them and readers buy them. Between 2000 and 2013, for instance, Yamamoto published approximately forty-five books,[49] and

Figure 4.3.
Despite the readers'
critical responses,
some of Yamamoto's
books have achieved
the #1 position on
Amazon's ranking of
best-selling books.

in 2018, her new tutorial introducing readers to trading virtual currencies (2018) became a #1 bestseller on amazon.co.jp.

While readers might not find trading tutorials helpful in their projects to become successful online traders, they seem to enjoy reading them as career porn. This might be because these tutorials tirelessly repeat the message that trading is fun, easy, and a path to the good life. They present online trading as an opportunity to earn an income (and possibly even to develop a career).[50] It is in this sense that I see the labor women invest in writing these tutorials and promoting online trading as a form of affective labor that integrates both feminized affective labor and intellectual labor.

Seminars and lectures sponsored by securities firms also illustrate how female traders are mobilized to feminized affective labor. I attended a lecture by Ikebe Yukiko, who earned fame when the National Tax Agency imposed a penalty of approximately $4 million on her for neglecting to pay taxes on her earnings from online trading (Ikebe 2008, 2009, 2010). I am not sure whether it was the amount that captured the popular imagination or the rumor that Ikebe paid the fine in cash straight out of her safe when the tax collector showed up at her home unannounced.

Ikebe did not fit the stereotype of amateur female traders. Unlike other female traders who authored tutorials, she started trading through brokers in the late 1980s. She came from a wealthier family than most women who turned to trading during the 2000s. Although she did not fit the image of the female traders who appeared in the media to promote online trading, Ikebe, too, was mobilized to inspire women to invest their savings using online trading platforms. Owners of these platforms and the media probably found Ikebe's tax evasion scandal too savory to pass up. Although it was common among traders to disclose how much money they earned from trading, most did not have concrete evidence to back up their claims, unlike Ikebe.[51] She told me that when she started trading, she relied on (and learned from) professional brokers. She followed the news and instructed her broker to make changes to her investment portfolio based on what she understood about the economic performance of certain companies and credit ratings of particular countries. The development of online trading platforms helped her cut out the middlemen. Her decade-long experience of trading through brokers made her transition to online trading seamless.[52]

Kanetsu FX Securities sponsored a lecture by Ikebe that I attended, which Tokyo TV recorded. After the lecture, a television producer for Tokyo TV's financial news interviewed Ikebe. I was invited to be present at the interview, during which the producer also asked me a couple of questions about the "global" view on Japanese housewives who pursue online trading. Before the interviews, however, Ikebe gave a lengthy PowerPoint presentation, which was a mix of trading charts and photos of her visiting exotic tourist destinations. The presentation worked affectively. It did not offer trading tips but did forge an association between online trading and the good life. The travel photos also legitimated Ikebe as a competent trader whose opinion one could trust when selecting an online trading platform. Dark-suited employees of Kanetsu FX Securities were conveniently available to answer questions about their services and to recruit potential clients from the fully packed lecture hall.

Ikebe entered the popular imagination as the "kimono trader" because she never appeared in public wearing anything other than exquisite kimonos. Yamamoto, Wakabayashi, and Ikebe playfully reflected upon their own media personas, describing themselves and others to me as the "the trader-comedienne" (*owarai-kei torēdā*), "the sexy-trader" (*sekushii torēdā*), "the trader beauty" (*bijin torēdā*), or the "kimono [i.e., classy] trader" (*kimono torēdā*). Occasionally, women traders grumbled about their stereotypical representations in the media but went along with them because cohesive public personalities opened opportunities for them to publish books, give lectures, and develop ca-

Figure 4.4.   Yamamoto Yuka giving a lecture with fellow traders about her new interest in virtual currencies.

reers unrelated to trading. The excessive feminization and self-feminization of these women traders, however, played an important role in the ultimate demise of the trader boom.[53] By mobilizing female traders to feminized affective labor, the media and the finance sector undermined a perception of women as serious traders and foreclosed opportunities for them to continue earning an income as financial educators and advisors. What the media and the financial sector celebrated as women's natural talent for finances remained tied to their traditional gender roles, which, in turn, reconfirmed that women remained amateurs on the margins of the world of finance.

Women's Aspirations beyond Trading

Women traders offered consistent stories to the media to describe their paths to online trading and what this endeavor meant to them. During interviews with me, Yamamoto Yuka and Wakabayashi Fumie recited many of the stereotypes that the media circulated about them. Listening to the stories of how these women began trading made me think that a stable media persona might have been indispensable to securing a flow of book contracts, lecture commitments, and interviews. A closer inspection of their narratives, however, revealed slight inconsistencies, which I view as expressions of how these women strategically positioned themselves vis-à-vis the opportunities they were trying to seize.

Among the women amateur traders who became celebrities, Yamamoto was the most prolific writer. The media frequently turned to her for an insider's view about the women trader trend, and her voice became one of the most prominent. When I asked her what she envisioned for her future, however, she shared plans unrelated to trading. I got the impression that she did not believe it was viable to continue playing the role of the amateur trader. Rather, she was thinking of translating her celebrity status into writing mystery novels, which is what she had originally wanted to do. Yamamoto was sharp and had a great sense of humor. She told me that most women traders played the "sexy-smart" image, but she thought of herself as a trader-comedienne (*owarai-kei torēdā*). Directing attention to her humor may have been a technique she employed to separate herself from the feminization of women traders. When I inquired whether I could ask her questions that pertained to her life beyond online trading, she responded that I could ask her any question other than her weight and waist size.

I learned from a magazine interview with Yamamoto that she turned to trading after she gave birth to her first daughter and became a homemaker.[54] She started looking for work and discovered online trading as a source of income she was able to pursue from home while raising her daughter. Initially, she set a modest goal for herself: she wanted a monthly disposable income of only $200. She taught herself trading and developed a method that worked with her responsibilities as a mother and a wife. As her trading skills improved, she upped the ante, but never to the point at which trading would interfere with her responsibilities as a homemaker. With a goal to earn 10 percent in profits, she limited both the time she spent trading and the goals she set for her investments.

Her story suggests that the middle-class ideal of family—which consisted of the working father, a stay-at-home mother, and children—was increasingly hard to maintain in the aftermath of a long recession. Online trading was certainly a strategy to sustain the very postwar gender roles that many young women (like Wakabayashi Fumie) wanted to get away from, but to which many others remained attached (like Yamamoto Yuka, Torii Mayumi, Mayuhime).

In my interview with Yamamoto, she told me that she originally wanted to become an academic, but in high school she hung out with the wrong crowd and neglected her schoolwork. As a result, she failed her entrance examination to the university she wanted to attend. After graduating from Kitasato University (still a renowned private university), she became a teacher in a vocational school, where she taught science. She also worked as a volunteer in a biotech lab at the University of Tokyo as a technician in charge of experiments with liver cells. She married a colleague in the same lab and quit her position because of a conflict of interest. She wanted to write mystery novels but was unable to find a publisher. When one publisher heard that Yamamoto was pursuing online trading, he advised her to write trading tutorials. The fact that Yamamoto contemplated a career in academia did not appear in printed interviews with her. The reason for this might have been that this fact conflicted with her media image, that she was an average housewife from the suburbs, which I do not think is an accurate description. Her ability to translate complex economic processes into simple language and her determination to develop her career made her anything but an "average housewife."

Inconsistencies such as these reveal that these women not only understood how to sell foreign currencies but also how to develop self-brands. For instance, when Yamamoto described her trading method, I learned that she adhered to a research-oriented approach. She used various data sources to gather information about companies whose stocks she was considering trading. To explain what she meant by research-oriented approach, she offered the following example. When she heard that the price of gasoline was going up, she immediately checked stock prices—not only of electronic automakers but also of sugar-producing factories because she knew that ethanol was made from sugar cane and was a potential substitute for gasoline. She emphasized not only the importance of doing research but also of cross-referencing information to ensure that her information was reliable.

This story includes an important element that does not fit Yamamoto's media persona. It is that she draws on her background in research when trading, which contradicts her insistence that she had no relevant training and was only an "average housewife from the suburbs." Media images that highlighted Yamamoto's inexperience reinforced the idea that even women who lacked preparation could succeed in online trading. Yet her experience illustrates that online trading is a lot more labor intensive than the popular media present it.

Yamamoto described herself as a person who did not give up on things easily. For instance, it took her a while to digest the criticism posted on social networking sites and BBS sites, such as *nichanneru* (2channel, www.2ch.net). These comments criticized her for encouraging other women to get engaged in something as risky as day trading. People called her a "high-risk housewife" and said they felt sorry for her husband and would never marry someone like her. She said that reading such criticism hurt her feelings, but she derived encouragement from all the other women who came to her rescue and responded to these critics on her behalf. She said that the criticism that came from the old business elite was especially hard to swallow and mentioned one article that made her feel particularly bad. It claimed that she and Livedoor's former CEO Horie Takafumi were examples of people who would only make the Japanese economy more volatile.[55] She admitted that day trading was not necessarily good for economic stability, but she also did not think that economic stability was sustainable.

She reasoned that women traders attracted media attention because they challenged the prevalent stereotype that portrayed Japanese homemakers as risk-averse—people who preferred to keep their savings in fixed deposit accounts even if those accounts did not yield interests. She thought that keeping money in low-interest savings accounts was irresponsible, and that financial speculation was not risky as long as it was done responsibly. She lamented that salaries were stagnating in the aftermath of the recession. Her husband, for example, made JPY300,000 ($2,738) a month, which was not enough for a family of four living in the suburbs of Tokyo. She stressed that she wanted to increase her family's income and had no choice but to pursue online trading from home. She emphasized that she always kept some savings that she never touched and with which she never "gambled." She believed that it was the people unwilling to learn the business of trading that *were* the gamblers: they were the ones who lost money.[56]

She also shared her opinion with me that many women became celebrities not because they were successful traders but because they had the necessary looks and personalities. These celebrity traders did some trading and were successful to a certain degree, but then they became "campaign girls" for securities firms. Yamamoto commented that the women who wrote only one or two books were rarely serious traders. When I first met her in 2010, she had been writing trading tutorials for ten years and had published forty of them. She defined her human capital value not in terms of her expertise in online trading but in terms of her celebrity status, which she saw as a flexibly investable form of capital that she would be able to transform into new money-making opportunities. I gather from the resumes Yamamoto has posted on various websites offering her services as a financial advisor and financial educator that she is not only remarkably talented but also exceptionally entrepreneurial.

On a Japanese database of lecturers,[57] for example, Yamamoto is introduced as follows:

> She graduated from the Faculty of Sciences at Kitasato University and worked in Kanagawa Prefecture's Third Center as a research fellow. She participated in a research project that aimed to develop a hybrid artificial liver and to preserve liver cells. After the project ended, she served as a curriculum coordinator in a vocational school. She taught courses on animal cell engineering and vegetable tissue cultures. She was also in charge of preparatory courses for exams on handling poisonous and toxic substances. In a continuing education program, she also earned a degree in applied psychology and worked as a school counselor in a vocational school. After that employment experience, she worked as a counselor for a project that aimed to develop health management systems for corporate employees. She coordinated the drafting and writing of project proposals.

Her pursuit of various careers illustrates that she was undoubtedly more ambitious than the average homemaker and that she positioned herself as a celebrity unique enough to attract event organizers who aimed to fill lecture halls; at the same time, she needed to make herself seem ordinary enough to readers of trading tutorials who needed to imagine themselves in the author's shoes in order to gain the courage to start trading.

Wakabayashi Fumie was another celebrity trader I interviewed, and she also appeared in the *Financial Times* article I mentioned earlier. Wakabayashi began trading at age twenty. When she was preparing for her college entrance exam, her father's small construction and engineering business went bankrupt. She had to give up her dreams of earning a college degree and becoming a nurse. Instead, she held several part-time positions until she landed a job as an office lady at the investment consultant company E-Capital. At E-Capital, she became interested in the stock exchange and began trading—in her free time, not as part of her paid work.

Wakabayashi did not have anything flattering to say about being employed as an office lady. In *I Love Stocks* (2004), she recounted that she found the work excessively demanding and the rampant sexism disturbing. Among other responsibilities, Wakabayashi was assigned to recruit new clients over the phone. The five percent who did not immediately hang up on her insulted her with comments such as the following: "Why should I listen to you? Women cannot understand stock trading"; "If you do this kind of work, no one will ever marry you"; and "Instead of the stock prices, tell me your price." Wakabayashi decided that if she learned trading, she could quit her job and would not have to deal with dirty old men (*kuso oyaji*) ever again. She bought a few trading tutorials but did not understand them. She felt dispirited, but then a male colleague took pity on her. He lent her his trading account so she could try trading herself. Wakabayashi says that when she started trading, all the pieces of the puzzle aligned into a coherent picture (2004, 22).

She published nine trading tutorials and a Nintendo DS investment game between 2004 and 2007, after which she stopped writing tutorials. Her publications earned her invitations to appear on radio programs and television shows, including Tokyo Broadcasting System's *Sunday Japon* and Tokyo Television's *Asa wa Vitamin*. In 2005, Wakabayashi founded F&D Ltd. with three million yen in capital [roughly $30,000] and sixty issued stocks. According to Wakabayashi's website, the firm operates stock investment; publishes trading tutorials; conducts seminars; manages restaurants; designs, manufactures, and sells character goods; and administers a pet shop.

Between 2007 and 2012, Wakabayashi also served as an adjunct economics professor at Tokuyama University, where she taught "Contemporary Stock Market Theory." Additionally, Wakabayashi offered a course entitled "First Step to New Stock Investment" at Meiji University's Liberty Academy, which is a continuing education program separate from the university's curriculum. On the program's website, Wakabayashi is listed as an adjunct professor at Tokuyama University, but according to Wakabayashi's Japanese-language Wikipedia entry, her contract at Tokuyama University was cancelled in 2012 for what the Wikipedia entry alludes to as Wakabayashi's questionable entrepreneurial ethics, evidenced by her use of such titles as "adjunct professor" when she only finished high school.[58]

Of all the women traders, Wakabayashi has become the most popular because of her weekly appearance on Tokyo TV's afternoon variety program *Go ji ni Mucchū!* She accepted an invitation to be a regular guest on the show on Wednesdays in 2005, but in 2008, a blog-related copyright infringement (she repurposed information from an affiliate of *Nihon Keizai Shinbun* on her Ameba blog) forced her to withdraw. She returned to the show a year later and was paired with cross-dressing essayist Matsuko DeLuxe. The show runs every weekday and has two regular hosts accompanied by two regular guests that participate one day a week. Wakabayashi and Matsuko DeLuxe are the regular guests on Mondays. In the show, Wakabayashi is introduced as a "stock trader." Her Wikipedia entry mentions that the media scooped her up because she was a "trader-beauty" (*bijin torēdā*) and that the distinguishing feature of her tarento persona was her amateurishness as a celebrity, manifested in mistakes observers described as cute. An example of such a slip-up was when she thought a discussion about the American singer Beyoncé was about some up-and-coming celebrity from South Korea named Bee Yon-Se.[59] Not knowing Beyoncé could have been interpreted as charmingly geeky, but clearly the tension between the expectations to convey authority and to project an image of accessibility found its expression in curious ways.

In her interview with me, Wakabayashi was bitter about women's limited career opportunities in Japan and the feminization (if not sexualization) of women traders in the media. Both Wakabayashi and Yamamoto used the same expression (*chiyahoya sareta*) to argue that securities firms, publishers, and the media exploited amateur traders for their own benefit.[60] Wakabayashi also criticized Japan for its stubborn attachment to conservative gender roles established in the postwar period, its fetishization of lifetime employment as the dominant form of socially recognized work, and its preoccupation with educational credentials. She told me that she found the world of finance fascinating and that she would have been happy to pursue a career in finance. She, however, found show business more welcoming than the financial sector.

Conclusion: Amateur Trading and Affective Labor

In this chapter, I argued that owners of online trading platforms (supported by publishers) mobilized women to the financialization of daily life. Women's role in promoting online trading, however, did not make the professional world of finance more inclusive and accessible to women. They still remain at the margins of the financial world, in which they participate mainly as retail investors. Karen Ho insightfully remarks that "employee liquidity" is an organic part of work culture in the financial sector. In her view, the hyper-casualization of employment, endemic job insecurity, and instantaneous and absolute downsizing are key features of work conditions on Wall Street (2009).[61] While work in the financial sector is similarly insecure in Japan (Miyazaki 2012), it is even more unstable for women who would like to enter the professional world of finance via learning how to trade online. These individuals have a better chance to develop a career from selling their expertise as amateur traders than they do from actually trading. Furthermore, they do not have access to the system of mentoring, benefits, and bonus payments that professional traders enjoy.[62]

The media representations of female traders as amateurs *and* homemakers—even though many of them were single or divorced—played an important part in the mobilization of women to a new regime of feminized affective labor in the digital economy. The housewife signified a historically specific relationship to money; it was a trope for responsible investment pursued in the interest of social reproduction—just like the way the little girl in Yamamoto's book invested her savings. The association of the female trader with the position of homemaker reinforced the expectation that respectable women should engage in trading only as amateurs because such a configuration of work would not compromise their principal responsibility for ensuring the well-being of their families. Somewhat ironically, female traders at the same time exposed the fact that the postwar model of sustaining a middle-class family on the male breadwinner's family wage was no longer viable. Rather than exacerbating the already record high unemployment rates by forcing women into the labor market, digital technologies like online trading were promoted as tools that enabled women to maintain their families' middle-class status by working from home.

Christian Marazzi underscores the role of gender in mediating the shift from a manufacturing-driven growth model toward financialization. He writes, "[I]n the sense that it enters directly into the sphere of the circulation of capital, that is, in the sphere of exchanges of goods and services, it is a question of extending the processes of extracting value from the sphere of reproduction and distribution—a phenomenon, let it be noted, for a long time well known to women" (2010, 50). Like bloggers, women traders also mediated the crumbling of lifetime employment. By promoting the idea that digital technologies allowed women to help complement their husbands' income, they effectively relieved employers from their responsibility to pay their salaried employees a family wage, which was the standard practice during the postwar period. As the rise of online trading accounts from 296,941 in 1999 to 7.9 million in 2005 testifies,[63] women did not take long to internalize the ideology of the possible as a responsibility to find ways to improve their own or their families' conditions, even if that entailed such risky endeavors as gambling with their or their families' meager savings.

By emphasizing that female traders were amateurs, the media also contained the labor of these women under the category of feminized affective labor. And as women went along with this particular representation of their labor, they found themselves trapped in their roles as amateur traders. Similar to the labor of net idols and bloggers, the affective labor of women traders extended the feminized affective labor of women from the postwar period into the twenty-first century. While female traders helped promote online trading, the new association between women and financialization did not make it easier for women to enter the professional world of finance. They remained retail investors. Rather than fighting to make the financial sector more gender inclusive or the world of professional work more accessible to women, female traders contributed to making their own labor invisible. By emphasizing that online trading was an easy way to make money from home, women might have succeeded in sublimating anxieties about the erosion of Japan's mass middle-class society—a theme I will engage in the last chapter—but they also undermined their own access to work that did not involve feminized affective labor.

Dreamwork

CELL PHONE NOVELISTS, AFFECTIVE LABOR, AND PRECARITY POLITICS

The cell phone novel phenomenon emerged in the early 2000s and peaked in 2007, when cell phone novels topped literary bestseller lists and the number of these novels hit the one million mark on the popular cell phone novel platform Maho no i-rando (Yoshida 2008). Cell phone novels are composed on flip phones and uploaded to platforms that were redesigned (Maho no i-rando) or specifically developed (No-ichigo) to accommodate the writing and reading of these novels.[1] They dwell on themes of suffering and pain that arise from unrequited love, the obstacles to true love, teenage pregnancy, miscarriage, abortion, rape, bullying, social injustice, drug abuse, incestuous relationships, or incurable disease. The exploding popularity of these novels puzzled critics. While some surmised that cell phone novels persuasively captured young people's sense of hopelessness (Honda 2008; Sugiura 2008), others interpreted them as efforts by young women to project themselves into the future (Hayamizu 2008a, 2008b). In this chapter, I adopt and expand upon the latter perspective. I argue that the first cell phone novelists began articulating a politics of precarity, and they did so not only in their novels, but also in their commentaries about their work as novelists. Owners of cell phone novel platforms, however, transformed this political impulse into a project of social reproduction, which was more conducive to selling ad space.

By 2009, approximately 35 percent of young workers between the ages of fifteen and thirty-four were employed in temporary positions.[2] In the same year, an additional 9 percent of the same age group was unemployed.[3] As evidenced by the curious revival of Kobayashi Takiji's 1929 novel, *Crab Cannery Ship*, the disenfranchisement of youth in the realm of labor fed a sense of betrayal among young people. A popular activist of the freeter generation,[4] Amamiya Karin, famously noted that *Crab Cannery Ship*'s description of excessive exploitation on the open sea, where no regulations protected the workers, aptly mirrored "the current desperate situation of young workers" (Field 2009, 4). The economic downturn hit women especially hard because they had already been in a vulnerable position in the labor market before the burst of a real estate bubble sent Japan's economy into a long recession. It was not a coincidence, therefore, that irregular workers (overwhelmingly women) started writing cell phone novels in the early 2000s.

The employment available to young women—especially to those who came from lower-middle-class and working-class backgrounds—was irregular and located primarily in the service industries.[5] Amamiya Karin, who was a precarious worker herself, described the jobs she was able to land as positions from which "she could be fired anytime, the pay was minimal, rarely was she addressed by name, and the work could be done by anyone." She concluded that "[a]s a worker, and human being, she was disposable" (Allison 2012, 356). Although irregular service work lacks a career structure, opportunities for skill enhancement, and benefits, it still demands that workers invest their personality in the work process. Not surprisingly, the more a regime of unfulfilling labor embraced young women in Japan's service industries, the more desperately these women sought work they perceived as meaningful. Many of these women turned to the digital economy in search of more rewarding job opportunities.

In this context, online platforms like Maho no i-rando aggressively promoted the writing of cell phone novels as an opportunity for young people to become best-selling authors.[6] Publishing companies that acquired or developed cell phone novel platforms further nurtured this dream by printing in book format the novels that readers ranked the highest on cell phone novel platforms. What is more, publishers and cell phone novel platforms made the writing of cell phone novels competitive by organizing annual contests that offered prizes up to $100,000. In reality, however, only five or six novelists won prizes each year, and the highest number of cell phone novels published in one year (2007) was ninety-eight (Galbraith 2009). These are very small numbers given that hundreds of thousands of novels are uploaded to cell phone novel platforms every year. While pursuing the dream of getting a book contract, novelists reported that they also found pleasure in forging emotional connections (*kokoro no tsunagari*) with their readers.

Michael Warner argues that texts produce publics whose existence is contingent on readers' attention "however notional or compromised, and not on its members' categorical classification, objectively determined position in social structure, or material existence" (2002, 61). Thinking more specifically about how individuals develop political consciousness, Stuart Hall claims that objective economic conditions do not transform individuals into political subjects (1996). Rather, processes of articulation—the production of links between individuals and the enunciation of a common ground that results from this network of links—constitute individuals as subjects of politics. Lastly, network theorists have identified digital media as sites for the emergence of new modes of political engagement. Tiziana Terranova claims that digital media offer a potential for political expression by enabling the dynamics of capillary communication[7] to produce a common ground (2004).

Early cell phone novels, I propose, articulated a common ground that crystallized around the experience of precarity—an ethical domain of politics Judith Butler compellingly describes as the recognition that "our shared exposure to precarity is but one ground of our potential equality and our reciprocal obligations to produce together conditions of livable lives. In avowing the need we have for one another, we avow as well basic principles that inform the social, democratic conditions of what we might still call 'the good life'" (2015, 218). Early cell phone novels and proletarian literature may not have the same intentions, but they resonate with similar effects. Norma Field asserts that the *Crab Cannery Ship* boom "issued from and feeds a hunger for collectivity and activism amid the loneliness and cynicism produced by neo-liberal callousness" (2009, 7). By posting cell phone novels online, the first cell phone novelists opened new channels of communication and forged new political publics. What seemed to be an emerging politics of precarity, however, did not evolve into a political movement. Owners of online platforms, in the end, transformed this political impulse into a project of social reproduction, which was more in alignment with their interest in selling ad space.

Cell Phone Novelists and Affective Labor

At the end of 2002, 79.2 percent of cell phone users subscribed to the internet through their cell phones. In the same year in the United States, the percentage was only 8.9 percent (Matsuda 2005). According to a survey, more than 98 percent of Japanese people between the ages of ten and twenty-nine used cell phones in 2006 (Takeuchi and Kawaharazuka 2011). Young people in Japan rely on their cell phones rather than personal computers to access the internet to find entertainment, to shop, to play games, or to seek work. Not only has the digital economy responded to this trend by developing entertainment for cell phones, but precariously employed young people have also recognized the lucrative potential in producing content.

The author of the first cell phone novel was a man named Yoshi. Like most cell phone novelists that followed him, he concealed his identity from the public, revealing only that he was a "thirtysomething freeter." With an investment of JPY100,000 ($913), Yoshi launched a website, where he posted his novel in 2000. To promote his novel, he distributed leaflets to young women in Shibuya. News of his novel spread by word of mouth, and within three years, the site had received twenty million hits. In 2002, armed with a sizeable box of fan mail, Yoshi convinced a small publisher (Starts) to print his novel, which he entitled *Deep Love* in English (2002). Starts sold 2.5 million copies of *Deep Love*, which set the publisher on its path to becoming the number one publisher of cell phone novels in Japan. Starts also launched its own cell phone novel platform, No-Ichigo.

Deep Love is a story of a teenage girl who contracted AIDS in the course of sex work, which she turned to so that she could pay for her boyfriend's heart surgery. The story was adapted as a graphic novel, a movie, and a serialized television drama. Matsushima Shigeru, Yoshi's editor at Starts, told me that Yoshi was successful because he was a clever entrepreneur. Yoshi invested heavily in promoting his novel and the genre of cell phone novels more broadly.

It is curious that Yoshi uses the story of a woman (in this case, a fictional character) to build his career. The drama of the female protagonist in *Deep Love* represents an exaggerated version of the gender role and gender division of labor that the young women in my case studies strove to escape by trying to develop new careers in the digital economy. Yoshi's novel depicts the life of a young woman who gives up her life and labor for her man. This type of gendered sacrifice is a staple element in the melodramatic repertory of cell phone novels. The discrepancy between female authors writing cell phone novels to gain access to professional work and their stories of women who do not fight their victimization might play a part in undermining the potential of the genre to empower women. While these stories can be read as a critique of labor precarity, as I will suggest later, the ambivalence encoded in the narratives also resonates with the net idols' critiques of cute culture. Recall that the success of net idols was contingent on performing cuteness, but their embrace of cute looks and behaviors did not help women dissociate themselves from feminized forms of affective labor.

Inspired by the sweeping success of *Deep Love*, Maho no i-rando, a platform that had offered a service to design and host homepages, created an application that allowed users to upload their novels to the site. By drawing on Yoshi as a model, the platform promoted the writing of these novels as a path to becoming a best-selling author. Despite the fact that the first cell phone novelist was a man, acquisition editors claim that the majority of writers who followed in Yoshi's footsteps were women in their twenties. It is difficult to get an accurate demographic profile of cell phone novelists because most use pen names when they begin writing, and they remain anonymous even after their novels become best sellers. Writers claim that they had no choice but to conceal their identity from the public to protect the privacy of the people, including themselves, they wrote about. At the same time, sexually explicit scenes and content that critics describe as sordid are rampant in cell phone novels. Anonymity helps writers avoid having to deal with criticism from parents. According to an editor I interviewed at Take Shobō, many parents were worried that by reading these novels, their daughters would become more likely to accept the extreme forms of violence these novels often depict.[8] In cell phone novels, after all, protagonists acquire the strength to succeed in life by suffering through traumas, like rape.

It is a safe estimate that at least 70 percent of cell phone novel writers are women. The Japanese-language Wikipedia entry about cell phone novelists[9] lists the twenty-three most famous authors. Among them, six are men and seventeen are women.[10] The freelance writer Sasaki Toshinao, whom I also mentioned in chapter 3 in my discussion of nomad work, published a collection of interviews with some of the first cell phone novelists (2008a). Out of the ten authors the volume features, only one is a man. Indeed, Patrick Galbraith notes that many young men tried to distance themselves from cell phone novels, which they found "hilarious." He writes, "For their part, media-savvy 'otaku' are getting a kick out of cell phone novels—by piling on merciless lampoons and viciously critical rants. Regarding the enormously popular *Koizora* [Mika's first novel, *Love Sky*], for example, they point out that the self-styled 'true story' has a character in the advanced stages of cancer who fathers a child, the mother of whom miscarries after being pushed down by a female bully. These plot points are stretches, to say the least, and move to the realm of the comical when combined with grammar and vocabulary below the high school average."[11]

Galbraith's observation also supports the popular impression that the first cell phone novelists were predominantly from lower-middle-class or working-class backgrounds and often from rural areas of Japan. Sasaki's volume confirms this perception (2008a). Among the ten cell phone novelists he interviewed, one woman worked in the sex industry, another was employed in a hostess club, two were young, stay-at-home mothers, and five worked in the service industries (as a receptionist, an office lady, a beautician, and two sales associates). These novelists all described their day jobs as work they did not enjoy and/or considered to be "dead-end" jobs. The only male writer, Sinka, worked in a factory as a blue-collar worker.[12] The majority of the first cell phone novelists stressed that their stories were based on their own lives, and most stories dwelled on hardships they faced in high school.

These novelists commonly recounted that before they started writing cell phone novels, they had only read graphic novels. Many of them blamed their education for alienating them from reading and writing. Sinka confessed that creative writing was the subject he hated the most in school (Sasaki 2008a). In fact, before he started writing his cell phone novel, he had never written more than two sentences at a time. He claimed that he was attracted to cell phone novels precisely because the genre was a "democratic" form of cultural expression.[13] Sinka contrasted writing a cell phone novel to playing the guitar. As a self-taught guitar player, he stressed, he had to practice tirelessly to master the techniques that would enable him to express his emotions through music. On the other hand, clunky sentences and awkward wording were acceptable in cell phone novels, as these compositional infelicities only enhanced the authenticity of these novels. In other words, Sinka appreciated the cell phone novel as a genre available to anyone regardless of class and educational background through which one could share his or her feelings with others. The cell phone novel, he concluded, was a genre that did not make success contingent on the practice of writing (Sasaki 2008a, 111–12). This is an insightful point, but as we will see later, it did not hold true for writers who approached writing cell phone novels as a career opportunity. These writers worked hard on improving their writing skills.[14]

When asked about their experiences writing cell phone novels, authors never failed to enumerate the sacrifices they made. Sleep deprivation was high on the list of grievances, as writers worked on their novels after they finished their day jobs. Mizushima Riko noted that she slept as little as three to four hours a day for weeks when she was writing her first novel (Sasaki 2008a, 43). She also chose a lower-paying job, one that allowed her to go home after work as opposed to requiring her to work overtime and drink with colleagues after work. Completing a cell phone novel demanded sustained commitment. A cell phone novelist named Rin reported that it took her six months to finish *If You*.[15] Yet another novelist, Chaco, said she tapped the keyboard of her cell phone, which was a flip phone, literally until her fingers started bleeding (Sasaki 2008a). Writing a cell phone novel, however, was not only physically trying. Many writers claimed that they started writing their novels to "confront their past" (*shippitsu wa jibun no kako to mukiau tame*), by which they referred to facing and coming to terms with traumatic events they experienced in their adolescent years.

Writers often juxtaposed the labor of writing cell phone novels to the labor their day jobs required. Many of them said that writing novels demanded what they were unwilling to invest in their day jobs: their souls. Cell phone novels were expected to feel authentic (*riaru*),[16] and novelists tried to generate this effect by writing in the first person and stressing that their novels were based on traumatic experiences they or their friends had suffered. I found it curious that reviewers on amazon.co.jp overwhelmingly evaluated these novels based on whether the novels succeeded in making them cry. A television commercial for Mika's *Love Sky* draws on this perception of cell phone novels. It features a female high school student who suffered an accident. The commercial says, "If you want to cry, read a cell phone novel." I noted in my book about 1990s Japanese television dramas that television producers firmly believed in the correlation between viewership and what they called their ability to push the crying button (2010a). Cell phone novelists certainly kept their index finger on the crying button. An editor at Starts Publishing, Matsushima Shigeru, confirmed this when he told me that the keywords of the genre were "stories that make you cry" (*nakeru yōna hanashi*) and "stories that make you want to work harder to succeed" (*gambaru yōna kimochi*).

Authoring cell phone novels involved not only writing and completing research but also maintaining relationships with readers. The writing of cell phone novels thus exposes how deeply affective labor draws on one's personality. It also sheds sharp light on the continuity between the genres of labor Michael Hardt and Antonio Negri distinguish as affective and intellectual labors (2004). The labor that novelists invested in engaged not only the writers' emotions but also their life experiences, ethics, and political sensibilities. By exposing this tendency in affective labor, I illuminate why this genre of labor has emerged as the emblematic form of labor in the digital economy. Unlike other nontraditional forms of labor, such as emotional or phatic labors, affective labor expands sources of value extraction by inviting individuals to invest multiple aspects of their personality simultaneously as the raw material of valorization. That is, affective labor taps into what constitutes a person as a unique individual.

Linking a worker's sense of self with work is not new. Throughout the postwar period, Japanese employers demanded an intense commitment, but only from their male employees, whom they rewarded with lifetime employment. In the context of labor market deregulation, employers switched from carrots to sticks, that is, to controlling their employees by reminding them of their disposability. My interviews with cell phone novelists reveal why young women so readily accepted the invitation to pursue unpaid affective labor in the digital economy. These novelists accentuate the perils of a labor market that allows dignity to be purchased through unpaid affective labor. When I asked Chaco if she enjoyed working as a cell phone novelist, she said the following:

> In terms of the time investment, writing cell phone novels is not all that different from my previous jobs. I worked as a sales associate and a receptionist. Although I was paid to work forty hours a week, I ended up working much more, and my work spilled over to my days off. I did unpaid overtime every day, and when I was not busy with work, my boss asked me to follow up with our customers on earlier sales. I was thinking about work all the time. Since I started writing cell phone novels, not much has changed. When I am not working, I am still thinking about work. Well, work is always hard for me, because I try to do things conscientiously. But when I am writing a novel, I feel, "Hey, I really love doing this," and this feeling makes an enormous difference.[17]

Mika (the novelist mentioned earlier) offered the following insight:

> Before I became a cell phone novelist I worked in the service industries. Communication, problem solving skills, and smiling practically without a break were key requirements for my line of work. When I am working on a novel, I am all alone. It is no longer a struggle with customers but a struggle with myself. For much of the time, I feel lonely and insecure. As a type of work, writing novels is better than any of the soul-sucking service jobs I've had, but it is also much more overwhelming because it demands my soul. But writing novels makes me much stronger. It helps me overcome my weaknesses. There is nothing more gratifying than this sense of achievement (*tasseikan*).[18]

The more a volatile economy requires workers to invest their souls in the work process, the more individuals long to attain employment they perceive as meaningful. In 2000s Japan, this paradox has affected the young more than any other segment of the working population. Although youth unemployment reached historic heights in the early 2000s, it was commonly dismissed as a voluntary choice. Young people were ubiquitously blamed for having a diminished sense of commitment to work, yet, the spectacular success of cell phone novel platforms suggests that young people were dedicated to work they perceived as meaningful.

As young Japanese women tore fictional couples apart in their cell phone novels, they sought their own romances—not with male lovers but with the idea of developing meaningful careers through writing. Angela McRobbie observed that in the United Kingdom in the 2000s, young women articulated a critique of precarious labor conditions when they strove to escape the drudgery of service employment with their search for self-directed work. She writes, "One way of understanding this is to suggest that the idea of 'romance' has been deflected away from the sphere of love and intimacy and instead projected into the idea of a fulfilling career. No longer looking for a husband as a sole breadwinner, young women romanticize the idea of career. They want to find work about which they can feel passionate. Passionate work in turn becomes a further mark of feminine intelligibility and success" (2016, 91). McRobbie concludes, "By in effect marrying her work, having devoted so much romantic energy into finding the right job, rather than finding the right man, the woman can uplift herself into a relatively undesignated middle-class category" (2016, 110).

This analysis resonates closely with young women's search for employment they perceived as meaningful in 2000s Japan. Stressing that the digital economy offered everyone the same chance to become best-selling authors, owners of novel platforms seduced young women to unpaid affective labor. In the Japanese context, technological utopianism—the portrayal of online platforms as spaces where everyone has equal access to the digital means of production—also played an important part in mediating the splintering of Japan's middle classes.[19]

Scholars observe that when labor increasingly draws on the worker's personality, there is a heightened likelihood that it will both produce surplus value and reproduce society (Hardt 1999; Lazzarato 1996; Negri 1991; Weeks 2011). Kathi Weeks summarizes this idea:

> The interpenetration of production and reproduction has deepened as domestically produced goods and services continue to be replaced with commodified forms, and as many modes of service and caring labor are transformed into waged forms of employment. Production and repro-

duction thus come to resemble one another more closely, in terms of both their respective labor processes and their outcomes. Second, not only is reproductive labor more clearly productive today, as evidenced by its many waged forms, but productive labor is increasingly reproductive in the sense that it often creates not only strictly economic goods and services but also social landscapes, communicative contexts, and cultural forms. (2011, 140–41)

Although this issue is pertinent to all previous chapters of the book, the cell phone novel phenomenon illuminates most clearly that the digital economy plays what Hardt and Negri (2004) conceptualize as affective and intellectual labors against each other while continuing to advance the erosion of the boundary between paid and unpaid work. Specifically, the digital economy enticed women to write cell phone novels by promoting this activity as an opportunity to become best-selling authors. The competition to stand out, however, was cutthroat, and the actual rewards women derived from writing remained intangible. These included the hope that writers' talents might be recognized or that writers might be able to forge emotional ties with their readers.

Dreamwork on Magic Island

The number of cell phone novels posted on internet platforms is in the millions. Maho no i-rando (Magic Island) was the first platform to develop an application that allowed users to upload their novels to a site. Launched in 1999, Maho no i-rando targeted internet users in their teens and twenties by offering them the opportunity to create their own websites. In the early 2000s, the designers of the platform developed an application that allowed users to upload their diaries (*nikki*) and novels (*bukku*, which became known as the cell phone novel). After Japan's largest cell phone operator (NTT DoCoMo) began offering unlimited text messaging for flat monthly rates in 2004, the culture of writing cell phone novels took off. By the end of 2007, Maho no i-rando had 5.7 million registered users. This figure indicates only how many people wrote or commented on novels; reading novels did not require registration. In 2007, users accessed the site 3.3 billion times per month—a figure that advertisers found enticing (Yoshida 2008). Inspired by the success of Maho no i-rando, other companies sought to harness young people's interest in writing and reading cell phone novels by launching new cell phone novel platforms and developing applications for these novels on social networking platforms. Examples include Gocco (which was launched in 2006); Mobagē Taun (Mobile Game Town, a free game and SNS site, which was established in 2007); Oricon (a cell

Figure 5.1. Maho no i-rando (Magic Island). The platform seduces its visitors to write cell phone novels by featuring a daily ranking of cell phone novels and by offering information about the cell phone novel contest Maho no i-rando sponsors.

phone novel site colaunched by Oricon, Goma Books, and Success Networks Cooperation in 2007); and No-ichigo (a cell phone novel site launched in June 2007 by Starts Publishing) (Yoshida 2008).

Not only have cell phone novels achieved unprecedented popularity on online platforms, they have also generated spectacular sales in print. The average sales of printed cell phone novels easily reached four hundred thousand copies per novel,[20] and even first-time authors enjoyed print runs of between fifty thousand and one hundred thousand copies.[21] Based on the number of cell phone novels in print, the cell phone novel trend peaked in 2007. In 2006, twenty-two cell phone novels were published, and a year later, it rose to ninety-eight.[22] An author named Bunny, whose first novel sold about 110,000 copies, disclosed that she made $611,000 from royalties.[23] Yoshida Satovi, an expert in cell phone commerce, claims that it is often fans who buy the printed books. She reasons, "Your fans support you and encourage you in the process of creating work—they help build the work. Then they buy the book to reaffirm their relationship to it in the first place" (Yoshida cited in Goodyear 2008).

Internet platforms such as Maho no i-rando enticed young people to write cell phone novels by forging a powerful association between writing such novels and the good life. Tominaga Masao, who designed the site, explained that his mission was to generate a space where magic happens and dreams come true.[24] He insisted that everyone had magic and invited young people to discover and work their own. In the wake of labor market deregulation, he summoned young people to become more entrepreneurial by shaping their own lives through the types of work they chose to pursue. To young people, this formulation was more appealing than the alternatives, which stressed the responsibility of the individual to succeed in a volatile economy. Young people found the latter formulation unsettlingly elusive. It provided no direction for how to make use of freedom and exercise responsibility. Tominaga, on the other hand, encouraged young people to share their life experiences with their peers on Maho no i-rando. He argued that young people who told their stories on his site could potentially attain financial stability and individual autonomy and thus gain access to the good life. Note the similarity between the idea of "telling one's life story" and the promise of blog tutorials that bloggers should transform their lifestyles (and personalities) into content.

Maho no i-rando was able to help, however, only a miniscule minority of cell phone novelists become professional writers. By deriving its revenues exclusively from advertising, Maho no i-rando followed the business model of commercial television, but it corrected one of the major structural problems in television production: escalating labor costs. The skyrocketing costs of professional labor in media production make the costs of content production exorbitant. When Maho no i-rando invites aspiring young novelists to present their work to the world, it deploys a highly efficient cost-cutting measure. By promising them the opportunity to pursue careers as professional novelists, Maho no i-rando seduces amateur writers to invest unpaid affective labor into writing novels. It secures a free supply of highly diversified content[25] that is likely to offer something appealing to everyone. Maho no i-rando and other sites also feature search engines designed specifically for these platforms that help readers find the novels that reflect their sensibilities and moods.[26]

Cell phone novel platforms encourage readers to communicate with writers, which enables them to draw readers into the writing process. The designers of novel platforms understood that the lack of communication between producers and consumers was a major flaw in the production of mass media, so they designed platforms that facilitated communication between them. A key feature of this design is the bulletin board (*keijiban*), a space where writers and readers can communicate with each other. To encourage interaction between authors and readers, platform designers (Maho no i-rando, in particular) have also developed diary and blog applications (Yoshida 2008).[27] Links to the personal blogs and diaries of authors are posted alongside their novels.

Unlike the first cell phone novels that were marketed as autobiographical, novels written after 2005 are more likely to be fiction. Authors often emphasize that they derive inspiration for their stories from readers' comments. An employee in the content department of Maho no i-rando stressed to me that the cell phone novel was becoming a genre that is increasingly produced collaboratively by writers and readers, and the latter has the power to change the plot or the ending of the story.[28] On the one hand, access to authors helps readers appreciate cell phone novels as more personal than mass-produced entertainment fare such as television dramas (Sano 2007). On the other hand, by encouraging readers to provide writers with feedback, novel platforms draw readers into the writing process and inspire them to write their own novels.

Capitalizing on the growing appeal of DIY careers among young women, these platforms promote the writing of cell phone novels as a type of dream-work—work that is both meaningful and lucrative. No-ichigo, the second largest cell phone novel platform owned by Starts Publishing, features a "celebrity meter" that indicates that by 2012, the site had helped 106 amateur novelists attain celebrity status. No-ichigo lists the names of these writers along with links to their novels and blogs. Promoting the novelists whose books were published in print is only one of the various strategies platform owners employ to encourage amateur novelists to envision themselves as best-selling authors. They also "educate" novelists about copyright laws so that they are prepared to negotiate when a publisher or a television network approaches them with a proposal to republish their stories (as novels or graphic novels) or to develop a serialized drama based on their novels. Discussing copyright issues helps writers envision the possibility that their novels might become best-sellers. After all, educating authors about protecting their copyrights suggests that acquisition editors and television producers are browsing the site in search of new content.

No-ichigo also inspires novelists to envision themselves as celebrity authors by enabling and encouraging them to communicate with editors at Starts. At the same time, the platform offers sophisticated applications to help writers promote their novels.[29] Through their mail magazines, cell phone novel platforms encourage readers to rank cell phone novels. They emphasize that readers could help their favorite authors publish books in print by submit-

Figure 5.2.　No-ichigo promotes cell phone novels as an opportunity to become a professional writer. The site emphasizes the cell phone novel competition the platform sponsors.

ting votes. They offer examples such as Chaco's *Tenshi ga Kureta Mono* (*The Gift from Heaven*) that Starts published in 2005 after the readers ranked the novel number one on Maho no i-rando.[30] These ranking systems are important tools to enhance competition between cell phone novelists and encourage writers to strive for popularity (as opposed to writing novels for the pleasure of communicating with readers). As a result, fan management has become an important part of the writer's work, as writers are encouraged to inspire their readers to vote for them. Writers can do this by investing in communicating with their readers, listening to them, and being respectful of them.

Most pertinent to my argument that online platforms make the writing of cell phone novels competitive is that cell phone novel platforms forged business tie-ins with publishers. Ascii Media Works, for example, purchased Maho no i-rando (and Kadokawa Corporation acquired both in 2013), while Starts launched No-ichigo. Ranking systems help publishers identify popular novels and thus transform online platforms into content farms that supply novels for print. These portals, of course, also bring in revenue from advertising. At the same time, online platforms and publishers team up to inspire young people to write these novels by sponsoring extravagant annual cell phone novel contests.[31] These contests are open to anyone registered with the sponsoring platform.

In 2006, Maho no i-rando, Starts, and the Mainichi Newspapers Co. organized the first contest, the Nihon Keitai Shōsetsu Taishō (Japan Cell Phone Novel Grand Prize). The next year, Maho no i-rando created its own annual contest, the Maho no i-rando Award. Other companies quickly followed suit. Mobagē Taun, for example, introduced the Mobagē Shōsetsu Grand Prize in 2007. In addition to publishing contracts, these annual contests offer generous cash prizes to finalists selected by a jury.[32] In December 2007, Goma Books created its own cell phone novel contest and offered the winner the largest prize to date, JPY10 million ($913,000).[33] The increasingly lavish prizes suggest that publishing cell phone novels is a lucrative business. These prizes are enormously appealing to freelance writers who are developing their careers. What is even more enticing is that the prizes also come with publishing contracts that chart a career trajectory for amateur writers to become professional cell phone novelists. The popular "professional" cell phone novelists Yoshi and Mika sold more than 2.5 million copies of their novels *Deep Love* and *Koizora* (*Love Sky*), respectively. In other words, the real prize is dreamwork. From royalties and licensing fees, best-selling authors can earn millions of dollars.

In the late 2000s, these figures prompted millions to write cell phone novels. But, as stated previously, only a few writers actually make money from these novels. Instead, promoting the ideology of the possible, the digital economy molds young people into subjects of labor that Paolo Virno calls opportunists: "Those who confront a flow of ever-interchangeable possibilities, making themselves available to the greater number of these, yielding to the nearest one, and then quickly swerving from one to another. . . . It is a question of a sensitivity sharpened by the changeable chances, a familiarity with the kaleidoscope of opportunities, an intimate relationship with the possible, no matter how vast" (2004, 86). Although publishers buy only a tiny percent of the novels that are posted to cell novel platforms, these platforms promise novelists a path to the good life. In reality, however, the digital economy only socializes young people into a volatile labor market by encouraging them to embrace the idea that unpaid labor (in the form of affective/hope labor) is instrumental to developing careers.

To become a best-selling author is a powerful dream, evidenced by the fact that cell phone novel platforms continue to make profits from selling ads. As they write their novels and communicate with their readers, cell phone novelists bring to life communities that platform owners sell to advertisers. In the previous section, I demonstrated that the first cell phone novelists were able to forge new readership because they gave visibility to a growing sense of vulnerability among young people. In this sense, early cell phone novels encoded a political impulse, but online platforms transformed this impulse into the more advertising-friendly idea that the genre was a project of revitalizing social ties. With the commercialization of the genre, labor precarity was recoded into social viability, and the cell phone novelist appeared in the recognizable form of a young woman participating in social reproduction. The figure of the cell phone novelist was detached from such associations as rape victim, juvenile delinquent, and cutthroat entrepreneur who made a fortune writing shoddy romance novels.

Before concluding the chapter with an analysis of two of the most popular cell phone novels written by Mika and Chaco, I want to highlight that online platforms and publishers were able to recode cell phone novels as a project of social reproduction not only because the stories of disposability resonated with the readers' experiences. As a particular technology, the cell phone also played an important role in reinterpreting the genre as a project of social reproduction. Mizuko Ito noted that in the early 2000s, the cell phone in Japan was an intimate technology. Young people used their cell phones not as a phone but as a texting device. Moreover, it was common among young people to exchange text messages with only three to five friends and family members. In other words, young people used their cell phones to maintain their existing relationships with the closest people in their lives (2005).

In the early 2000s, researchers were skeptical about the capacity of the cell phone to build relationships between people who never meet face-to-face. The cell phone novel trend suggests that this skepticism was unfounded, that young people actually drew on the intimate character of the cell phone to rebuild social ties. Cell phone novels generated a sense of intimacy not only by sharing personal stories of suffering but also through the technologically determined stylistic features of cell phone novels that were instantly and intimately familiar to young people (Kim 2012; see also Mizukawa 2013).[34]

Some writers used personal computers to write cell phone novels, but editors claimed that these novels were less well received. An editor at Goma Books, Kanematsu Keiko, remarked, "When a work is written on a computer, the nuance of the number of lines is different, and the rhythm is different from writing on a cellphone."[35] The rhythm of the reading was an important element in identifying the writer as a member of a generation that grew up texting on their cell phones. Indeed, I asked an editor to comment on the speculations that some editors also authored cell phone novels. The secrecy around the personalities of some cell phone novelists nurtured suspicions that these writers did not even exist. The editor reassured me that the writing style and especially the rhythm of cell phone novels were so unique that editors in their forties would not have been able to replicate them.

Cell Phone Novels and Precarity Politics

The allegedly personal stories of suffering and pain also added a sense of intimacy to the consumption of cell phone novels. I argued that early cell phone novels encoded a political impulse in that they articulated a sense of socioeconomic vulnerability and insecurity that was widespread among youth. Marilyn Ivy uses the term *parapolitics* to describe the ways Nara Yoshitomo incorporates his fans into the production of his work. She writes, "this parapolitics is based on shared affects and affections and generates forms of association and communality difficult to establish in late capitalist Japan" (2010, 23). My textual analysis of two early cell phone novels—*Koizora* (*Love Sky*) and *Tenshi ga Kureta Mono* (*The Gift from Heaven*) reveals that cell phone novels initially encoded a similar form of politics with comparable effects.

In *Love Sky*, Tahara Mika, a freshman in a high school in Kyushu, falls in love with the delinquent hero, Sakurai Hiroki (Hiro). The novel centers on the couple's evolving relationship and troubles. Hiro's ex-girlfriend (Saki) incites a group of men to rape Mika. Then Saki pushes Mika down the stairs. Mika consequently suffers a miscarriage and loses Hiro's child. After Mika attempts suicide in response to being bullied in school, Hiro finally breaks up with her. As if to hurt Mika intentionally, he starts dating her friends. Mika then begins dating Yū, with whom she goes to college. One day, Hiro's friend Nozomu reveals to Mika that Hiro is terminally ill with lymphoma. When Mika visits Hiro in the hospital, the two realize they still love each other. Mika marries Hiro, who passes away shortly after their wedding ceremony. Hiro's mother gives Mika his diary, from which she learns that Hiro never stopped loving her. He had broken up with her to spare her the pain of his loss. *Koizora* seems sensational, but it was marketed as a novel that was based on true events. Mika, however, never revealed precisely what parts of the story came from her real life.

Like *Koizora*, Chaco's *Tenshi ga Kureta Mono* was also promoted as a novel based on real events from the author's life. Mai is a freshman in a high school in Osaka. She does not have any friends and feels lost. When Mai gets introduced to a circle of friends who congregate after school, she meets Kagu. Over time, she develops feelings for him. Kagu has a complicated family background: his father abandoned the family, leaving them with huge debts. Kagu takes over the role of breadwinner and refuses to forgive his father when he returns. The father commits suicide, causing Kagu to drop out of school and move to Wakayama prefecture to work to repay his father's debts. The responsibility of providing for his family consumes him, preventing him from cultivating his relationship with Mai. Although Mai starts dating someone else, she cannot forget Kagu. One day she calls him to tell him she loves him, but on his way to meet her, he dies in a car accident.

Both of these stories, as well as other cell phone novels, are derivatives of the shōjo genres[36] of the 1990s. Unlike previous shōjo genres that offered stories of middle-class romance, one can conceptualize the cell phone novel as a response to the socioeconomic disenfranchisement many young people experienced, especially youth who came from lower-middle-class and working-class backgrounds. A brief analysis of how the cell phone novel differs from earlier shōjo genres, however, reveals how cell phone novelists confront the weakening of emotional ties—a trend that has prompted critics to describe Japan of the 2000s as "a society without relationships" (*muen shakai*) (Tachibanaki 2010). Unlike earlier shōjo stories, cell phone novels rarely offer a happy ending. In the 1990s, "happily ever after" stories solved the imminent crisis and existential dilemma of the shōjo heroine by securing her entry into a stable and secure middle-class lifestyle (Lukacs 2010a). The shōjo of the 1990s appeared in a transitional stage of her life, moving from adolescence to adulthood.

The cell phone novel heroines of the 2000s are also transitioning out of adolescence, but they never reach adulthood. In cell phone novels, uncertainty and vulnerability extend from adolescence into young adulthood. In these novels, previously intimate spaces (family and school) no longer function as realms of nurturing and protection. Instead, they emerge as emblems of authoritarianism that lost their foundational meaning; they only discipline, they do not offer protection. In cell phone novels, formerly familiar territories are unfamiliar, and formerly safe zones become spaces of struggle for survival.

The hero serves as the key to the socioeconomic security of the shōjo heroine, and his death in cell phone novels can be read as a reference to the waning power of the state and the faltering industrial system. That is, the young woman's loss of her boyfriend represents the inability of the state to protect its citizens from the destructive forces of an unregulated economy and the withdrawal of corporations from the provision of job security. The heroine wavers over whether she sees herself as entitled to the normative ideal of middle-class security, but she then resolves her identity crisis when she insists on her pursuit of the hero. Through this perseverance, she wins his heart. While the shōjo heroine of the 1990s sought true love to help her overcome feelings of socioeconomic insecurity, the uncertainties of the heroine in cell phone novels are more deeply rooted, and the options available to her are not as clear. The death of the hero confirms what she has long suspected: she is on her own in the world. Cell phone novels typically end on this despairing note of self-awareness.

Most novels, however, frame this ending in epilogues that usher the reader from the heroine's narrative present to the novelist's real present. Whereas the narrative present is the denouement of the heroine's past, the real present is a closure to the author's past and a foundation of her future. Most prominently, these epilogues encourage readers to live meaningful lives (*ima wo seiippai ikirō*), create connections with others (*kizuna wo tsukurō*), and be positive about the future (*maemuki ni narō*). A curious aspect of these messages is that the authors do not derive these conclusions from experiences of suffering described in their novels. Rather, novelists insist that they learn these lessons from their readers. Cell phone novelists open their epilogues by pointing out that without the encouragement of their readers, they would not have been able to complete their novels. They insist that it is the readers who helped them "regain their strength to be forward-looking" (Mone 2007, 299) and to leave behind their past selves. The following are a few examples of ways novelists have described their past lives: "I was full of anxieties" (Mika 2006, 363); "I hated myself so much that I wanted to die" (Nana 2009, 253); or "I entirely lost the will to live" (Mone 2007, 298). These novels, however, are not purely therapeutic. BeaHime, the author of *Teddy Bear*, aims to raise consciousness when she writes: "We have the right for livable lives. We are not disposable (*iranai ningen*)" (2006, 213). The significance of "livable" is connected to the realm of employment, in that disposability refers to being superfluous in economic terms.

The trope of disposability is key to understanding the excessive eventfulness and melodramatic excess that characterize cell phone novels.[37] I interpret this excess as symptomatic of a fixation on social relevance. Cell phone novels do not focus on how the protagonist feels about her social world and the individuals that surround her; instead, they center on the heroine's experience of being intensely loved or hated. This perspective expresses the heroine's insistence that she is not irrelevant, at least in social terms. In parallel, the novelist comes to the same realization in the process of writing her novel. She realizes that she is able to inspire her peers to look forward to a brighter future (and for meaning in work) despite her economic vulnerability—a result of the unwillingness of employers and the inability of the government to invest in young people's future, which is an issue I discussed in chapter 3 in relation to Tanimoto Mayumi's book *Career Porn Is a Waste of Time*.

Lauren Berlant posits that when growing economic precarity undermines the capacity of the family and the nation to maintain an experience of belonging, intimate publics emerge to fulfill that role (2011). These intimate publics "provide the feeling of immediacy and solidarity by establishing in the public sphere an affective register of belonging to inhabit when there are few adequate normative institutions to fall back on, rest in, and return to" (2011, 226). By generating cell phone novels, young Japanese people have produced an intimate public. Cell phone novels are responses to the experience of precarity, but they articulate more than the minimalist optimism of the defeated who, according to Berlant, struggle on "to stay attached to life from within it, and to protect what optimism they have for that, at least" (2011, 10). Through the very act of communicating with their fans, cell phone novelists insist that economic precarity should not necessarily equal social precarity.

But cell phone novels are not just a response to socioeconomic uncertainty in recessionary and postrecessionary Japan. They also call attention to the precarious situations of Japanese women who have long been mobilized into unpaid work in the domestic sphere. In her analysis of drag performance as a playful subversion of gender-based exclusion, Judith Butler writes, "Significantly, it is in the elaboration of kinship forged through a resignification of the very terms which effect our exclusion and abjection that such a resignification creates the discursive and social space for community, that we see an appropriation of the terms of domination that turns them toward a more enabling future" (1993, 137). Early cell phone novels resignified feminine intelligibility by disconnecting the figure of the young woman from a regime of feminized affective labor and what Lee Edelman calls reproductive futurism— the "absolute privilege of heteronormativity" that renders unthinkable a future not anchored to the image of the Child (2004, 2).[38] In early cell phone novels, young women expressed a view that a future built on heteronormative sociality that anchors women to the domestic sphere is less and less attainable. By writing about rape, miscarriage, and nonreproductive sex, the first cell phone novelists created a space where they experimented with new forms of feminine intelligibility. The commercialization of the genre, however, transformed young women's experiments with new subjectivities into a project of social reproduction.

Early cell phone novels did encode a political impulse even if it was no more than what Ivy calls parapolitics (2010).[39] The commercialization of the genre, however, recoded this impulse into much less radical messages about the importance of revitalizing social and emotional ties. In 2010, Mika said the following: "The weakening of social ties (*muen shakai*) saddens me deeply.

What we have to realize is that emotional ties (*kokoro no tsunagari*) or connectedness (*kizuna*) with others is not something one can develop by one's own effort. We have to work on these collectively. Even if you are in a place where you feel that you are so lonely that you no longer have the strength to reach out, remember that many others feel the same way. I hope that over the next years to come, cell phone novels will become tools to help us connect with each other."[40] Michael Hardt sees a potential in affective labor to foster new forms of sociality, which can be a means to subvert dominant power relations (1999). In conjunction with the commercialization of the cell phone novel trend, however, the project of exposing the increasingly dominant condition of disposability was transformed into a much less radical project about fighting a collective crisis in sociality—an effect of an ailing economy's destabilization of normative relationships and forms of belonging. As Mika's comment from 2010 suggests, cell phone novelists' acceptance of their mobilization to this project reconnected women to feminized affective labor.

Conclusion: Dreamwork

Early cell phone novelists produced a juncture at which writers and readers came to understand themselves as new publics and began to develop critical insights about their lives and futures. With the enormous commercial success of the genre, however, these critical insights were folded into a more commercially viable project of revitalizing social and emotional ties in a recessionary social context. The feeling of betrayal that the first cell phone novels voiced so forcefully was repurposed to reconnect social relationships. Novelists emphasized that the massive sympathy they received from their readers helped them understand that they were not alone. Cell phone novel platforms were developed to encourage communication between writers and readers. Accordingly, the first cell phone novelists uploaded their novels to cell phone novel platforms chapter by chapter and communicated with their readers during the writing process. Although writers often complained that their readers pressured them to be more productive, they also admitted that they found it rewarding to bring a community to life. Writers described this feeling as so powerful that they were willing to compromise on the themes they would tackle in their novels. Mizushima Riko, for instance, revealed that she did not enjoy reading or writing romantic stories. Her readers, however, loved them, so she felt she had no choice but to write them (Sasaki 2008a).

When writers talked about their readers, they commonly articulated a sense of responsibility. They claimed that they often struggled to keep up with the demands of their readers because they became busy with their day jobs or simply lost interest in writing. They felt an obligation to their readers, however, whom they did not want to betray. Not wanting to be disloyal to readers resonates with the sense of betrayal that prompted young people to write cell phone novels in the first place. Many novelists talked about their readers as their new families. Chaco, for instance, who dropped out of high school and thus lost access to people of her generation, stressed that her readers became her new family (Sasaki 2008a).

Silvia Federici claims that the power of collective experiences helps overcome a sense of powerlessness and inability to move forward (2012). She writes, "The new enclosures ironically demonstrated that not only commons have not vanished, but new forms of social cooperation are constantly being produced, also in the areas of life where none previously existed, as for example the Internet" (2012, 139). Similarly, Isabell Lorey argues that the experience of precarity in neoliberal conditions inspires individuals to create new apparatuses of security (2015). Unlike Judith Butler, who sees precarity as an essential characteristic of the conditions of living beings who are *all* vulnerable and dependent (2004), Lorey argues that neoliberal reforms in particular make life more precarious and force individuals to create new practices of securitization. She stresses the paradox at the heart of the precaritization process: the subject is promised freedom to self-actualize but is also subjugated to the normalization of risk and uncertainty. A positive effect of neoliberal restructuring is that while it commercializes care work, it also generates possibilities for new care communities (2015). That is true, but it is also true that *women* are assigned more responsibility in maintaining these new care communities, and women for the most part, are *not paid* for the work they invest in social reproduction.

Digital technologies mediate these processes in ways that make their duplicitous character amply evident. Cell phone novel platforms promise writers the opportunity to develop careers as professional writers, but in actuality, they mobilize their users to the unpaid affective labor of online content production. As I have suggested throughout the book, patriarchal gender biases are encoded in the designs of online platforms, and cell phone novel platforms are no exception. The applications offered on these platforms that enable authors to communicate with their fans, for example, are far more sophisticated than the ones that help contributors improve their own writing skills.

Social responsibility has remained a central theme in the accounts cell phone novelists offer to explain why they were drawn to the genre and why they continue writing cell phone novels. By the late 2000s, however, the tension became more palpable between platform owners' interpretation of social responsibility as an expression of writers' willingness to perform the feminized affective labor of social reproduction and writers' use of the notion of social responsibility to describe themselves as professional novelists. Chaco, for instance, related her experiences of writing as follows:

> I am ashamed of this now, but I hated books my entire life. I loved stories, but I satisfied my craving for them from movies, television dramas, and graphic novels. I started reading books only after I decided to pursue writing as a career. I spent an enormous amount of time memorizing dictionaries (Japanese language, thesaurus, etc.) to increase my vocabulary. At the same time, the more I embraced a sense of responsibility, the more demanding my work became. I wanted my books not only to be well written but also to be factually correct. I thought a lot about social responsibility, how I could avoid endorsing irresponsible and unethical behavior. I spent a lot of time doing research for my novels and consulting experts to ensure factual correctness. Professional writers do all this, but I never learned to write, so the whole process was very painful for me. *This job feeds me* and puts a roof over my head. Of course, I work extremely hard to do it well. And the better I am, the more I enjoy writing.[41]

Like Chaco, many young women turned to writing cell phone novels in the early and mid-2000s. The most successful novelists—Chaco, Mika, Saori, Rin, Miho, Nana, Nanase, Mone, BeaHime, Ayaka, Asuka, Saoya Kanoko, Kagen, Tsumugi, Towa, Paapuru, Fujiwara Aki, Mizushima Riko, Mei, Yui, Megumi, Miyu—wrote cell phone novels between 2005 and 2007, and most of them stopped writing before 2010. Younger generations of women continue writing these novels, however, and cell phone novel platforms continue making profits from selling communities of writers and readers to advertisers. According to the profile page that No-ichigo maintains to promote its site to advertisers,[42] it is female middle school and high school students who now read and write cell phone novels.[43] The participation of middle school students in the digital economy makes one wonder how early socialization to feminized affective labor will shape young people's relationship to work.

Digital Labor, Labor Precarity, and Basic Income

I have argued in this book that young women's projects to sculpt DIY careers have fueled the development of the digital economy in Japan. While gender hierarchies supplied the workforce that built Japan's digital economy, in other contexts, other affiliations of identity played equally important roles. In the United States and Europe, for instance, age was just as relevant as gender. In these regions of the world, it was young people who turned to the internet to build new careers, hoping to translate their intimate familiarity with social media and content sharing platforms into new life projects. The widespread impression that such careers are incomparably more lucrative and enjoyable than conventional forms of employment have only increased their appeal. The YouTube celebrity Markiplier (aka Mark Fischbach), for example, is reputed to have made millions of dollars from his hilarious gaming videos, and he appears to be having fun with what he is doing. When YouTubers like Markiplier, PewDiePie (aka Felix Kjellberg), DanTDM (aka Daniel Middleton), and Jacksepticeye (aka Seán William McLoughlin) make hefty sums of money wedding play with cold hard cash, parents lament that it is increasingly difficult to convince children about the value of education and job security.

It is not only the widespread speculations about the wealth of YouTube celebrities that make these careers appealing to young people. Governments also proactively promote self-styled careers in the digital economy to mediate and sugarcoat labor market deregulation. Angela McRobbie's analysis of the shifting valuation of creative work in the United Kingdom (2016) resonates with the ways owners of online platforms and the popular media promoted DIY careers in 2000s Japan. McRobbie observes that in the United Kingdom, young people also joined the creative class in massive numbers during the 2000s. Although they understood that they would not have access to job security, they turned to the creative industries because they hoped to find meaningful work there. The British government, in turn, celebrated them as the new vanguard of entrepreneurship—success stories of young people who invented new careers and occupational identities for themselves. McRobbie suggests that the British government's new support for creative labor is an example of labor reform that facilitates a shift from traditional job security toward DIY careers that do not come with labor protections (see also Gill and Pratt 2008; Song 2007).

The careers that young people develop using digital technologies, however, are often tied to the profitable life cycles of these technologies. Arguing that capitalism tends to intensify cycles of innovation, Bernard Stiegler proposes that we need to think about "how to overcome the short-termism that we have been led to by a consumerism intrinsically destructive of all genuine investment— that is, of investment in the future—a short-termism which has systematically, and not accidentally, been translated into the decomposition of investment into speculation" (2010, 6). Careers such as the ones YouTube allows its users to develop come with a short shelf life. These careers might offer temporary solutions to young people's immediate problems with employment, but they certainly do not solve our broader problems with waning job security.

What Eran Fisher calls technological utopianism made DIY careers in Japan uniquely seductive in the late 1990s and 2000s (2010). Fisher defines technological utopianism as a belief that digital technologies enable a more democratic, participatory, and inclusive mode of production while making work more humane and fulfilling. Owners of online platforms, authors of self-help tutorials, and the popular media in Japan all promoted the idea that careers in the digital economy were more rewarding than employment available in the traditional labor market. The hope to attain purposeful employment, in turn, foreclosed discussions about how the digital economy developed its business model by drawing on young people's (and especially young women's) willingness to perform what Kathleen Kuehn and Thomas Corrigan call hope labor—unpaid or underpaid labor that individuals are willing to perform "in the hope that future opportunities may follow" (2013, 19).

All forms of employment involve some degree of unpaid hope labor, but the case studies in this book demonstrate that digital media entrepreneurs in Japan have systematically capitalized on this form of labor to develop online platforms. The fact that the digital economy evolved as part of the commercial media complex was also not conducive to conceptualizing the online activities of internet users as labor. Rather, owners of online platforms characterized these activities as practices of consumption and entertainment. Platform owners in the United States, by contrast, reason that internet users should consider the cutting-edge digital tools of self-branding and exposure to large audiences as in-kind or indirect forms of compensation. The case of the Huffington Post (huffpost.com) illustrates that discussions of compensation have advanced further in the United States than they have in Japan.

In February 2011, Arianna Huffington sold huffpost.com to AOL for $315 million. Bloggers were understandably upset: they argued that the articles they had posted to the site for free were essential to the development and rising valuation of the platform. They sued AOL for one third of the purchase price, but US District Court Judge John Koeltl dismissed their case. Arianna Huffington—whom the lead plaintiff and labor activist Jonathan Tasini described as a "slave owner on a plantation of bloggers"—commented that bloggers were never promised direct compensation and did receive ample indirect compensation in the form of television appearances, paid speech opportunities, and book deals.[1] Judge Koeltl closed the case with the following statement: "The principles of equity and good conscience do not justify giving the plaintiffs a piece of the purchase price when they never expected to be paid, repeatedly agreed to the same bargain, and went into the arrangement with eyes wide open."[2]

In this book, I propose that Japan's digital economy was built on innovating Marx's labor theory of value. Rather than paying workers only for socially necessary labor time, however, owners of online platforms generate profits by not recognizing the online activities of platform users as labor. Consider, for example, the case of the growing global demand for click farms. In June 2017, three Chinese men were arrested in Thailand for importing cell phones without paying customs. Immigration officers learned that the men owned 476 cell phones and approximately 347,200 SIM cards that they used to operate a click farm. Specifically, they used the phones to run up "likes" and page views of WeChat, a Chinese social media application that offers instant messaging, commerce, and payment services. Immigration officers also learned that what the men were paid was based on how many likes and page views they generated. Their click work earned them between $2,950 and

$4,400 a month. How the men were able to obtain so many SIM cards from Thailand's largest cell phone provider is unclear, but what is relevant to my discussion is that there are people who are, indeed, paid for their click work, while most of us do it for free.[3]

Content farms like Demand Media (now Leaf Group) in the United States offer a similar example. Wikipedia defines a content farm as "a company that employs large numbers of freelance writers to generate large amounts of textual content which is specifically designed to satisfy algorithms for maximal retrieval by automated search engines."[4] That is, content farms produce content that will be sufficiently interesting to prompt readers to click on links that will then deliver them to advertisers. The quality of the writing is so questionable that some call the content produced on these farms "churnalism." Content farms have also been criticized for underpaying their freelancers. They pay as little as $3.50 per article, but at least they recognize digital labor as productive labor. Millions of bloggers, on the other hand, produce content worldwide for free.

Trebor Scholz writes that, "Currently, digital labor appears to be the shiny, sharp tip of a gargantuan spear of neoliberalism made up of deregulation, economic inequality, union busting, and a shift from employment to low-wage temporary contracts" (2017, 2–3). He sees Amazon's Mechanical Turk—an online labor brokerage platform—as "an influential template for the future of work" (2017, 16). MTurk is a platform that allows requestors to hire "Turkers" to perform human intelligence tasks. It does so because it would be more expensive to develop algorithms to complete the task than to hire Turkers. An example of this is cataloguing shoes by color, a function that image recognition software cannot accurately complete. Scholz describes MTurk as a new business model to "get all the work done without the workers" (2017, 26). It is a crowd-sourcing platform (Howe 2008) that breaks up assignments formerly completed by salaried employees into what Lilly Irani calls "microwork"— smaller tasks that can be assigned to underpaid (and, in many cases, unpaid) volunteers (2015a, 2015b).

Drawing on the premise that innovation in code is also innovation in social relations, Irani argues that digital labor normalizes labor precarity. It does so by relying on automated management techniques that treat issues of worker management as a computational problem and human labor as a computational service, thus concealing the fact that real individuals complete the requested tasks under highly exploitative labor conditions (2015a). The anonymity that MTurk normalizes in the realm of work is but one of the multiple effects and expressions of labor market deregulation that is gradually widening a wedge between capital and labor, transforming quasi-familial relationships between employers and employees into distant and amorphous linkages.

The digital economy intensifies two interrelated trends in the realm of work. One is the extraction of value from labor without entering into contractual relationships with workers, while the other is the strategic blurring of the boundary between production and reproduction.[5] This book builds on the works of the Italian Autonomists, who were among the first to theorize labor and exploitation by rethinking Marx's wage-centric conceptualization of value. Deriving inspiration from Marx's idea of the general intellect, the Italian Autonomists argued that while capitalists continue extracting profit from the labor of individual workers, they are simultaneously and increasingly tapping unpaid labor as a source of value. As long as individuals think and speak, says Paolo Virno, they contribute to the general intellect from which capital appropriates surplus value (2004). Virno argues that under post-Fordism, machines are not dead labor. Rather, they participate in generating and circulating knowledge by plugging workers into the general intellect. Similarly, Hardt and Negri propose that exploitation under post-Fordist capitalism is no longer primarily the expropriation of value from the labor time of individual workers but rather the capture of value from cooperation among workers, which emerges from the productive energies of labor itself (2004, 2017).

While the theory of the general intellect examines how the sociality of production is becoming a source of private appropriation, the concept of the social factory, which I use in this book, investigates how capital extracts value from activities it does not recognize as productive labor. More so than the theory of the general intellect, feminist scholars found the idea of the social factory helpful to argue that women's unwaged work in the domestic sphere also produced profit for capital (Dalla Costa and Dalla Costa 1999; Dalla Costa and James 1975; Federici 2012; Fortunati 1995, 2007; Jarrett 2017). The Wages for Housework movement built on the theory of the social factory to propose that the concept of labor should be retheorized and expanded beyond labor's waged forms (Weeks 2011).[6] The starting point of this movement was the position that Marx's labor theory of value concealed the fact that capital extracted surplus value not only from labor expended in contractual relationships but also from the unwaged labor women were mobilized to invest in reproducing labor power.

The Wages for Housework movement, Kathi Weeks astutely observes, has accentuated the point that "gender difference and hierarchy are also constituted and reproduced through laboring practices, and that specific gender divisions of labor are part and parcel of contemporary capitalist labor formations" (2011, 118). More specifically, Fordist capitalism drew on a division of labor based on gender within which men worked for a family wage, while women were responsible for taking care of their families. As such, Fordist capitalism drew the institution of the family directly into the sphere of production by recruiting women to become housewives. Mariarosa Dalla Costa and Selma James argued that Fordism transformed the family from being a refuge from the cold reality of capitalism into an essential part of the factory system (1975).[7]

Although Fordist capitalism gave way to post-Fordist accumulation in the 1970s, the gender division of labor that characterized Fordism survived this shift in Japan. Women remained assigned to unwaged reproductive labor and irregular forms of wage labor. And gender inequality in the conventional labor market paved the way for women to the digital economy. While gender discrimination in hiring practices is more prominent in Japan than in other advanced capitalist countries, the link between women and ambiguously defined work is not unique to Japan. Andrew Ross notes that in the United States in the early 2000s, 77 percent of unpaid internship positions were assigned to women (2012, 24). Ross writes, "The sacrifices, trade-offs, and humiliations entailed in interning are more redolent of traditional kinds of women's work, whether at home or in what used to be called the secondary labor market (to distinguish it from the family wage generated by the primary market)" (2012, 24). Angela McRobbie observes the same tendency in the United Kingdom, where she sees women transitioning from constituting a reserve army of labor to entering "the heartland of new forms of work" (2016, 30).[8]

It is hardly surprising that the Wages for Facebook initiative has developed its manifesto drawing on the programmatic statement of the Wages for Housework movement. These manifestos expose the common roots of digital labor and feminized forms of unwaged labor (Jarrett 2017). The Wages for Housework movement has made the following declaration: "The crime against us internationally, from which all other crimes against us flow, is our life sentence of housework at home and outside, servicing men, children, and other women, in order to produce and reproduce the working class. For this work we are never paid a wage. This crime of work and wagelessness brands us for life as the weaker sex and delivers us powerless to employers, government planners and legislators, doctors, the police, prisons and mental institutions as well as the individual men for a lifetime of servitude and imprisonment."[9]

The Wages for Facebook manifesto reads as follows:

They say it's friendship. We say it's unwaged work. With every like, chat, tag or poke, our subjectivity turns them a profit. They call it sharing.

We call it stealing. We've been bound by their terms of service far too long—it's time for our terms. . . . It is important to recognize that when we speak of Facebook we are not speaking of a job as other jobs, but we are speaking of the most pervasive manipulation, the most subtle and mystified violence that capitalism has recently perpetrated against us. True, under capitalism every worker is manipulated and exploited and his/her relation to capital is totally mystified. The wage gives the impression of a fair deal: you work and you get paid, hence you and your boss are equal; while in reality the wage, rather than paying for the work you do, hides all the unpaid work that goes into profit. But the wage at least recognizes that you are a worker, and you can bargain and struggle around and against the terms and the quantity of that wage, the terms and the quantity of that work.[10]

Thinking about the Wages for Housework movement in retrospect, Silvia Federici declares, "We want to call work what is work so that we can rediscover what is love and create our sexuality, which we have never known" (2012, 20). The manifesto of the Wages for Facebook initiative concludes similarly, "We want to call work what is work for that eventually we might rediscover what friendship is."[11]

The manifesto drives home the point that the digital economy expands and normalizes practices of extracting value from activities it does not recognize as productive labor. As such, online platforms are also eroding salaried and waged employment, a trend echoed in the aspirations of the online company workmarket.com. Aiming "to power the future of work," the company's five-year plan is to facilitate a shift from a labor market characterized by full employment and jobs for life to a market dominated by freelancers, part-timers, and independent contractors (Scholz 2016, 66).[12] Many have expressed concern about the digital economy propelling such shifts in labor. In assessing how digital labor affects the world of work, the largest metal workers' union in Germany (IG Metall) sees digital labor as a force that breeds a pervasive moral decline in the workplace. Correspondingly, the German Association of Unions describes digital labor as "modern slavery," which "drives competition to the bottom" (Scholz 2016, 67). Not surprisingly, among the five major investors of WorkMarket, we find SoftBank—Japan's largest telecommunications and internet company.

Focusing on the period between the late 1990s to the late 2000s, I argue that Japan's digital economy evolved by harnessing and reproducing existing inequalities in the local labor market. My case studies demonstrate that rather than enabling women to develop meaningful careers, the digital economy mediated a shift from employment security to irregular work arrangements. While my book documents the first decade of this trend, scholars more recently began exploring resistance to digital labor and its tendency to foment labor precarity. Trebor Scholz proposes that as microwork is becoming a standard means to earn an income and individuals assemble livelihoods by working for multiple employers simultaneously, governments need to develop systems of portable benefits for workers. By extension, the notion of employment should be expanded to include the diverse realities of today's working populations. Employee-like rights should be extended to everyone who performs what they view as labor. Scholz suggests that sites like turkernation.com should build a worker-owned, apps-based labor platform that would advocate for the recognition of currently invisible or obscure forms of work as employment (2017). Such a platform would also be able to inform workers of their rights, challenge the institution of independent contracting, document unfairness, advocate a living wage, and campaign for guaranteed basic income.[13]

A more fundamental question, in Scholz's view, is why we accept the commercialization of the internet. Instead, we should develop democratically governed service platforms and online marketplaces that are owned and operated by the people who rely on them. At the same time, we should create the equivalents of labourleaks.org and home.coworker.org that protect the rights of individuals who pursue digital labor. I agree with Scholz's conclusion that a system of basic income might be able to counterbalance the shift from job security to the pervasive insecurity that microwork is unleashing (2016, 71).

It is indeed symptomatic of the growing flexibilization of work arrangements that discussions about the universal basic income have recently gained new traction (Aronowitz and DiFazio 1994; Ferguson 2015; Gorz 2009; Hardt 2000; Hardt and Negri 2000; Standing 2017; Van Parijs and Vanderborght 2017; Weeks 2011). Focusing on South Africa, James Ferguson has observed that in the wake of the waning ability of governments to generate employment, systems of social protection are increasingly assuming the form of cash payments to the poor (2015). According to Ferguson, when wage labor no longer constitutes the privileged foundation for citizenship, governments should guarantee the right to a minimum income the same way that they recognize mandatory education as a basic right of citizenship. A justification for introducing a system of basic income could be that citizens own their country and therefore should have access to their homeland's wealth.

Although mass unemployment, informal livelihoods, and highly fluid domestic groups that Ferguson sees as prominent features of everyday life in

South Africa are not yet mainstream characteristics of life in Japan, Anne Allison compellingly demonstrates that poverty is no longer a fringe phenomenon in Japan either (2013). With the Japanese government abandoning its full employment policy, Allison argues, the character of unemployment shifted from frictional to structural unemployment. As a result, she observes, vulnerable segments of the population such as youth, women, and the elderly are sliding into poverty. In Japan, a growing percentage of the population, including working-age people, is excluded from salaried employment, which itself is rapidly shrinking. As I argue in this book, the emergence of the digital economy has further advanced the precaritization of Japan's labor market by expanding practices of extracting value from labor without entering into wage relationships with individuals. It seems to me that in this context, discussions of a universal basic income might indeed be relevant to rethinking how we define employment and what new system of protections could compensate for the erosion of job security.

My case studies demonstrate that labor market deregulation intensifies existing inequalities in the realm of work. Echoing Paul Willis's classic study of how the school system in the United Kingdom channeled working-class students into jobs that reanchored them to working-class status (1977), gender hierarchies and discriminatory employment practices in the traditional Japanese labor market delivered women into a new regime of unpaid labor in the emerging digital economy. Rather than demanding access to salaried employment, women sought work they saw as meaningful, which I attribute to the legacy of postwar developmentalism.[14] Between the early 1950s and the late 1970s, Japan's gross national product (GNP) grew significantly faster than the GNP in other OECD (Organization for Economic Cooperation and Development) countries, prompting Chalmers Johnson to call Japan a "miracle modernizer" (1999, 48). The developmental state's legitimacy was rooted not in its capacity to ensure the autonomy and freedom of its citizens but rather in its capacity to secure the economic well-being of the citizenry. In exchange for lifetime employment (a family wage, opportunities for skill development, job security, and pension benefits) corporations demanded loyalty from their employees and willingness to adopt a lifestyle devoted to work. Decades of paternalistic and, in the Japanese case, patriarchal laborism, in turn, have discredited job security, which is why the women whose stories I present in this book prioritized fulfilling work over employment security.

The story of Namba Tomoko—the only woman among the ten most successful owners of online platforms in Japan—suggests that criticism of gender discrimination is expanding. Yet even critics like Namba who encourage employers to support work-life balance seem reluctant to denounce the pervasive ideological support for laborism and preoccupation with economic growth. The 2018 labor reform, for instance, which introduced a cap of one hundred hours a month on overtime work, was discussed simultaneously as a response to the growing number of deaths caused by work stress (*karoshi*) and a strategy to increase labor productivity.

The policies companies have implemented in recent years suggest that it is the employees themselves who are to blame for sustaining a culture of workaholism. To discourage workers from putting in overtime, some employers introduced drones that fly around in offices blasting "Auld Lang Syne" to remind workers to stop working after standard work hours. Another company requires its employees to wear a purple cape with yellow stars to "embarrass" them when they violate the company's "no overtime day once a month" policy,[15] while other employers simply encourage their workers to cry. They reason that crying relieves stress by relaxing autonomic nerves.[16] While these examples are multiplying, a more pointed and critical inquiry into the ascendance of laborism has yet to emerge. Namba Tomoko's story illustrates the difficulties in questioning the normativity of workaholism.

Before founding DeNA, Namba worked at the management-consulting firm McKinsey and Co. In an interview, she recounts that she worked as hard as she could and slept as little as humanly possible in order to fulfill her dream of becoming a successful businesswoman. While she was working at McKinsey and Co., she rarely got home before 4:00 or 5:00 in the morning, and she was never late to start the next day at 9:00 a.m. On weekdays, she seldom slept more than two to three hours a day. She began to feel burned out and, hoping for better work conditions, decided to seek employment in the digital economy. After establishing DeNA, she soon found out that if she wanted to succeed, she had to work just as hard as she used to at McKinsey and Co. Not being one to settle for mediocre results, Namba continued leading a work-oriented lifestyle.[17]

Her husband, whom she met at McKinsey and Co., was just as focused on work. The couple never once ate a meal together in their home. But in April 2011, Namba's husband was diagnosed with cancer, and Namba decided to step down as CEO of DeNA. She told the media that she wanted to take care of her husband. Her decision puzzled the public not only in Japan but also worldwide. An article in the *Wall Street Journal* describes Namba's story as follows: "When Tomoko Namba, one of Japan's most powerful businesswomen, announced in May that she was resigning as CEO from the mobile-games company she founded, shocked shareholders sent the company's shares down 4 percent. Tech darling DeNA Co. was experiencing meteoric growth, after all. And since she was a female chief executive in a country where less than 2 percent of business leaders are women, the reason for resigning was all the more baffling: Take a traditional female role of caregiver for a sick husband."[18]

Curiously, during her tenure at DeNA, Namba did not advocate equal opportunities for men and women in the realm of work. Rather, she was vocal about criticizing the system of lifetime employment, which, in her view, stifled innovation. Since her resignation from DeNA, however, Namba has emerged as a powerful voice demanding that employers support their employees' efforts to balance work with life. She encourages employers to accommodate their workers when they need to take a leave of absence to care for their children or ailing family members. She stresses that women's position in the labor market will not get better when they alone are tasked with raising children and caring for the elderly. Namba encourages employers to allow male employees to take paternity leave and be more involved in their children's lives.

These demands are of critical importance. They do not, however, question the pervasive attachment to laborism that had established gender inequality in the realm of work in the first place. Namba's propositions do not problematize the belief that economic growth serves the social good and enables individuals to attain the good life. This is puzzling because Namba Tomoko's story clearly illustrates that the fusion of life and work can be just as alienating as the split between them. I agree with Kathi Weeks, who suggests that in addition to reinstating a firm boundary between life and work, we should also consider new distinctions, such as work time and nonwork time, work and antiwork, and work and postwork (2011). After all, the hopes the digital economy dangled in front of young women remained largely unfulfilled. Instead, young women's search for meaningful work revitalized the postwar ideology of laborism in a new ideological guise I call the ideology of the possible. Drawing on this ideology, the digital economy has redefined work as a fluid arrangement that floats on a continuum between salaried employment and unemployment. Promises such as meaningful work and the good life are all too enticing even when we recognize that their pursuit advances the expansion of that continuum.

Introduction: Labor and Gender in Japan's Digital Economy

1 Examples include *Blade Runner* (1982), *The Terminator* (1984), *The Matrix* (1999), *I, Robot* (2004), and *Wall-E* (2008).

2 Sony resumed production of Aibo at the end of 2017. The new Aibo features more advanced artificial intelligence capabilities than its predecessors. It develops its own personality over time and is able to recognize different members of the family. It interacts in more nuanced ways with family members who pet it more often.

3 Guy Standing makes a distinction between waged workers and salaried employees. The concept of wage worker refers to piece-rate and time-rate laborers, while the concept of the salaried employee refers to workers who receive not only their monthly salaries and yearly bonuses but also benefit from company-specific training, pension plans, health insurance, sick leave, and paid holidays (2011). The salaryman (*sararīman*) in Japan is what Standing calls a salaried employee. In this book, I adopt Standing's distinction between salaried and waged workers.

4 Brian Larkin remarks that infrastructure studies tend to focus on the materiality of infrastructures (2013). Infrastructure studies are less compatible with my approach to the internet, as this literature reinscribes a dichotomous relationship between humans and technologies. By contrast, I stress that humans are central to the development and maintenance of infrastructures.

5 See Marie Hicks's insightful analysis of how the British computer industry lost its edge by excluding women from technological innovation (2018).

6 Scholars agree that the recession began around 1990 after a real estate bubble burst in the late 1980s (Yoda 2006). There is less agreement, however, on whether the recession ended in the late 2000s or in the early 2010s. Joseph Stiglitz argues that during the 2010s, per capita economic growth in Japan has been stronger than in the United States, Great Britain, Germany, and Australia (2015). This means that inequality is still less pronounced in Japan than in some other advanced capitalist countries. What seems difficult to question, however, is that employers used the recession as an excuse to streamline their workforce, which has affected young people, and especially women, more than any other segment of the population.

7 I agree with Ursula Huws, who argued that the notion of "labor market" can only be used for contexts characterized by "corporatist politics, historically strong internal labor markets, considerable employer investment in training and tightly defined occupational demarcations, and a welfare system closely linked

to employer-based plans" (2014, 36). Japan fits this characterization. Furthermore, the highly structured character and unique culture of the labor market in Japan also justifies using the concept of the labor market in the Japanese context. This structure and culture evolved in the postwar period when large and midsize firms hired their employees straight out of school and for a lifetime (Cole 1972). Schools employed job counselors who cultivated relationships with particular firms and helped students find employment. See Mary Brinton's discussion of how this mediation between schools and employers started breaking down in the wake of the recession (2010).

8 As in the United States, the first generation of internet architecture was developed by researchers in Japan. The founder of the internet in Japan, Murai Jun, lamented that the lack of government funding was conducive to the rapid commercialization of the internet (Murai et al. 2008). The first IP network (JUNET) was launched in 1988 to facilitate communication between computer specialists working at Keio University, Tokyo Institute of Technology, the University of Tokyo, and Iwanami Publishing Company. In 1993, Internet Initiative Japan Ltd. and AT&T JENS started a commercial internet service. Nippon Telegraph and Telephone (NTT) quickly followed suit and emerged as the dominant internet provider in the 1990s offering a dial-up (ISDN) service, which was up to 64 kbit/s. Throughout the 1990s, the subscription fees were so high that after 11:00 p.m., when NTT offered a flat-rate service, the volume of internet traffic increased conspicuously. Service charges decreased only after the government deregulated NTT by separating the company's mobile, landline, and internet services in 1999. Although cable television operators began offering broadband products in the late 1990s and Tokyo Metallic Communications Corporation started offering Asymmetric Digital Subscriber Line (ADSL) service in 1999, the internet was still expensive, and internet infrastructure was not on a par with that of other advanced capitalist nations. Mori Yoshirō's "e-Japan" initiative in 2001 was a policy initiative to address this problem. In 2001, SoftBank started a price war by offering a 12 Mbit/s ADSL service for a monthly subscription fee of about $30, while NTT's slower ISDN dial-up service cost twice as much. By 2004, Japan had developed the best cost-to-performance ADSL service in the world.

9 In 1993, NTT DoCoMo (Do Communication Mobile) introduced the personal digital cellular (PDC) system. In 1999, NTT launched i-mode, which was the first commercial internet service that used cellular phones as end terminals. Two other carriers, KDDI (au) and J-Phone (which was acquired by Vodafone and then by SoftBank), started offering similar services shortly after NTT launched i-mode. By the mid-2000s, i-mode by NTT DoCoMo, EZweb by KDDI (au), and Vodafone Live by SoftBank emerged as the major mobile internet service providers.

10 See Wikipedia, https://en.wikipedia.org/wiki/Honda; Rakuten, http://global .rakuten.com/corp/investors/financial/indicators.html, both accessed May 30, 2018.

11 See Rakuten, https://global.rakuten.com/corp/about/overview.html, accessed May 30, 2018.

12 See Mixi, http://mixi.co.jp/company/; DeNA, http://dena.com/intl/company

/overview/; GREE, http://corp.gree.net/jp/en/corporate/summary/, all accessed May 30, 2018.

13 The digital economy evolved in a context that scholars theorized as financialization (Krippner 2011) and rentier capitalism (Harvey 2014; Piketty 2014). These concepts refer to a shift in balance in the mode of accumulation from wealth accrued from labor to wealth generated from capital. According to Thomas Piketty, capitalists responded to the rising price of labor by developing new strategies to extract surplus value from capital. The problem with investing in assets (e.g., real estate, companies, financial constructs, intellectual property rights, brands, etc.), Piketty observes, is that it channels investment away from innovation, which drives the creation of new jobs (2014).

14 See Wikipedia, https://ja.wikipedia.org/wiki/ライブドア; https://ja.wikipedia.org/wiki/堀江貴文; YouTube, https://www.youtube.com/watch?v=Exvg0_9MqKc, all accessed May 30, 2018.

15 See Jun Hongo, "Horie handed 2 1/2 years: Upstart Founder of Livedoor Facing Real Time in a Cell," *The Japan Times*, March 17, 2007, accessed May 30, 2018, http://www.japantimes.co.jp/news/2007/03/17/national/horie-handed-2-12 -years/#.V4GepVfqqno.

16 Today, Line Corporation—a Japanese-Korean internet business that developed line messaging services and the Naver Japan search portal—operates the Livedoor blog service and IPS.

17 Wagyu comes from crossbreeding four different breeds of cattle. What is known as "Kobe beef" is one variety of wagyu.

18 See Aya Takada and Hiromi Horie, 2017, "Japan's Internet Maverick Has New Global Target: $180 Steaks," *Bloomberg*, October 15, https://www.bloomberg.com /news/articles/2017-10-15/japan-s-internet-maverick-has-a-new-global-target -180-steaks.

19 See Rakuten, http://corp.rakuten.co.jp/about/overview.html; Wikipedia, https:// ja.wikipedia.org/wiki/三木谷浩史; https://ja.wikipedia.org/wiki/楽天, all accessed May 30, 2018.

20 Interview with Mayuhime posted on Mayuhime's web page, http://mayuhime-fx .com/, accessed October 1, 2018. The term *office lady*, or OL, is appropriated from the English language and refers to young women who hold non-career-track positions in the context of white-collar employment.

21 Jacques Donzelot demonstrates that whereas discussions of what constitutes meaningful work commonly emerge from criticisms of exploitative employment practices, employers often appropriate these discussions to improve the productivity of their workforce. Donzelot interprets the discourse of pleasure in work in 1970s France as a new management strategy to address the high social costs borne by the persistent pursuit of productivity in advanced capitalist economies. He remarks, "While work had hitherto been seen as serving the satisfaction of needs, these needs had themselves been multiplied by the frustrations inherent in work, thereby paradoxically accentuating the need not to work" (1991, 253). The discourse of pleasure in work, Donzelot concludes, aimed to neutralize this

problem by recoding work as a site where economic and social needs can both be satisfied.

22 Meaning in work, of course, was also discussed outside the context of lifetime employment. Dorinne Kondo observes that in a small, family-owned confectionary factory where she conducted her fieldwork, workers did not consider work simply as a means to an end. Rather, they saw work as an activity that enabled them to belong to a community while also allowing them to realize their own human potential (1990). Beyond the criteria of belonging and self-determination, however, different workers interpreted the idea of meaningful work differently. The owners of the company saw their work as meaningful because it enabled them to fulfill their duties to their families and "derive a sense of their own competence" (1990, 277). Male workers, on the other hand, saw work as a means to reinforce their masculinity. Kondo also observed a strong connection between work for wages and perceptions of social utility, which—in addition to financial necessity—put enormous pressure on people to work.

23 Paul Roquet suggests that in the period of rapid economic growth, background music that helped increase the productivity of employees was in demand. In the recessionary period, however, the demand shifted to ambient music that imparted a sense of security and sensory cohesion (2016).

24 Within this system, promotion is based on the length of tenure with the company (*nenkō*), which made it difficult for employees over thirty to change jobs. This was because it was less expensive to hire new employees who had just graduated and could be trained to acquire the specific skills the company needed.

25 William Kelly noted that mass middle-class society was more of an aspirational ideal than a reality; only one third of the population had access to lifetime employment, which secured one's position in the middle class (1986).

26 *Freeter* is a hybrid of the English word *free* and the German word *Arbeiter*. It refers to young people who drift from one short-term job to another.

27 Her Japanese-language Wikipedia entry describes Wakabayashi as a "financial/investment critic (*kabushiki hyōronka*), day trader, and tarento." The business card Wakabayashi gave me said that she was a stock market critic, while her books introduce her as "trader and financial advisor" (*torēdā, fainansharu adobaizā*). See Wikipedia Japan, http://ja.wikipedia.org/wiki/%E8%8B%A5%E6%9E%97%E5%8F%B2%E6%B1%9F#cite_note-11, accessed on May 30, 2018. Yamamoto called herself "money advisor" (*manē adobaizā*) (2009b) and "chief fund manager" (*chīfu fando manējā*) (2007b).

28 When discussing what constitutes good work, scholars offer such criteria as job security, protection against economic downturns, good pay with annual increases, opportunities for promotion, the possibility of advancement to better jobs, access to fringe benefits such as health insurance and pension plans, a pleasant work environment, a sensible balance between life and work, flexibility in scheduling work, recognition of merit, the ability to make decisions about one's work conditions, the importance of autonomy, the ability of workers to achieve

self-actualization, and the ability to experience one's job as interesting, challenging, and meaningful (Kalleberg 2013; Scholz 2017).

29 I take this insight from Kathi Weeks's work (2011).

30 Similarly, Luc Boltanski and Eve Chiapello also see the discussion of meaning in work—articulated as a humanist critique of alienation in work—as a transformative force in the realm of work (2007).

31 See Investopedia, http://www.investopedia.com/ask/answers/111015/when-did-facebook-go-public.asp, accessed May 30, 2018.

32 Trebor Scholz argues that in the United States, the disappearance of public spaces and a media-generated culture of fear (stranger-danger) force young people to socialize online (2017, 88). danah boyd makes the same argument. She observes that teens spend time on social media because parents generally discourage them from spending time with their friends in public (2014).

33 Ursula Huws questions the conceptualization of digital labor as cognitive or immaterial labor, stressing that a growing proportion of digital labor is actually low-paid and menial labor (2003, 2014). Similarly, Ayten Aytes suggests that the expanding practices of crowdsourcing erode the line between industrial and cognitive labor, as crowdsourcing is contingent on work organization and a division of labor that is akin to industrial production (2012).

34 These scholars ask what kind of labor is expended, what kind of commodities are produced, and what means of production are used in processes of extracting surplus value.

35 Juliet Schor argues that in the absence of commercial alternatives to the housewife's labor, women's time became an artificially undervalued resource in the United States. What Schor describes for the United States unfolded in a similar fashion in Japan (1993).

36 Hardt writes, "Health services, for example, rely centrally on caring and affective labor, and the entertainment industry and the various culture industries are likewise focused on the creation and manipulation of affects. To one degree or another, this affective labor plays a certain role throughout the service industries, from fast-food servers to providers of financial services, embedded in the moments of human interaction and communication. This labor is immaterial, even if it is corporeal and affective, in the sense that its products are intangible: a feeling of ease, well-being, satisfaction, excitement, passion—even a sense of connectedness or community" (1999, 96).

37 Hardt and Negri write that intellectual labor is "labor that is primarily intellectual or linguistic, such as problem solving, symbolic and analytical tasks, and linguistic expressions. This kind of immaterial labor produces ideas, symbols, codes, texts, linguistic figures, images, and other such products" (2004, 108).

38 Developed by rational choice theorists in the 1960s, human capital was a theory to assess the relationship between education and employment security (Becker 1964). Emerging from the economics of education, the theory of human capital aimed to measure how investment in education and training affected the kind of employment one was able to attain.

39 Follow-up email communication (May 17, 2016).

40 Aramis was a project to develop a system of personal rapid transit in France. The planning of the project started in 1969, while the actual implementation began in 1974. The project aimed to do away with the automobile by developing a train system that was able to break up into individual cars, which then would go separate ways to transport their passengers to their destinations. The idea was to develop a system of personal rapid transit that was as intimate and personalized as a taxi but as secure and inexpensive as public transportation. Latour asked what roles such factors as technological feasibility, economic viability, and social acceptability played in the failure of the project.

41 Lisa Parks and Nicole Starosielski stress that while the owners of infrastructures are usually public entities or private companies, infrastructures emerge out of negotiations among such nonhuman and human actants as "design schemes, regulatory policies, collective imaginaries, and repetitive use" (2015, 5).

42 In a different context, Melissa Gregg has discussed how new media technologies increase the workload of salaried professionals by transforming work into an intimate experience. She suggests that the imperative to be connected normalizes a style of work that bleeds into spaces of nonwork and reinforces associations between technology, flexibility, mobility, and freedom (2011).

43 Katherine Hayles (1999) and Rosi Braidotti (2013) have discussed how the decreasing distance between humans and machines affects humans.

44 *Enterprise*, Season 2, Episode 4. See IMDb: Ratings and Reviews for New Movies and TV Shows, http://www.imdb.com/title/tt0572198/, accessed May 30, 2018.

45 Stiegler suggests that capitalism accelerates cycles of innovation that, in turn, create distance between culture and technics. As a result, technics start following different rhythms of evolution, emerging into technical systems that Stiegler defines as "stable interdependencies at a given time or epoch" (1998, 26). Similarly, Gilbert Simondon theorized the relationship between humans and machines via critiquing Marx, who he viewed as too unyieldingly attached to the problem of labor. Such an inflexible focus on labor becomes an obstacle to grasp the transversal relations between humans and machines (2017). Unlike Marx, Simondon sees the real source of alienation in the fact that human beings see themselves as superior or inferior to machines rather than existing in equality alongside machines (2012). I would be more sympathetic to this claim if human beings existed in equality with one another in the first place.

46 Tarleton Gillespie observes that algorithms are represented as impartial and objective, but they always encode the value judgments of their designers (2014). Similarly, proposing that authority is increasingly expressed algorithmically, Frank Pasquale asks why search engines do not consider whether restaurants give their workers health benefits in ranking restaurants (2015). See also Chun 2008, 2013; MacKenzie 2006; Manovich 2013; Parisi 2013; and Striphas 2015.

Chapter 1: Disidentifications

1 In Japanese, the terms used are *onna no ko sashin* (girl/girly photo) or *gāri photo* (girly photo). Because the concept of "girly" photography is commonly used, I will not abandon it. I will, however, use this label in quotation marks as a reminder that I consider "girly" a misnomer that reproduces gender inequalities. The quotation marks also aim to index the unfavorable reception of this label among women photographers. I use the terms *women photographers* and *female photographers* to discuss the photographers that male critics in Japan called "girly" photographers. In my view, "women's photography" does not constitute a genre. I do not see sufficient stylistic or thematic overlap among the works of women photographers to justify lumping them together under the category of "girly" photography. What Iizawa called "onna no ko shashin" was a discursive construct formulated and held together by patriarchal laborism that assigned women to feminized affective labor.

2 Canon Inc., Canon's global website, New Cosmos of Photography, "Akiko Ozawa: A Day (Women of Thirty Years)," http://global.canon/en/newcosmos/gallery /grandprix/2005-akiko-ozawa/index.html, accessed May 14, 2018. See also Wikipedia Japan, https://ja.wikipedia.org/wiki/ガーリーフォト, accessed May 14, 2018. I am not saying that critics all represented one coherent position, but there was significantly more coherence in the critical response than in women's photography itself.

3 See Safiya Umoja Noble's book on how commercial systems of information management, such as Google, reproduce a culture of racism and sexism through algorithmically driven mismanagement of data (2018).

4 Shinoyama Kishin, "Interview with Nagashima Yurie: Ikikata no Tsuyosa ga Shashin ni Deru," *Kōkoku Hihyō*, January 2001, 125–34.

5 ZoneZero: Photographic Convergence, Takeuchi Mariko, "Photography in Japan," 2008, http://v1. zonezero.com/magazine/articles/takeuchi/o2.php, accessed May 14, 2018.

6 See YouTube, https://www.youtube.com/watch?v=jp9eA9fZsow; https://www .youtube.com/watch?v=dgeeX9Z3guE; https://www.youtube.com/watch?v =s3kfY6oJPRw, all accessed May 14, 2018.

7 Canon Inc., Canon's global website, New Cosmos of Photography, "List of Past Winners," http://global.canon/en/newcosmos/index.html, accessed May 14, 2018.

8 In 1992, 483 entrants submitted 5,552 photos to the competition. In 2006, 1,505 applicants submitted 46,170 photographs. Canon Inc., Canon's global website, New Cosmos of Photography, "List of Past Winners," http://global.canon/en/newcosmos /index.html, accessed May 14, 2018.

9 Recruit Holdings Co., Ltd., Guardian Garden, Artist Search, http://rcc.recruit.co .jp/gg/artistfile/, accessed May 14, 2018.

10 Personal interviews with Nagashima Yurie (September 20, 2012) and Ninagawa Mika (September 18, 2012) in Tokyo.

11 Nagashima completed her master's thesis in 2015 and is currently revising it into a book.

12 Iizawa developed this idea in 1996 building on Miyasako Chizuru's 1984 book *Female Principle and "Photography."* He quotes Miyasako saying, "The 'male principle' offers the 'world' a meaning to life, but the 'female principle' receives from the 'world' a value of living." He continues quoting Miyasako, "The 'male principle' has the freedom to dissimilate the 'world,' but the 'female principle' has the freedom to assimilate with the 'world.' The 'male principle' is careful of things due to its nihilism, but the 'female principle' is careful of people due to its optimism." Iizawa concludes, "Comparing and contrasting in this way, it is clear how rich a potential 'female principle' photography carries, supported by assimilation and optimism, whereas 'male principle' photography has been poisoned to the nick by dissimilation and nihilism" (1996, 167–68). According to Miyasako, the ideal would be an androgynous marriage between the female and the male principles in photography. Iizawa does not search for androgyneity in women's photography. He was, of course, not the only critic to gender women photographers. For instance, the world-renowned photographer Araki Nobuyoshi similarly attributed the accomplishments of women photographers to their gender. He commented the following at an award ceremony: "In the last few years, the idea of 'winners and losers' has become very popular. The 30-year-old women that appear in these photos capture the vibrant essence of the feminine strength of today's women and show that they are undoubtedly among life's winners. . . . Those photos show women living their lives to the fullest. A man could never take such pictures—they are terrific. Photography itself has to have masculinity, but women appear to have more masculinity than men these days." See Canon's global website, New Cosmos of Photography, http://global.canon/en/newcosmos/gallery/grandprix/2005-akiko-ozawa/index.html, accessed May 14, 2018.

13 See Maho Kubota Gallery, https://www.mahokubota.com/wp/wp-content/uploads/2016/05/MKG-yurie_nagashima-about_me-en.pdf, accessed May 14, 2018.

14 See Nakamura Toyomi's personal website, http://toyomi.org, accessed on May 12, 2018.

15 In May 2018, when I visited her Instagram page, I saw that Suzuki introduced herself as a "cultural influencer" or, more specifically, "Cultural Influencer/Artist, Model, Writer, Photo & Design." See Suzuki Junko's Instagram account, https://www.instagram.com/junkosuzuki/?hl=en, accessed on May 12, 2018.

16 The techno-social assemblage of "girly" photography has also inspired social networking sites in the early and mid-2000s to develop photo applications (Mixi Photo Album and Yaplog's Photo Mail) and has facilitated the emergence of such photo-hosting sites as Hatena Photo and Photozou—the Japanese versions of Instagram, Photobucket, Pinterest, and Tumblr.

17 Another notable example is Kawauchi Rinko's *Cui Cui* (2005), which I analyze elsewhere (Lukacs 2015c).

18 Some art photographers such as Shinoyama Kishin have also viewed *Kazoku* as a celebration of familial intimacy and trust. See, for instance, "Ikikata no Tsuyosa ga Shashin ni Deru," *Kōkoku Hihyō*, January 2001, 125–34.

19 The award was sponsored by the Parco Gallery in Tokyo. Although Nagashima never published *Self-Portraits*, she included some of the photographs from this series in her photo book entitled *Past Time Paradise: 1992–2000* (2000).

20 Nagashima graduated from Musashino Art University in 1995 with a BA in visual communication design. She later earned an MFA from the California Institute of the Arts.

21 Shimamori Michiko asks Nagashima in an interview whether her family protested being photographed naked. Nagashima explains that *Self-Portraits* was her project to test the love of her family toward her (*aijō no kakunin*). See Shimamori Michiko's interview with Nagashima Yurie in *Kōkoku Hihyō*, April 2001, 110–14.

22 See Maho Kubota Gallery, http://www.mahokubota.com/wp/wp-content/themes /mahokubota.com/assets/MKG-yurie_nagashima-about_me-en.pdf, accessed on May 14, 2018.

23 In an ongoing book project, Ann Cvetkovich analyzes Rachael Shannon's inflatable tent installations. Arguing that sovereignty is an embodied practice that must be learned and experienced collectively, Cvetkovich looks at the works of artists who create built environments that generate new experiences of sociality. See University of Pittsburgh website, http://www.body.pitt.edu/sites/default/files /p-27cvetkovich8.5x11. pdf, accessed May 14, 2018.

24 Iizawa (2010). See also Yamauchi Hiroyasu's interview with Ume Kayo, "Nichijōni Uzumaku 'Warai' no Shattā Chansu," *Bijutsu Techō*, July 2007, 18–21; "Ume Kayo: Sono Toki no Arinomama no Funiki ga Shashin ni Dereba Ii Nātte Omou," *Bijutsu Techō*, August 2008, 152–67.

25 In Ume's photo book, Ume's Japanese-language comments are also translated into English. I have lightly edited parts of the comments for clarity.

26 See Maho Kubota Gallery, http://www.mahokubota.com/wp/wp-content/themes /mahokubota.com/assets/MKG-yurie_nagashima-about_me-en.pdf, accessed May 14, 2018.

27 Indeed, these three photographers all debuted with self-portraits: Nagashima with *Self-Portraits* in 1993, Hiromix with *Seventeen Girl Days* in 1995, and Ninagawa with *Happiness: Self-Portraits* in 1996.

28 In the overview of a photography workshop Nagashima held entitled "Photography as a Subversive Tactic: Being the Other," she writes, "When a society categorizes certain people under a common label, there is always a political undercurrent. By defining a group's characteristics as different from what is considered 'normal' or 'standard,' they can be made into the 'Other,' marginalized or isolated. For example, in a traditional gender-based power relationship a woman is often treated and expected to behave as a Model (object) in relationship to the Photographer (subject). It is important for all photographers to learn how to identify themselves with the 'Other' and to approach the norms imposed by society critically." See International Summer School of Photography 2014, Riga,

Latvia, http://www.issp.lv/en/education/summer-school/2014/masters-workshops #Yurie%20Nagashima, accessed May 14, 2018.

29 According to Louis Althusser, ideology is embodied in ideological and repressive state apparatuses. "Interpellation" (or hailing) is a practice that transforms individuals into subjects of these state apparatuses (2001).

30 I asked Nagashima about the reception of the photo book, as I was curious whether it was received as she intended it to be. I interpreted the desexualized images in the volume as reminders that the sexualized images were parodies. Yet I wondered whether the desexualized images did not become resexualized simply because they were situated in the context of sexualized images. I learned that the volume had a short shelf life. Soon after its publication, the publisher, Fuga Shobō, went bankrupt and was not able to pay for storage. Most copies of the photo book were destroyed.

31 Later, Nagashima pushed this idea further when she portrayed herself smoking while expecting her son. If gender is performance, she was thinking with Butler, then within the practices of repetitive signifying, the subversion of identity becomes possible (1990).

32 I do not agree with Iizawa, who writes the following: "For them, the device called photography was meant neither to create an unexisting 'alternative world' according to one's aesthetic nor to record a rare and special event" (1996, 159).

33 See Canon's global website, New Cosmos of Photography, http://global.canon /en/newcosmos/gallery/grandprix/1995-hiromix/index.html, accessed May 14, 2018.

34 See Canon's global website, New Cosmos of Photography, http://global.canon/en /newcosmos/gallery/grandprix/1995-hiromix/index.html, accessed May 14, 2018.

35 Nancy Baym and Theresa Senft define the selfie as "a photographic object that initiates the transmission of human feeling in the form of a relationship" and "a gesture that can send, and is often intended to send, different messages to different individuals, communities, and audiences" (2015, 1589). Similarly, Paul Frosh conceptualizes selfies as "gestural images," which say not only "see this, here, now" but also that "see me showing you me" (2015, 1610). Selfies show a self that is enacting itself and invite spectators to reflect on the "very instability of the term 'self'" (2015, 1621). As he argues, "the selfie invites viewers, in turn, to make conspicuously communicative, gestural responses" (Frosh 2015, 1622).

36 Iizawa writes the following about Hiromix's Girls Blue (1996): "It certainly is a photo book that gives a sense of extreme cheerfulness, like children enjoying their everyday lives innocently. However, it also seems that the bright lights are not the only things that are captured in the photographs. The feeling of wanting to keep 'the day that only exists today' that passes in a blink; the melancholic feeling of 'blue,' characteristic of adolescent years. The linking of these feelings might have made this volume appealing to young people" (2012, 196).

37 See Richard Lloyd Parry, "Hiromix Is as Big in the East as Madonna Is Here, and When She Throws a Tantrum, You'd Better Duck: Richard Lloyd Parry Meets a Typical Product of Nineties Japan," Independent, January 31, 1999, http://www

.independent.co.uk/life-style/real-people-interview-hiromix-portrait-of-the
-artist-as-a-little-madam-1077349.html, accessed May 14, 2018.

38 Honma Takashi's interview with Nagashima Yurie, *Kōkoku Hihyō*, April 2001, 115–19.

39 Women photographers mentioned in interviews that carrying around equipment in the city is a challenge, as a couple of cameras weigh four to five kilograms.

40 Kaori Shoji, "Young Women behind the Camera Craze in Tokyo," *New York Times*, January 16, 1999, http://www.nytimes.com/1999/01/16/style/16iht-photog.t .html, accessed May 14, 2018. We do not know whether the author of the article is actually quoting Hiromix or imagining a "typical" response Hiromix might have given. If Hiromix actually said this, she might have wanted to reproduce the image of the "silly girl" to keep the boundary between male critics and female photographers.

41 Hiromix worked with Araki as a model and compiled *Seventeen Girls Days* under the advisement of Honma Takashi, who was Araki's assistant at the time. Hiromix's diary-style photography was influenced by Araki's diaristic work, such as *Pseudo Diary* (1980), *The First Years of Heisei* (1990), *A Photomaniac's Journey* (1992), and *Sentimental Journey: Winter Journey* (1991). Her visual style was characterized by a rough and often out-of-focus capture of the everyday; it was akin to the works of photographers, especially Moriyama Daido, who gathered around the short-lived photography journal *Provoke* in 1968 and 1969 (Sas 2011).

42 Interview with Hiromix: Suguni Toranaito Maho ga Tondeiku, *Kōkoku Hihyō*, June 1998, 66–77.

43 Ninagawa Mika, "Ninagawa Mika ni yoru Ninagawa Mika," *Bijutsu Techō* 60, no. 915 (November 2008), 44–45.

44 Ninagawa, "Ninagawa Mika ni yoru Ninagawa Mika," 44–45.

45 Ninagawa, "Ninagawa Mika ni yoru Ninagawa Mika," 44.

46 Ninagawa, "Ninagawa Mika ni yoru Ninagawa Mika," 45.

47 Ninagawa Yukio was a renowned stage director who became famous for his exuberantly scenic stage productions and directions of Shakespeare plays with actors wearing costumes from Japan's feudal (Tokugawa) period (1600–1868). He passed away in May 2016.

48 Ninagawa, "Ninagawa Mika ni yoru Ninagawa Mika," 45. Ninagawa's statement supports critics' proposition that women's work is more related to their intuition than men's. However, Ninagawa does not connect intuition to femininity. Instead, she talks about the dichotomy between art and science and does so without gendering this dichotomy.

49 Canon Inc., Canon's global website, New Cosmos of Photography, "Masafumi Sanai: Stoned and Dethroned," http://www.canon.com/scsa/newcosmos/gallery /1995/masafumi_sanai/index.html, accessed June 14, 2016, now defunct.

50 After realizing that not all young women practiced "girly" photography while some male photographers did, Iizawa modified his argument by shifting to a discussion of the male and female principles in photography (2010).

Chapter 2: The Labor of Cute

1   Alice Marwick defines microcelebrity as a state of being famous to a niche group of people, "a self-presentation strategy that includes creating a persona, sharing personal information about oneself, constructing intimate connections to create the illusion of friendship or closeness, acknowledging an audience and identifying them as fans, and strategically revealing information to increase or maintain this audience. Social media technologies are an intrinsic part of this process" (2013, 117). Net idols drew on strategies similar to the ones microcelebrities use to build an online presence. They, however, were not able to benefit from social media technologies, as the net idol trend had peaked around 2004, before these technologies became available. I do not conceptualize the net idols as microcelebrities because becoming an internet celebrity was not the ultimate goal of net idols. They instead strove to develop a variety of careers that were not tied to social media. When net idols achieved (or failed to achieve) their goals, they shut down their web pages.

2   Mario Tronti defines the social factory as follows: "At the highest level of capitalist development social relations become moments of the relations of production, and the whole society becomes an articulation of production. In short, all of society lives as a function of the factory and the factory extends its exclusive domination over all of society" (1962, 9).

3   Unlike women photographers, net idols had to please their fans—*otaku*—whose interest in cute culture scholars have insightfully documented (Galbraith 2013; LaMarre 2009).

4   One of the photo books that featured the most popular net idols was entitled *Net Idol Secret File: Netto Aidoru Shashinshū* [Net Idol Secret File: Photo Book Featuring Net Idols] (Tokyo: Geibunsha, 2002). The title refers to the secrecy around net idol careers. The author is Makihara Susumu, a male photographer; he writes his name in katakana or romaji (English script) and has been publishing photo books of nude young women.

5   The first telecom deregulation took place in 1985 when the Japanese Telecom Business Law was amended and Nippon Telegraph and Telephone (NTT) was privatized. In 1999, to further the deregulation of the communication industries, NTT was divided into NTT holding company, NTT Communications (long-distance and global), NTT-East (local telephone), and NTT-West (local telephone). This deregulation was called the second telecom deregulation. See Fuke Hidenori, "Structural Change and Deregulation in the Telecom Industry," 2000, http://park12.wakwak.com/~kobakan/contents/0007structuralchangederegulation_intelecom_R.html, accessed May 14, 2018.

6   In 2001, Yahoo! BB of SoftBank began offering an internet service with 8Mbps connection for a monthly flat rate of 3,017 yen ($27). Until then, other ADSL services provided 1.5 Mbps connections for a monthly fee of 4,000 to 6,000 yen ($36–$54). Wikipedia Japan, https://ja.wikipedia.org/wiki/Yahoo!_BB, accessed May 14, 2018.

7   To create a web page, users had to learn at least a basic level of HTML. Infoseek's how-to page offers tutorials that explain, for example, what HTML is, how to input text, break lines, etc. See http://infoseek_rip.g.ribbon.to/iswebmag.hp.infoseek.co.jp/, accessed May 14, 2018.

8   Geocities provided web space and web page building tools. It was easy to use, but the web layouts were rudimentary. Goo.ne.jp was a search engine, but it also offered space and tools for creating personal websites. See Wikipedia Japan, http://www.geocities.jp/seidy_seidy/goo/kihon.html. Freeweb was similar to Geocities. It was bought by Infoseek, a search engine like Goo, and became a web space service called Isweb. It closed in 2010, while Geocities is still available. See https://ja.wikipedia.org/wiki/Infoseek_isweb, both sites accessed May 14, 2018. Livedoor also started offering web space around 2000. In 2002, the company bought an online diary service for women. See Internet Watch, http://internet.watch.impress.co.jp/www/article/2000/0925/zerodoor.htm, accessed May 14, 2018.

9   In the early 2000s, social networking sites (SNS) and blog services began proliferating; this further simplified the building and maintenance of personal web pages. These included Mixi, http://mixi.jp/; Nichanneru, http://www.2ch.net/; Livedoor, http://blog.livedoor.com/; Cosme, http://www.cosme.net/top/index; and Ameba, http://gg.ameba.jp. In 2004, Rakuten Inc. introduced a new service to build personal web pages, Zenryaku Purofiru, http://pr.cgiboy.com/, all accessed May 14, 2018, except the last one, which is now defunct. This service was more popular than social networking and blog sites because it provided users with URLs. Personal web pages created through social networking and blog sites were accessible only to other registered members of the same site. By contrast, private websites are open to all internet users.

10 The rationale behind hiring an agent lay in the belief that agents would protect the privacy and personal safety of net idols. In many cases, however, these agents recruited young women for work in the cybersex industry. A popular net idol agent was Minowa Keiju. Other net idol agencies include Net Idol *candy* and Sweet Netoa Jimusho Ōdishon (Sweet Net Idols Audition Agency). See http://group.ameba.jp/group/7agl-vvrIzq3/, accessed September 30, 2017, now defunct. Net Idol *candy* was launched on February 5, 2011. In order to get a contract from this agency, one had to go through an audition. In 2011, the agency managed the careers of thirteen net idols. Sweet Netoa Jimusho Ōdishon was launched on January 28, 2011, and in the same year, it managed the careers of eighteen net idols. Ameba—a free website service, which later became Japan's largest blogging platform—hosted both Net Idol *candy* and Sweet Netoa Jimusho Ōdishon, both sites accessed June 4, 2011, now defunct. In addition to net idol agents, Virtual Net Idol: Chiyu 12 Years Old was launched in 2001. This site featured news and the diary of an animated character. It had a significant impact, inspiring the development of other VNI sites such as Uron no Hitorigoto (Uron's Monologue) and Okome 777's Loop Lights Loom. These VNI sites paved the way to the development of blog sites by blurring the boundary between news sites and diary sites. See Chiyu's website, http://tiyu.to; Sakuraba Uebu Bunka

Kenkyūshitsu, http://websitemap.sakura.ne.jp/monograph/monograph03.html; Wikipedia Japan, https://ja.wikipedia.org/wiki/%E3%83%90%E3%83%BC%E3%83 %81%E3%83%A3%E3%83%AB%E3%83%8D%E3%83%83%E3%83%88%E3%82%A2% E3%82%A4%E3%83%89%E3%83%AB, all accessed May 14, 2018.

11 Authenticity also seemed to matter to fans. Alice Marwick notes that audiences expect microcelebrities to be more authentic than traditional celebrities, perhaps because microcelebrities did not emerge from the usual processes of star making. While some argue that authenticity has to do with consistency, others suggest that the key to authenticity is to reveal one's inner life—"honesty without pretense" (2013, 120).

12 See Net Idol Search, http://www.netidolwosagase.com/, accessed May 14, 2018. Other net idol ranking sites include Net @ Idol, http://www.maeweb.com/netidol /a.html; https://web.archive.org/web/20041015093833/http://www.maeweb.com /netidol/a.html; Net Idol Support Club, http://netooidol.gooside.com; http:// netidol-company.sakura.ne.jp/; Net Idol Cosplay, https://web.archive.org/web /20100510154825/http://netidol-company.sakura.ne.jp/; http://virus.s1.xrea.com (defunct and no archived screenshot available). Note that I also listed the archived versions of defunct sites., all accessed May 14, 2018.

13 See Zakzak Online News, http://www.zakzak.co.jp/tsui-sat/tsuiseki/contents /0826_01.html, accessed May 14, 2018.

14 See Net Idol Search, https://web.archive.org/web/20010410063606/http://www .netidolwosagase.com/contentu/help.htm, accessed May 14, 2018.

15 See Net Idol Search, https://web.archive.org/web/20001110012700/http://www .netidolwosagase.com/index.html, accessed May 14, 2018.

16 These photo books featured the most popular net idols of 2000–2001. According to my survey, these books featured a total of 288 net idols whose profiles included their web addresses. In 2010, 274 of these websites were defunct, and I did not find any trace of 259 of these net idols.

17 Net Idol Information Guide, https://web.archive.org/web/20140409205219/http:// net-idol.j-guide.info/, was part of Suzuki's website (Media Net Japan), which aimed to promote search engine optimization (SEO), accessed April 9, 2014, now defunct. The Net Idol Information Guide was a registration-based portal. Registration was free. The instructions said, "We are accepting registration to Net Idol Information Guide for free. You can register your website instantly, for free. Note: The website that does not fit the themes cannot be registered." The site featured the following themes: Ranking, Goods, Costume Play and Costume, DVD, Photo Books, Shopping, Music Albums, Blogs, Event Information, Related Books, Information Portal, and Links. Suzuki's idea was that net idols who wanted to promote their websites would register on his site. Under "Photo Books," a registration from 2006 said, "Cosplay photos of anime and more! Please visit my page and take a look at my photo book!" Under "Blogs," another registration from 2006 said, "Haruka: A Regular Girl of Our Days! Net idol Haruka's website. There Are Photos, BBS, and Links (laugh). Looking for Net Idol Friends? Email Me!" Given the small number of registrations, it seems that Net Idol Information

Guide was not very successful. The portal was active until 2012. See Minako's Cosplay Site, https://web.archive.org/web/20080501125008/http://www.geocities.jp/minako_love_p/, and Haruka's Net Idol Site, https://web.archive.org/web/20141004224552/http://www.flexmegu.com/haruka/, accessed May 14, 2018.

18 See Net Idol Academy, http://www.net-idol-academy.com/, accessed September 24, 2018.

19 Fans become visible in the net idol universe not only via the comments they post to net idols' websites but also via the gaze that informs what content net idols will produce. See Ivy (2010) and LaMarre (2009) for luminously insightful analyses of how fans are incorporated into productive processes.

20 I am thankful to Gavin Wittje for bringing the relevance of the cute face to my attention.

21 See Wikipedia, http://en.wikipedia.org/wiki/Ebihara_Yuri, accessed May 14, 2018.

22 "Ebi-kawaiku Ikitai!" *AERA* 10, 19 (17), April 2006, 38–41, 41.

23 See Tanaka Eris's Twitter account, https://twitter.com/eris_inko and Tanaka Eris's blog on Hatena Blogging Platform, http://erisinko.hatenablog.com; http://mixi.jp/view_community.pl?id=110533, all sites accessed May 14, 2018.

24 See Tanaka Eris's website, Eris in Wonderland, http://www.kinokopress.com/inko/top.html, accessed February 28, 2013, now defunct.

25 See Tanaka Eris's website, Eris in Wonderland, http://www.kinokopress.com/inko/top.html, accessed February 28, 2013, now defunct.

26 See Tanaka Eris's website, Eris in Wonderland, http://www.kinokopress.com/inko/top.html, accessed February 28, 2013, now defunct.

27 The title is a playful reiteration of Yamada Yoji's hit television series *It's Hard to Be a Man* (*Otoko wa Tsurai Yo*, 1969–95).

28 See also Shiokawa (1999).

29 Ngai writes that "the formal properties associated with cuteness—smallness, compactness, softness, simplicity, and pliancy—call forth specific affects: helplessness, pitifulness, and even despondency" (2005, 816). Equally illuminating, Marilyn Ivy (2010) suggests that Nara Yoshitomo's paintings of creepy-cute children play with the semantic boundaries of *kawaii*. She writes, "The modal requirements of the *kawaii* have been pushed past the limits of vulnerable malleability, disclosing the aggressive dimension always implicit in the cutified aesthetic relationship" (2010, 15).

30 The contemporary entertainment industry primarily uses *iyashi-kei* to refer to young female idols of every stripe, from mainstream tarento to bikini models. "Iyashi Būmu no Kōsatsu [Discussion of the Iyashi Boom]," http://machika.oops.jp/healingframe.htm. See also the Japanese Wikipedia on "iyashi," http://ja.wikipedia.org/wiki/%E7%99%92%E3%81%97; first site is now defunct, second site accessed May 14, 2018.

31 Examples include Kozue Haruna, Sakai Rika, Nagaike Natsuko, Yoko, and Tsukimiya Usagi. See http://ameblo.jp/kozueharuna/, accessed May 14, 2018;

http://www.sakai-rika.com/profile.html, accessed August 20, 2011, now defunct; Wikipedia Japan, http://ja.wikipedia.org/wiki/%E6%B0%B8%E6%B1%A0%E5 %8D%97%E6%B4%A5%E5%AD%90, accessed April 18, 2019; http://blog.livedoor .jp/yokochannel/, accessed April 18, 2019; and http://usagi-moon.com/prof.html, accessed May 14, 2018.

32 Examples are Suzuki Yasuka, Mii, Hina. See http://www.yasuka.cc/, accessed August 20, 2011, now defunct; http://ameblo.jp/isseiko193/, accessed May 14, 2018; http://www.blogmura.com/profile/00490936.html, accessed May 14, 2018; and http://hina2008.jugem.jp/, accessed May 14, 2018.

33 An example is Sakurai Ryon, aka Yamamoto Akari. See http://www.jah.ne.jp /~ryoryo/akari.html, accessed August 20, 2011, now defunct.

34 An example is Inozuka Shino. See http://again789.fc2web.com/index.html, accessed August 20, 2011, now defunct.

35 Examples include Nakamura Toyomi, Mizunagi Ren. See http://www.toyomi.org/ and http://www.page.sannet.ne.jp/hatue/index.html, both sites accessed May 14, 2018.

36 Examples include Kikōden Misa, Hōjō Rara. See http://blog.dmm.co.jp/actress /kikouden_misa/, accessed September 30, 2017, now defunct.

37 See Inui Yoko's Net Idol site titled YokoEgg, http://www.yokoegg.com/index .html, accessed May 14, 2018.

38 Nakamura's photos of flowers are reminiscent of the centrality of flowers to Ninagawa's work. She named her website that is dedicated to her career as an art photographer www.toyomix.com, which evokes the name of the famous "girly" photographer, Hiromix; accessed May 14, 2018.

39 See Nakamura Toyomi's personal website, http://loversdesign.com, accessed May 14, 2018.

40 A recently updated introduction on the website Nakamura dedicated to photo-therapy introduces Nakamura as follows: "I was a stage actress before entering the world of photography. My first stage appearance was when I was 12 years old. For reasons beyond my control, I left the stage; yet my heart was still restless. I was looking for something that can replace theater and I encountered 'photography.' Photography accommodated all of my feelings and thoughts. It allows me to be a screenwriter, a director, and an actor. I find the genre of self-portraiture particularly appealing. Similar to how each line that describes a character's life in a play is relevant, I want every photo I take to express my thoughts and feelings. Photography is a drama without movement and sound. That is what makes it fun. And yet, I still would like to stand on a stage. With my body, my voice, my words, I want to create a true light. My trials and errors continue." See http://loversdesign.com. Nakamura has another website dedicated to developing her career as an art photographer, http://toyomi.photo/art/. She frequently updates the blog section of the web page http://toyomi.photo/art/?page _id=36. Lastly, Nakamura also has a work-only Instagram account: https://www .instagram.com/toyomi.photo/; all sites accessed May 14, 2018. To develop her

career as an art photographer, Nakamura is currently apprenticing with Tokoro Yukinori.

41 In addition to her own websites, http://loversdesign.com; http://www.toyomi .org/; and http://toyomi.photo, Nakamura currently maintains accounts on Facebook, Twitter, Tumblr, and Instagram; all accessed May 14, 2018.

42 See http://toyomi.photo/art/?page_id=40, accessed May 14, 2018. Nakamura wrote the following in an email to me. "Being born as a woman, I want to be desired as woman until I die. . . . How do women experience their womanhood in the city? The number of unmarried women is increasing, the birth rate is dropping, and women are wearing their fingers to the bone for work. They live their lives pretending they are not making significant sacrifices. I shoot photographs of women in this harsh world superimposing them onto decaying flowers. Flowers that are torn off, withered, dried out. I name each one of them, call them, and sprinkle milky white liquid on their petals. These flowers are the proofs that women have been loved as women. I want women to remember that. Women are allowed to desire the love and the gaze until they turn into ashes, until flowers return to earth. Shibuya, where I live, is said to have the highest rate of unmarried women in Japan. I am one of these women. Through photography, I will continue expressing the feelings and thoughts of women who desire love in this lonely corner of the metropolis." (Email communication, May 17, 2016).

43 In a television commercial, we see Ebihara trying on different white hats for fifty seconds of a fifty-three second television commercial. We understand only in the last three seconds that the ad is for McDonald's when the golden arches appear and Ebihara exclaims, "I am loving it!" Sianne Ngai offers sharp insights to unpack the associations between eating, cute, and power. She writes the following: "In its association with food, the dinner plate does more than merely supply a material support for Nara [Yoshitomo]'s images of mutilated or injured children. Evoking the expression, 'You're so cute I could just eat you up,' Nara's use of food-related objects for his interrogation of kawaii becomes extended and exaggerated in Fountain of Life, a sculpture in which seven of what appear to be disembodied dolls' heads are stacked on top of one another in an oversized tea cup with accompanying saucer, with tears/water flowing out of their closed eyes. Underscoring the aggressive desire to master and overpower the cute object that the cute object itself appears to elicit, the tie between cuteness and eating that Nara's work makes explicit finds its consumer culture counterpart in the characters generated by San-X, an edgier and more contemporary incarnation of Sanrio, the company that invented the iconic Hello Kitty" (2005, 820).

44 Technological developments, the rising wages in advanced capitalist countries, the fragmentation of the consumer market, and competition from developing countries are commonly offered to explain the shift to post-Fordism.

45 Kambayashi, Takehiko, "Women Work Way Up in Japan; Entrepreneurial Spirit Helps Lift Ailing Economy," *Washington Times*, July 26, 2002, A17.

46 When the school system is not equipped to prepare young people to adapt to the

capriciousness of an ailing economy (Brinton 2010), digital technologies acquire new relevance. The architects of the digital economy take over the responsibilities of teachers and career counselors. Many young people perceive unpaid work in the digital economy as the only possibility for finding work.

Chapter 3: Career Porn

1   Vincent Mosco calls this the myth of the digital sublime (2004).
2   Bloggers embodied the homo oeconomicus that Michel Foucault described "as entrepreneur of himself, being for himself his own capital, being for himself his own producer, being for himself the source of [his] earnings" (2010, 226).
3   See Wikipedia, http://ja.wikipedia.org/wiki/%E3%83%96%E3%83%AD%E3%82 %B0%E3%81%AE%E5%A5%B3%E7%8E%8B, accessed May 15, 2018.
4   See Ameba Media Guide, http://stat100.ameba.jp/ad/mediaguide/2015_1-3/2015 _1-3_Ameba_MEDIAGUIDE.pdf. Among the registered users of the Pig Games, women account for 65 percent and men for 35 percent (Game Age Sōken 2012), accessed May 15, 2018.
5   In descending order, these include (1) AI's Gaishi-kei OL AI no Kyō no Kōde Burogu, http://ameblo.jp/nyprtkifml/, (2) Itsutake's Official Blog: Puchi-pura Kōde Mama Fasshon Blog Arigato, http://ameblo.jp/yuuyaismyself/, (3) Mie's Fasshon to Ryōri to Kaji Nikki, http://ameblo.jp/miemio6/, (4) Noriko's Noricoco Rūmu: 365 Nichi Kōdinētā Nikki, http://ameblo.jp/noricoco1023/, and (5) Masaki's 30dai Mama Fasshon ya Shumi no Burogu: Sengyō Shufu Masaki no Burogu, http:// blog.livedoor.jp/masakiblogg/, all accessed May 15, 2018. The top five food bloggers are also women. These include (1) Shiori's Fūdo Kōdinētā SHIORI no Burogu: Tsukutte Agetai Kare Gohan, http://ameblo.jp/karegohan/, (2) Yukko's Fūdo Kōdinētā, Yukko no Oishii 365+, http://ameblo.jp/yukkosan-514/, (3) Fūdo Anarisuto Hirabayashi Remi's Official Blog Remi's Charming Restaurant by Diamond Blog, http://www.diamondblog.jp/official/remi_hirabayashi/, (4) Ayaka's Fūdo Kōdinētā Ayaka-san no "My Recipe Book," http://www.recipe-blog.jp /profile/59571, and (5) Hatsu's Ebisu/Ginza Daisuki Shinmai, Fūdo Kōdinētā Hatsu no Burogu, http://ebisu-gourmet.blog.jp/, all accessed October 1, 2017. The top five bloggers that write about issues pertaining to family and child-raising are women as well. These include (1) LICO's Kodomo no Kokoro ga Odayaka ni Sodatsu Mahō no Ikuji-ō, http://ameblo.jp/licolily/, (2) Surume's Surume blog, http://surume.hatenablog.jp, (3) NTV's Mama mo Ko mo Kosodate Burogu, http://www.ntv.co.jp/mamamocomo/blog/, (4) Sonoda's Obieru Kosodate Nikki Manga, http://obieru767. blog.fc2. com/, and (5) Hebubu's Tōdai-sotsu Sengyō Shufu no Kosodate Burogu, http://hebubu.seesaa.net/. Even in the category of entrepreneurship and technology, we find women among the top five most popular bloggers. (Except for the last link, which is now defunct, all links were accessed May 15, 2018.) The top five list includes (1) Oteki no Burogu, https:// ohtedaiki.wordpress.com/, (2) 31sai Sakuma Minoru Sarariiman Kigyōka Burogu, http://sakumaminoru.net/, (3) 23sai Kigyōka Ayumi no Burogu, http://

ameblo.jp/shine—1/, (4) Josei Kigyōka Ono Yukika no "Official Blog," http://ameblo.jp/tokyo-trust/, and (5) Globis Hori Yoshito no Burogu, Kigyōka no Fūkei/Bōgen, http://blog.globis.co.jp/, except for #3, all accessed May 15, 2018.

6 The most popular themes of blogging on Ameba in June 2015 were topics that seem more appealing to women, including "diary," "capricious life," "raising children," "take it easy," "thinking out loud," "happy life," "high school students," "middle school students," "music," and "fashion." See Ameba, http://ranking.ameba.jp/, accessed May 15, 2018. The most popular blog news site, for instance, Dokujo News (http://www.officiallyjd.com/), targets women with celebrity gossip, but the owners and producers of the site are not women; accessed May 15, 2018. The company that owns the site, JSquared Inc., owns Girls Channel—a BBS that also centers on celebrity gossip and is linked to Dokujo News. Girls' Channel is similar to Nichanneru, but the topics focus on celebrities, fashion, makeup, and romance. Clearly, these are topics that envision women as the audience.

7 Net idol sites were online diaries or text sites, which are websites whose pages are stored on a private or rented server. Owners or renters of text sites use website-making software to edit the HTML, and each HTML file is uploaded via FTP. Text sites usually feature an index or top page that lists updates of new articles, allowing visitors to click on each article. The characteristics of text sites include repeated line breaks that serve to punctuate the text and varying font types, colors, and sizes to make the design more inviting. Within the broader genre of text sites, diary sites feature content that is about the site owner's daily life. Diarists strive to develop a style that readers will find enjoyable and produce content that is entertaining and informative. Another genre of text sites was news sites, such as A! Netto (1997), Smallnews! (1998), Henjinkutsu (HJK), Moo No Rōkaru, J-o no nikki, and TECHINSIDE.NET. In May 1999, Ura News (later renamed as Renpō) and itoya_laboratory*net_news were launched. Both published column-like short articles in the style of what later became blogs. Hyakushiki was launched in January 2000. Some of the most popular individual news sites, such as Tentative Name, Katoyūke Danzetsu, Music Distribution Memo (Ongaku Haishin Memo), moved on to blogging platforms.

8 BBS used Common Gateway Interface (CGI), which needed to be hosted on a server. Many rental websites had their own BBS CGI, but there were also rental BBS services available. There were several styles of BBS. Nichanneru, for instance, uses the thread float system, where multiple threads can be opened under a single BBS, placing the most recent entry at the top. Major BBS services use a simpler "thread" system, where one BBS is treated as one thread. Each entry is numbered, and the most recent entry appears at the top of the list. There were other types, such as the tree-system (users can reply to a post and the replies are nested under the original post), one-line response system, a post has a character limit, usually consisting of one line), and a forum (each user can open a new "room," the list of rooms is presented on the top page, and the responses are not nested).

9 Tsuda was forced to shut down this ranking due to trolling by a competitor, Bauwau, who developed another diary service called Nikki Enjin (1996–2000),

renamed in 2000 as Nikki Saito (2000–2007). To help navigate the growing number of online diaries, a new genre of diary evolved that offered commentaries about diaries (Nikki Yomi Nikki).

10 The contributors remained anonymous by leaving their handles blank. By 1998, trolling became so widespread on Ayashi World that Shiba, the founder of the site, was forced to close it.

11 In 2015, Nishimura bought 4chan from Christopher Poole.

12 Blogroll comes from combining blog and logrolling. It is a blogger's list of hyperlinks to other blogs that the blogger recommends. A permalink is an archived URL of a specific web page, frequently blogs. Originally, all hyperlinks were permalinks, as it was not possible to change content. A permalink is a link to a specific version of a web page. When web pages are used as sources of content, permalinks are recommended so that the source remains unchanged.

13 In the mid-2000s, the most popular blog platforms were Livedoor Blog (November 2003), Cocolog (December 2003), Jugem (February 2004), Ameba Blog (September 2004), So-net (September 2004), and FC2 (October 2004). Some of these blogging portals also overlapped in terms of the services they offered with social networking sites, such as mixi (1999) and GREE (2004). Wordpress, Facebook, and Twitter are also used in Japan. Yahoo offers a blogging service as well. Other platforms were crossover portals between blogging portals and diary sites. Hatena Diary (January 2003) is the most prominent example of this continuity between online diaries and blogs. On Hatena Diary, users create their own diary pages, but the architecture of the portal is configured in a way that individual diaries are immediately tagged and thus made searchable for the Hatena community. Users who are tagged under the same keywords read each other's diaries to see how other users use the same tag. Azuma Hiroki notes that it is common that users force each other to change their tags, thus expanding the available tags and drawing more users to the site. The tag war also makes people more involved in the Hatena community (Hamano 2008, 117). Kondo Junya, founder of Hatena Co. Ltd., explains that the trackback system, which was developed in the United States, is less popular in Japan. It allows bloggers to track back posts and communicate with each other. Kondo feels that Japanese internet users are more reluctant to directly communicate with each other. They feel more comfortable to speak up in spaces such as the ones the tagging system generates (Hamano 2008, 118–19).

14 Examples include Wakatsuki Chinatsu and Manabe Kaori. See Wikipedia, http://ja.wikipedia.org/wiki/Category%E2%80%90%E3%83%8E%E3%83%BC%E3%83%88: %E3%83%96%E3%83%AD%E3%82%AC%E3%83%BC, accessed May 15, 2018.

15 See IT Media Mobile, http://www.itmedia.co.jp/mobile/articles/0601/25/news090.html; Celebrity Blog Ranking, http://www.talentblog.jp/tllink/tllink.php?mode=rank; Ameba, http://official.ameba.jp/ranking/day/accessRankingCategory 0-1.html; Naver Internet Content Service Company, http://matome.naver.jp

/odai/2133371919025777401; Six Apart Japan, http://www.sixapart.jp/news/2012
/03/12–1000.html; and Blogos News Portal, http://blogos.com/article/65664/, all
accessed May 15, 2018.

16 Trebor Scholz discusses the algorithmic optimization of stories in the interest of
    maximizing advertising revenue. The themes of stories and videos are calculated
    based on algorithms that determine what themes will receive the highest number
    of hits. The Leaf Group (formerly Demand Media) buys content from seven thou-
    sand independent contractors (2017, 34). Scholz also notes that YouTube hires
    consultants to better understand how to trigger the participation of the crowd.
    They are paid to help management understand how they can get unpaid produc-
    ers to create value (2017, 87).

17 Tiziana Terranova writes, "it is a question of attracting and individuating not
    just this free labor, but also in some way various forms of possible surplus-value
    that can capitalize on the diffused desires of sociality, expression, relation. In this
    model, the production of profit by companies would take place over and against
    the individuation and capture of a 'lateral' surplus value (the sale of public-
    ity, and the sale of data produced by the activity of users, the capacity to attract
    financial investments on the basis of visibility and the prestige of new global
    brands like Google and Facebook). In many cases, surplus value resides in the
    saving of costs of this very labor since the latter becomes 'externalized' to users
    (the externalization of analysis and beta testing of videogames or technical sup-
    port to users)" (Terranova cited in Marazzi 2010, 55–56).

18 In terms of Ameba's revenues, 51 percent comes from advertising, 30 percent is
    derived from games and other media (mainly people buying virtual goods and
    currency to play these games), 17 percent is from the sale of Ameba's stocks, and 2
    percent comes from investment development. See https://www.cyberagent.co.jp
    /ir/special/business_report/2014/ebook/index.html#page=56, accessed October 1,
    2017, now defunct.

19 Fujita founded CyberAgent when he was twenty-four years old. By 2014, he be-
    came Japan's forty-seventh-richest person. Fujita is reputed to be the youngest
    CEO in Japan who has listed a company on the Tokyo Stock Exchange. See
    http://www.forbes.com/profile/susumu-fujita/, accessed May 15, 2018.

20 See Ameba Media Guide, http://stat100.ameba.jp/ad/mediaguide/2015_1-3/2015
    _1-3_Ameba_MEDIAGUIDE.pdf, accessed May 15, 2018. Ameba functions as
    an affiliate service provider (ASP). Affiliate advertising means that bloggers can
    earn money by displaying ads on their blogs as affiliates for advertisers. To do so,
    a blogger has to register with an affiliate service provider, choose the banner ads,
    and add them to her blog. ASPs aggregate all businesses that wish to advertise on-
    line. It is the ASPs that pay bloggers using three common formulas: pay-per-click
    (the blogger is paid each time a visitor clicks on the advertiser's banner), pay-per-
    impression (the blogger is paid per page view), or pay-per-action (the blogger is
    paid each time a visitor makes a purchase). The last formula pays the most, but
    it requires bloggers to proactively promote products by writing reviews about

them. ASPs check the content of one's blog to confirm its appropriateness for advertising. If one passes the inspection, she can choose what to advertise. She will receive the banner to copy into her blog and sign a contract. Some ASPs are strict, so bloggers usually start with a less strict one, build a profile, and then challenge a stricter ASP. Some ASPs, like A8.net and Rakuten, do not do inspections, but A8.net requires users to pay bank transfer fees ($1–$8) after each transaction, while Rakuten pays only using the site's internal point system. Ameba also pays in Ame Gold, which can be used only on Ameba. According to a survey conducted by the NPO Association of Affiliate Marketing in 2005, 57 percent of respondents use blogs to participate in affiliate advertising (more than 70 percent for women in their twenties through forties). See Affiliate Program Survey 2005, http://affiliate-marketing.jp/release/release051214.html, accessed May 15, 2018. In 2005, Takamori Hideaki claimed that a blogger could make a few hundred to a few thousand dollars each month through affiliate advertising (2005a; see also 2005b, 2005c, 2006). Similarly, Hayashi Natsuki reported that within ninety days, he was able to increase his page views to a thousand a day and made JPY1 million/month ($9,100/month) from affiliate advertising (2006). According to the survey I cited above, more than 70 percent of affiliate program users earn less than JPY1,000/month ($9/month).

21 See *The Japan Times*, http://info.japantimes.co.jp/info/100-next-era-ceos/2010 /contents/093.html, accessed May 15, 2018.

22 See Sony Global, http://www.sony.net/SonyInfo/csr_report/employees/info/ and Statista: The Statistics Portal, http://www.statista.com/statistics/267275 /worldwide-number-of-honda-employees/, both accessed May 15, 2018; 47 percent of the workforce are in their thirties, and 49 percent are in their twenties. Only 4 percent are in their forties, 69 percent are male, 47 percent are professional engineers, and 53 percent work administrative jobs; 36 percent are married, and the rest are single; 82 percent of the female employees are not mothers, 7 percent are on maternity leave, and 11 percent are working mothers. Only 11 percent of female employees do not return from maternity leave; 23 percent of the managers are female, 48 percent are new graduates, and 52 percent are midcareer hires. See CyberAgent Inc., https://www.cyberagent.co.jp/ir/special/business_report/2014 /ebook/index.html#page=56, accessed October 1, 2017.

23 See also Blogos News Portal, http://blogos.com/article/158758/, accessed May 15, 2018.

24 Kuchikomi Tsunagari is a site that aggregates blog entries written about the same topic (the topics are determined by Blog Topics Management or Ameba Blog staff). Users can jump to other blog entries written about the same topic. Ameba management claims that blog topics (*burogu neta*) are effective promotional tools. See Ameba, http://prom.ameba.jp/mediaguide/201201–03/2012_1–3 _ameba_ad.pdf, accessed October 1, 2017, now defunct.

25 Ameba Guruppo is a community platform of Ameba, where members can form a group according to their common interests, such as hobbies, pets, music, cook-

ing, TV, movie, celebrities, sports, anime, and games. Guruppo Community hosts the bulletin board of Ameba Groups. This is similar to mixi communities and Facebook groups.

26 This is an aggregate news service like Google News. Ameba News simply pulls news from sites such as Eiga.com, MyNaviNews, Netorabo, or R25. The news comes from online sources and not from newspapers or television stations.

27 Ameba GG is similar to women's magazines. It features articles written by Ameba staff members about such topics as "beauty, fashion, cooking, lifestyle, and motherhood." It is affiliated with a magazine named *Ginger*.

28 Currently, Ameba offers only "Woman & Crowd," a classified ad service that specializes in advertising part-time jobs to stay-at-home mothers. It is a registration-based service and currently has fifty thousand users.

29 In addition to selling online advertising, CyberAgent offers social games, such as Ameba Pig, Pig Life, Pig Island, Pig Café, and Pig World, which are comparable to Second Life and Nintendo's Mii.

30 See Ameba, http://ranking.ameba.jp, accessed May 15, 2018.

31 Ameba offers a list of topics (*burogu neta*) to write about. This list is refreshed every two weeks. The link to the topics is included on the user's "my page," and it is also available within blog editor. The topics are accessible to readers not registered with Ameba. Once users select what topic to write about, they will include a link banner to the topics page, so that other writers and readers know that they are contributing to a particular topic. Contributions to these topics can help bloggers increase their page views. See Ameba, http://kuchikomi.ameba.jp/, accessed May 15, 2018.

32 See Ameba, http://ameblo.jp/ameba-ad-pr/, accessed May 15, 2018.

33 See Ameba, http://blog.ameba.jp/content/amepon/top.html, accessed May 15, 2018.

34 Ameba prohibits any sale of products directly from Ameba blogs. Bloggers can advertise products but may not sell them. A shop can have its Ameba blog, but it has to be "a diary," and the shop has to have its own retail page outside Ameba. Ameba deletes blogs that involve transactions of money. The site scans blogs for information on bank accounts and links for external sites of affiliate advertising.

35 The uncanny uniformity of these titles raises the question of how global information and communication technologies such as iPhone and iPad might fuel similar fantasies about the power of technologies.

36 Tools that automate moneymaking include the trackback system, which is a way to notify a blog that someone linked to it. This system also helps identify groups of people who have the same interest. Another tool is RSS feeds that enable bloggers to syndicate data automatically. Using RSS means that one's browser constantly monitors the web and informs the blogger of relevant information. SEO (search engine optimization) and Google Alert are similar tools.

37 The bloggers she interviewed included: Hokama Hideyuki, an internet business consultant and former IT engineer, http://www.goal-seek.net; Yokosuka Ter-

uhisa, a consultant specializing in how to establish IT related businesses, http://yokosukateruhisa.com; a blogger named CafeMoca—a man in his early forties who writes a food blog, http://tabelog.com/rvwr/000164503/; another food blogger named Kitanose, http://blog.kitanose.jp; Aoyama Naomi (pen name: Murayama Lamune), who is also a consultant on how to use IT in launching a new business, http://lamune.cocolog-nifty.com/stylebis/2004/10/post_2 .html; Iraishi Takashi, who is also a technology consultant, https://futureship. sec.tsukuba.ac.jp/crew/0152.html; Nakano Teruhiko, also a consultant whose motto is that one has to become the only expert in something to be successful, http://1stmarketing.cocolog-nifty.com; and Ando Tetsuya who is an expert in fathering, http://fathering.jp/instructor/%E5%AE%89%E8%97%A4%E5%93%B2 %E4%B9%9F, all accessed May 15, 2018. There were two additional women bloggers who I could not find.

38 Amazon Japan, http://www.amazon.co.jp/product-reviews/4798108707/ref=cm _cr_pr_btm_link_2?ie=UTF8&pageNumber=2&showViewpoints=0&sortBy =byRankDescending, accessed May 15, 2018.

39 Similar to blog tutorials, seminars that offered bloggers help to improve their blogging skills mushroomed in the late 2000s. The cost of such seminars ranged from $50 to $500.

40 James Ferguson argues that development projects tend to operate as antipolitics machines. In his study of a development project in Lesotho, Ferguson found that the project he analyzed depoliticized the question of poverty by reducing it to a technical problem that can be addressed via technical solutions. Development projects, Ferguson concludes, reinforce and expand bureaucratic state power rather than solve the problem of poverty (1994).

41 Ameba has a separate category for a blogger named Ichikawa Ebizo, who is a kabuki actor and "trouble maker." He writes about his daily life and family. He is too popular to be counted in the blog ranking, so he received the title of MVP, which means The Most Popular Blog of all time. See http://ameblo.jp/ebizo -ichikawa/, accessed May 15, 2018.

42 See Ameba, http://ameblo.jp/momo-minbe/entry-11508604743.html, accessed May 15, 2018.

43 The other women on the top-five list include Hokuto Akira (second place), who was a professional wrestler and became very popular through her blog about her family. The fourth is Ohbuchi Aiko, a celebrity lawyer who blogs about her children and television appearances. The fifth is Watanabe Minayo, who was a celebrity in the 1980s. She reemerged as a blogger who writes about her family, children, cooking, and fashion. See (1) http://ameblo.jp/momo-minbe/, (2) http:// ameblo.jp/hokuto-akira/, (3) http://ameblo.jp/saeko-doll/, (4) http://ameblo.jp /ohbuchi-aiko/, and (5) http://ameblo.jp/minayo-watanabe/, all accessed May 15, 2018. Ameba hosts blogs of celebrities who pursue stealth marketing. Examples include Fujiwara Norika and Takimoto Miori. Fujiwara Norika's Ameblo blog includes a diary, but the bulk of the blog's content is made up of Fujiwara's commercial promotion of her media appearances and fashion goods she endorses.

Miori is an actress whose Ameba blog is about television shows and movies in which she appears and which she recommends. She also promotes fashion goods. Ameba does not simply sponsor celebrity blogs. It also monitors their blogs for inappropriate comments that are not acceptable for readers under twenty. Celebrity bloggers such as the ones I have just described provide models of successful entrepreneurship to other bloggers. While early blog tutorials published in the mid-2000s saw the secret of a successful blog in appealing content and investment in communication with blog readers, the blogosphere had become saturated by the late 2000s, and the rules of establishing an online presence had become much more difficult. See also http://fulogabc.hatenablog.com/entry/2016/02/03/180000, accessed May 15, 2018.

44 I have followed the career of Suzuki Junko since 2010.

45 See Suzuki Junko's Ameba Blog, https://ameblo.jp/bluejunebird/page-468.html, accessed October 10, 2018.

46 See Suzuki Junko's Ameba Blog, https://ameblo.jp/bluejunebird/page-461.html, accessed October 10, 2018.

47 Suzuki launched her own website in 2010. See http://www.kawaiilabotokyo.com, accessed May 15, 2018.

48 See Suzuki Junko's Google+ Account. https://plus.google.com/+JunkoSuzuki/posts, accessed May 15, 2018.

49 See Suzuki Junko's Bloglovin' Account, https://www.bloglovin.com/blogs/kawaiilabo-2710283, accessed May 19, 2016.

50 See Suzuki Junko's Facebook Account https://www.facebook.com/kawaii.labo, accessed May 19, 2016.

51 See Suzuki Junko's Instagram account, https://www.instagram.com/junkosuzuki/?hl=en, accessed September 28, 2018.

52 Duffy and Hund borrowed this idea from Ashley Mears (2011).

53 See Suzuki Junko's Instagram account, https://www.instagram.com/junkosuzuki/?hl=en, accessed September 28, 2018.

54 See YouTube, https://www.youtube.com/watch?v=HG2J1PVjJdo, accessed October 12, 2018.

55 This site is used similar to Niconico Dōga in Japan, a video-sharing site that features videos that include comments overlaid onto the videos and synched to specific playback times.

56 See Tominaga Ayano's Facebook and YouTube accounts, https://www.facebook.com/ayanotdo2; http://www.facebook.com/AyanoTDO2; https://www.youtube.com/user/ayanotdo; and Tominaga Ayano's Twitter account, https://twitter.com/AyanoTDO, all accessed May 15, 2018.

57 The channel was launched in 2010. See UST Today, http://usttoday.jp/, accessed May 15, 2018.

58 According to the website of UST Today, the channel has 3,372 subscribers. The channel's introduction says "Monday 9pm [getsu ku] of the live streaming world" (Getsuku is Fuji TV's famous trendy drama slot). The viewers of the channel are regular users of social media who are interested in technologies. Viewers can

also be on the show, either invited to the studio or Skyped in. The equipment the team is using—multiple cameras and high-quality lapel microphones—is increasingly professional, and the news is recorded in a rental studio. See UST Today, http://www.ustream.tv/channel/usttoday, accessed May 15, 2018.

59 See Tominaga Ayano's Instagram account, https://www.instagram.com/ayanotdo /?hl=en, accessed May 15, 2018.

Chapter 4: Work without Sweating

1   Monex's CEO, Matsumoto Oki, posted the following message on the English-language site of the company: "Money generates value only when it is actually used, as with other public goods. The philosophy of Monex is universal—we wish to offer accessible financial services, in the same way as essential services like electricity and gas supply. To this end, we must create an improved capital market and provide even better 'money' services. It also means we need to fight old frameworks and systems by remaining faithful to our venture spirit." See http://www.monexgroup.jp/en/group.html, accessed May 16, 2018.

2   David Harvey writes, "The dismantling of the regulatory frameworks and controls that sought to curb, however inadequately, the penchant for predatory practices of accumulation has unleashed the *après moi, le déluge* logic of unbridled accumulation and financial speculation that has now turned into a veritable flood" (2011, 107).

3   Yamamoto observes that women leave their employment when they have their first child and return to the labor market as nonregular employees when their children grow up.

4   Akiko Takeyama notes that the Japanese term *puro* comes from the English word "pro" (i.e., professional), but the term is used differently in Japanese than it is used in English (2016). Takeyama writes, "The Japanese use of the word is more discursive and inclusive. Particularly, a *puro* has become, in recent years, one who willingly strives to continuously improve and pursue perfection" (2016, 93). For instance, Takeyama notes that the NHK documentary series entitled *The Professional*, which was launched in 2009, defines professionals as individuals who excel in a wide variety of fields, including entertainment, fishing, farming, retail, and even janitorial work (2016). In contrast, I am discussing the amateur/ professional dichotomy in this chapter not in the context of "puro" but in the English context of "professional." I do this because the professional/amateur binarism played out differently in the context of finance than in the context of blogging, for instance. In the context of finance, "professional" meant being employed in the financial sector as a waged employee.

5   David Pilling, "Japan's Fearless Women Speculators," February 20, 2009, *Financial Times,* http://www.ft.com/cms/s/0/6c1a6eb2-fc8b-11dd-aed8−000077b07658 .html, accessed May 16, 2018.

6   The heroine in Yamamoto Yuka's children's book is a reminder of how children

started learning saving habits by using their postal savings piggy banks that their parents received as a gift when they opened their own postal savings accounts.

7 Although credit cards were introduced in Japan in the late 1990s, Japanese credit card owners tend to pay their credit card bills in full every month (Garon 2006).

8 See Linda Yueh, "Japan's Savings Rate Turns Negative for First Time," 26 December 2014, *BBC News*, http://www.bbc.com/news/business-30603313, accessed May 16, 2018. In 2015, about 40 percent of unmarried adults and 30 percent of families in Japan were unable to save any money. In the mid-1990s, these percentages were 30 and 20, respectively. The article concludes that in 2014, the national household savings rate dropped to minus 1.3 percent. See Jonathan Soble, "Japan's Recovery Is Complicated by a Decline in Household Savings," March 19, 2015, *The New York Times*, http://www.nytimes.com/2015/03/20/business/international/japans -recovery-is-complicated-by-a-decline-in-household-savings.html, accessed May 16, 2018.

9 At the beginning of 2016, Japan's three largest banks, the Bank of Tokyo-Mitsubishi UFJ (BTMU), Mizuho Bank, and Sumitomo Mitsui Banking Corporation (SMBC), reduced their interest rates for fixed-term deposit accounts. BTMU, for instance, offers an interest rate of 0.025 percent for fixed-term (one month to ten years) deposits under JPY3 million ($27,384). See *The Mainichi English Language Online News Portal*, http://mainichi.jp/english/articles/20160206 /p2a/00m/0na/009000c, accessed May 16, 2018.

10 In 2013, the Tokyo Stock Exchange merged with the Osaka Securities Exchange to form the Japan Exchange Group (JPX). See http://www.jpx.co.jp/, accessed May 16, 2018. When Japan's economic bubble burst, the value and ranking of TSE started falling, but it is still the fourth-largest exchange based on market capitalization of listed shares.

11 Xiang Biao notes that Japan became one of the favored first destinations for Indian IT specialists after Japanese companies lifted the ban and allowed Japanese firms to hire engineers who did not earn their engineering qualifications in Japan (2006).

12 See Forex's Trading Platform, http://www.forex.com/forex-trading-platforms .html, accessed May 16, 2018.

13 However, Sassen argues that financialization also led to the consolidation of finances in particular cities. The reason for this, she argues, is the demand for resources (information) and talent that are concentrated in a network of financial centers (2006). The international interest in the women trader trend acknowledges Tokyo as one of the centers of global finance.

14 See Global Investor Group, http://www.fow.com/3502855/The-evolution-of -electronic-trading-and-regulatory-reform.html, accessed May 16, 2018.

15 Martin Fackler, "In Japan, Day-Trading Like It's 1990," *New York Times*, February 19, 2006, http://www.nytimes.com/2006/02/19/business/yourmoney/19day .html?ref=tokyostockexchange; Martin Fackler, "Japanese Housewives Sweat in Secret as Markets Reel," *New York Times*, September 16, 2007, https://www

.nytimes.com/2007/09/16/business/worldbusiness/16housewives.html, both accessed May 16, 2018.

16 Matsumoto had excellent credentials. He graduated from the Law School of Japan's top university, The University of Tokyo, and learned the ropes of trading in Japan at Salomon Brothers and Goldman Sachs. See Bloomberg, http://www.bloomberg.com/news/articles/2004–09–05/japan-logs-on-to-online-trading and http://www.bloomberg.com/news/articles/2013–06–05/japan-online-stock-trading-at-record-as-individuals-ride-swings, both accessed May 16, 2018.

17 GMO Kurikku Shōken, https://www.click-sec.com/, opened in October 2005. In the same year, the firm also launched FX Puraimu, https://www.fxprime.com/, both accessed May 16, 2018.

18 SBI Shōken, https://www.sbisec.co.jp/ETGate; Nomura Shōken, http://www.nomura.co.jp/retail/fx/; Himawari Shōken, http://sec.himawari-group.co.jp/; Gaitame Dotto Komu, http://www.gaitame.com/; Monex Shōken, http://www.monex.co.jp; Kawase Life, http://www.kawaselife.com/; Minna no FX, https://min-fx.jp/; Lion FX, http://hirose-fx.co.jp/; Yahoo Gurūpu FX, http://www.yjfx.jp/; Minna no Gaitame, https://fx.minkabu.jp/hikaku/cyber.html; Fōrando Onrain, which merged with FXCM Tenraku in 2011, http://www.fxcm.co.jp/; Central Tanshi FX, http://www.central-tanshifx.com/; Monex FX, http://www.monexfx.co.jp/; Ueda Harlow FX, http://www.uedaharlowfx.jp/; DMM FX, http://fx.dmm.com/fx/; Gaitame Online, http://www.gaitameonline.com/; Kanetsu FX Shōken, http://www.kanetsufx.co.jp/; FX Trading System's FX Broadnet, http://www.fxtsys.com/; Raifu Stā Shōken, http://www.live-sec.co.jp/; Kabu Dotto Komu, http://kabu.com/; Tenraku Shōken, https://www.rakuten-sec.co.jp/; Okasan Online Shōken, http://www.okasan-online.co.jp/; Matsui Shōken, http://www.matsui.co.jp/; Daiwa Shōken, http://www.daiwa.jp/; Tokai Tokyo Shōken, http://www.tokaitokyo.co.jp/; Musashi Securities, http://www.musashi-sec.co.jp/; Naito Shōken, http://www.naito-sec.co.jp/; Iwai Cosmo Shōken, http://www.iwaicosmo.co.jp/; Tachibana Shōken Netto Torēdo, http://t-stockhouse.jp/; HS Shōken, http://www.hs-sec.co.jp/; and Money Partners, http://www.moneypartners.co.jp/, all accessed May 16, 2018.

19 See IBM iX Blog: Insights on Business from Your Global Business Design Partner, https://www.ibm.com/blogs/insights-on-business/ibmix/oki-matsumoto/, accessed May 22, 2018.

20 See IBM iX Blog: Insights on Business from Your Global Business Design Partner, https://www.ibm.com/blogs/insights-on-business/ibmix/oki-matsumoto/, accessed May 22, 2018.

21 These included such sites as http://kakaku.com/fx/, http://www.sikyou.com/, http://kissfx.com/, and https://fx.minkabu.jp/hikaku/cyber.html, all accessed May 16, 2018.

22 These included http://foorex.com/ and http://zai.diamond.jp/fx, both accessed May 16, 2018.

23 Examples are http://www.lfx.jp/, which teaches beginners how to trade foreign currencies, and http://kabukiso.com/, both accessed May 16, 2018.

24 An example is Hitsujikai no FX Burogu. See http://kissfx.com/, accessed May 16, 2018.

25 Sassen writes that since 1980, the total stock of financial assets has increased three times faster than the aggregate gross domestic product of the twenty-three highly developed countries that formed the OECD (2006, 20). Correspondingly, Edward LiPuma and Benjamin Lee highlight the growing autonomy and authority of financial circulation. Circulation, they argue, is becoming the principal means of generating profit, absorbing the capital formerly directed toward production (2004).

26 In addition to circulation, which has become the new engine of the economy, another key feature of financialization is the development of abstract trading instruments. These two features also illustrate the decoupling of financial markets from the ordinary economy of production and consumption.

27 Krippner offers the example of the Ford Motor Company, which has in recent years generated its profits primarily from selling loans to purchase cars rather than from selling cars (2011).

28 This is not unlike what Greta Krippner calls portfolio income, referring to a tendency of nonfinancial firms to derive a growing part of their income from interest, dividends, and the like (2011).

29 Delineating a link between risk taking and masculinity, Caitlin Zaloom observes that aggressive risk taking is encouraged among Chicago pit traders. Traders use risk in their projects of self-creation, and greater risk brings more recognition (2006).

30 In Japan, there are professional financial analysts who are women. Examples are Otsuki Nana, who graduated from the University of Tokyo and earned an MBA from the London Business School. She is the executive director and chief analyst at Monex.

31 David Pilling, "An Unlikely Combo: Japanese Housewife and Superstar Forex Trader," *Wall Street Daily*, March 30, 2011, http://www.wallstreetdaily.com/2011 /03/30/retail-investors-in-japan/, accessed May 16, 2018.

32 Anne Allison observes that in Japan, mothers are held primarily responsible for the performance of their children in school (2000).

33 Yamamoto claims that she was able to work out a method that required her to spend only ten minutes a day on trading. This suggests that trading did not significantly figure into her home life. The anecdote she related to me (that I mentioned in the Introduction), however, contradicts this public statement. She told me that to ensure her good luck in trading, she always kept lemons around a cat figurine that is believed to bring good luck to its owner in Japan. This is similar to Caitlin Zaloom's description of the superstitious practices among Chicago pit traders, which include carrying talismans, appealing to the supernatural, avoiding parking in particular slots, or wearing lucky neckties. Zaloom notes that some traders even go as far as to refuse changing their socks or brushing their teeth when they are on a winning streak (2006).

34 Yamamoto Yuka, "Semete Hinto dake de Oshiete. Yamamoto Yuka san ga Jissenchū no 'Kabu ni Kanarazu Katsu Hōhō,'" *Da Capo*, July 20, 2005, 74–75.

35 See Livedoor News, http://news.livedoor.com/article/detail/4587744/?p=2, accessed May 16, 2018.

36 See Mayuhime's Personal Blog, http://mayuhime-fx.com/, accessed May 16, 2018.

37 See Yamane Akiko's website, http://www.yamaneakiko.com/, accessed May 16, 2018.

38 Financial speculation cannot be divorced from ideas of self-growth, self-fulfillment, and the good life. As such, I identify this form of labor as affective labor. Viviana Zelizer observes that we tend to treat economic and intimate relations as independent and even antagonistic realms of life; however, we constantly conflate economic and intimate relations (2007).

39 Interview with Mayuhime posted on http://mayuhime-fx.com/, accessed October 2, 2018.

40 Women trading online is not unique to Japan, and the representations of these women are often similar. Images show women in front of their laptops and surrounded by their children. See Madeline Thomas, "Online Investing and Women," *The Guardian*, June 19, 2010, http://www.theguardian.com/money/2010/jun/19/online-investing-women, accessed May 16, 2018.

41 The *New York Times* article mentions that Torii sponsors a support group for fellow traders, FX *Beauties Club*, which had forty members in 2007 (Fackler, "Japanese Housewives Sweat in Secret").

42 See Pure Edge: Torii Mayumi's personal website, http://www.pure-edge.org/, accessed May 16, 2018.

43 Nikkei CNBC Interview with Torii in 2014, YouTube, https://www.youtube.com/watch?v=oDbG2MVWPBE, accessed May 16, 2018.

44 The following site includes a list of charisma housewives whose blogs were turned into books. See Naver Internet Content Service Company, http://matome.naver.jp/odai/2134714600586297601, accessed May 16, 2018. The list suggests that celebrity status is the major factor in becoming a charisma housewife.

45 Yamamoto Yuka's FX-de Mōketai! See Amazon Japan, http://www.amazon.co.jp/%E5%B1%B1%E6%9C%AC%E6%9C%89%E8%8A%B1%E3%81%AEFX%E3%81%A7%E5%84%B2%E3%81%91%E3%81%9F%E3%81%84%EF%BC%81-%E5%B1%B1%E6%9C%AC-%E6%9C%89%E8%8A%B1/dp/4478620660/ref=sr_1_1?ie=UTF8&qid=1460594446&sr=8-1&keywords=%E5%B1%B1%E6%9C%AC%E6%9C%89%E8%8A%B1%E3%80%80FX%E3%81%A7%E5%84%B2%E3%81%91%E3%81%9F%E3%81%84, accessed May 16, 2018.

46 See Amazon Japan, http://www.amazon.co.jp/product-reviews/4478630941/ref=cm_cr_dp_see_all_btm?ie=UTF8&showViewpoints=1&sortBy=recent, accessed May 16, 2018.

47 See Amazon Japan, https://www.amazon.co.jp/%E3%80%8C%E6%A0%AA%E3%80%8D%E3%81%AE%E3%82%AA%E3%83%BC%E3%83%88%E3%83%A1%E3%83%BC%E3%82%B7%E3%83%A7%E3%83%B3%E3%83%88%E3%83%AC%E3%83%BC%E3%83%89%E3%81%A7%E5%84%B2%E3%81%91%E3%82%8B%E6%9C%AC-%E5%B1%B1%E6%9C%AC-%E6%9C%89%E8%8A%B1/dp/4478630941?ie=UTF8&*Version*=1&*entries*=0, accessed May 16, 2018. Twenty-four reviewers com-

mented on Yamamoto's book on automated trading (2004b). The reviews averaged a rating of 1.5/5. Out of the twenty-four reviewers, seventeen gave the book the lowest score of 1, two reviewers ranked the book as 2, one ranked it as 3, three ranked it as 4, and one reviewer gave it a score of 5. Most of Yamamoto's books received only a few reviews. Yamamoto's book entitled *Maitsuki 10man en wa Yume Janai: Kabu de 3000man en Mōketa Watashi no Hōhō* (It Is Not a Dream to Make $1,000 a Month: My Method of Making $300,000 from Online Trading) (2004a) received sixty-seven reviews, which is the highest number any of Yamamoto's books garnered. By comparison, a male trader, Hosono Masahiro, published a 2005 book entitled *Hosono Masahiro no Sekai Ichi Wakariyasui Kabu no Hon* (*Hosono Masahiro's The World's Easiest Stock Trading Tutorial*) that had 212 reviews.

48 Another reviewer states, "There is no point in reading this book. This author has written a lot of books, but she does not work in the financial sector and has no qualifications. Probably she made a little profit from trading in a market where even a monkey was able to make a profit. There are a lot of people around me who earned more money from online trading. There is no point in such amateur traders publishing books. It is outrageous to tell beginners to do margin trading of foreign currencies. That is an extremely risky genre of trading. She says that she only uses small amounts of money to trade. I wonder if it is not the case that she is only trading to be able to write trading tutorials. Regardless, I can certainly say that this is not a decent book." See Amazon Japan, http://www .amazon.co.jp/%E5%B1%B1%E6%9C%AC%E6%9C%89%E8%8A%B1%E3%81 %AEFX%E3%81%A7%E5%84%B2%E3%81%91%E3%81%9F%E3%81%84%EF%BC %81-%E5%B1%B1%E6%9C%AC-%E6%9C%89%E8%8A%B1/dp/4478620660 /ref=sr_1_1?ie=UTF8&qid=1460594446&sr=8-1&keywords=%E5%B1%B1%E6 %9C%AC%E6%9C%89%E8%8A%B1%E3%80%80FX%E3%81%A7%E5%84%B2%E3 %81%91%E3%81%9F%E3%81%84, accessed May 16, 2018.

49 See WorldCat: The Worlds' Largest Library Catalog, https://www.worldcat.org /search?qt=worldcat_org_all&q=%E5%B1%B1%E6%9C%AC%E6%9C%89%E8 %8A%B1, accessed May 16, 2018. In addition to trading manuals, Yamamoto also wrote a children's book (which I described at the beginning of this chapter), a couple of books about how to create one's own website, and a few self-help books about time management for housewives.

50 Similar to most other tutorials written by women, Wakabayashi's book, *I Love Stocks*, is premised on the idea that stock trading should be fun. She claims that a trader should not worry about what she does not know and what she has to learn. Rather, she should try her best and practice trading, which will definitely yield results (2004).

51 Women traders commonly shared how much money they earned from trading. Titles of trading manuals also routinely include figures that function as a mission statement and a call to action. Mayuhime, for instance, claims that the largest amount of money she made a month was JPY30 million ($27,384). Her first trading tutorial is entitled *Introduction to How to Make JPY10000 ($91) in an Hour per Day: Do Not Worry about the Recession! Earn a Steady Income from Scalping and*

Little Time Investment (2010). In an interview, Yamamoto claims that within a few years, she has transformed JPY1 million ($9,100) into JPY30 million ($274,000). In another interview, she claims that within six years, she made roughly half a million dollars. Yamamoto Yuka, "Semete Hinto dake de Oshiete. Yamamoto Yuka san ga Jissenchū no 'Kabu ni Kanarazu Katsu Hōhō,'" *Da Capo*, July 20, 2005, 74–75. Yamamoto Yuka, "6 nenkan de 5,000 man en. Kabu de Ie wo Tatemashita," *Da Capo*, December 20, 2006, 96–98. Torii Mayumi was introduced in the media—and her trading tutorials include this figure in their titles as well—as a trader who earned $150,000 in her first year of foreign-currency trading.

52 Securities firms drew upon Ikebe to attract senior citizens to online trading. Given that her path to online trading differed completely from the route taken by other women traders—because she had much more experience—the fact that securities firms paired her image with the premise that online trading was easy for retirees to learn teetered on the verge of irresponsibility.

53 Yamamoto, Torii, Mayuhime, and Wakabayashi no longer regularly update their websites. See Yamamoto Yuka's personal website, http://www.kabu-cha-yuka .com/, Yamamoto Yuka's Ameba blog, http://ameblo.jp/kabu-cha-yuka/, Yucasee Wealth Media Co., http://media.yucasee.jp/posts/index/171/4, Yamamoto Yuka's Facebook page, https://www.facebook.com/%E5%B1%B1%E6%9C%AC%E6%9C %89%E8%8A%B1-549589828502871/photos, and Wakabayashi Fumie's personal web page, http://www.fumie-w.com/, all accessed May 16, 2018.

54 Yamamoto Yuka, "5 Nen de 3000 Man Yen, Densetsu no Torēdā ni," *Fujin Kōron* July 7, 2006, 31–33.

55 Horie Takafumi, the CEO of Livedoor Co., was sentenced to 2.5 years in prison for falsifying financial statements and violating the Securities and Exchange Act. See *The Japan Times*, http://www.japantimes.co.jp/news/2007/03/17/national/horie -handed-2–12-years/#. U7rOvC9mD8A, accessed May 16, 2018.

56 See Jesook Song's brilliant analysis of the ways in which young women navigate the financialization of daily life in South Korea. Echoing Yamamoto's position, many of Song's interlocutors felt under pressure to invest their savings and take responsibility for their financial growth (2014).

57 See Personne's web page titled Kōenirai, https://www.kouenirai.com/profile/2441, accessed May 16, 2018.

58 In her book *I Love Stocks*, Wakabayashi says that after her father's business went bankrupt, it took her a while to get over the fact that she would not be able to earn a college degree. Her brother told her that in Japan, people were divided into three groups: the fortunate ones who landed jobs in large corporations, the less fortunate but still fortunate people who have jobs in mid-size and small firms, and people who do not belong to any firms. Wakabayashi's brother concluded by saying that just because one does not belong to any company, that does not mean that one is a failure. Whatever field one is in, she can do her best and rise to the top of that field. Wakabayashi worked different part-time jobs and kept reviewing

job ads looking for more lucrative job opportunities, but there were very few jobs available to someone who had only a high school degree (*gakureki no kabe wa yōsō ijōni takakatta*) (2004, 18–19).

59 See Wikipedia, https://ja.wikipedia.org/wiki/%E8%8B%A5%E6%9E%97%E5%8F %B2%E6%B1%9F, accessed May 16, 2018.

60 *Chiyahoya suru* means "pamper," "make a fuss of," and "spoil." I understood the expression as referring to the media lavishing too much, and sometimes unwanted, attention on women traders.

61 Ho also observes that employees see this work culture as justified. Individuals working on Wall Street consider performing in excessively insecure work environments to be a part of the game (2009).

62 See Kenny Mariasin, "In the Financial Sector, Women's Day Comes Only Once a Year," August 3, 2015, *Finance Magnates*, http://www.financemagnates.com /forex/analysis/financial-sector-womens-day-comes-year/, accessed May 16, 2018.

63 Fackler, "In Japan, Day-Trading Like It's 1990."

Chapter 5: Dreamwork

1 Some of the writers, like Nanase, disclosed that they actually used a computer to write their novels (Sasaki 2008).

2 *Kōseirōdōshō: Heisei 21-nen Jakunensha Koyo Jittai Chōsa Kekka no Gaikyo*, http://www.mhlw.go.jp/toukei/itiran/roudou/koyou/young/h21/jigyo.html, accessed May 16, 2018.

3 "Wakamonono Shitsugyōritsu 9%-dai," http://www.47news.jp/CN/201012 /CN2010120301000251.html, accessed July 25, 2012, now defunct.

4 The term *freeter* refers to young irregular workers.

5 *Kōseirōdōshō: Heisei 21-nen Jakunensha Koyo Jittai Chōsa Kekka no Gaikyo*, http://www.mhlw.go.jp/toukei/itiran/roudou/koyou/young/h21/jigyo.html, accessed May 16, 2018.

6 See Matsumura, Taro. 2006. "Mezasu wa Atarashii Karuchā wo Sasaeru Jenerēshon Mēdia maho no i-rando" (4), CNET Japan Blog, February 27, https:// japan.cnet.com/blog/matsumura/2006/02/27/entry__i4/, accessed April 22, 2019.

7 Terranova writes: "There is not simply an amorphous mass, but a fractal ecology of social niches and microniches. We are not living, that is, in a pure mass culture, but in a configuration of communication where a pure mass perception clashes and interacts with a fractured and microsegmented informational milieu" (2004, 144).

8 Interview with Kitano Hiroshi, Tokyo, June 21, 2010.

9 See Wikipedia, https://ja.wikipedia.org/wiki/%E3%82%B1%E3%83%BC%E3%82 %BF%E3%82%A4%E5%B0%8F%E8%AA%AC#.E3.82.B1.E3.83.BC.E3.82.BF.E3.82 .A4.E5.B0.8F.E8.AA.AC.E5.AE.B6, accessed May 16, 2018.

10 I synthesized this information from the profiles authors posted on cell phone

novel platforms and the gender-specific ways cell phone novelists used "I" in interviews when the author's profile did not include gender. In the Japanese language, women and men use different pronouns for first person singular.

11 Patrick Galbraith, "Screen Dreams: A Digital-Age Literary Form Has Become a Publishing Powerhouse," *Metropolis Magazine*, https://metropolisjapan.com /screen-dreams/, January 22, 2009, accessed October 6, 2017.

12 The ten cell phone novelists Sasaki interviewed included Mika, Mizushima Riko, Asuka, Nanase, Hasui Kūna, Sinka (the only male author in the volume), Miyu, Saori, Megumi, and Chaco. Four of these writers—Mika, Mizushima Riko, Saori, and Chaco—have become professional writers.

13 Sinka's characterization of the genre may not take into consideration the social complexities of cell phone usage. Cara Wallis uses the concept of "immobile mobility" to argue that having a cell phone in China's large cities might provide an illusion of mobility, but cell phones do not always function as devices of inclusion (2013). Young women who migrate to large cities from rural areas often feel culturally inappropriate and excluded from cosmopolitan modernity when, for instance, they use the wrong characters in text messages. Predictive writing does not make up for the limited education of these women. And even if owning cell phones allows young women to feel that they are modern and cosmopolitan, they cannot translate this sense of belonging into other forms of capital.

14 Cell phone novel portals also helped novelists improve their writing skills. The designers of Maho no i-rando, for instance, developed an application called IQ-mode, which is a composition aid integrated with a dictionary function.

15 See Norimitsu Ohnishi, "Thumbs Race as Japan's Best Sellers Go Cellular," *New York Times*, January 20, 2008, http://www.nytimes.com/2008/01/20/world /asia/20japan.html?_r=0, accessed May 16, 2018.

16 When discussing authenticity in these novels, Japanese critics use the word *riaru* (derived from the English word *real*). In Ishihara's view, what lends a sense of authenticity to cell phone novels is not that the described events actually occurred but that the suffering is real in the writers' imagination (2008; see also Sugiura 2008). Although not all cell phone novels draw on personal or real experiences of pain and trauma, *riaru* remains central to the marketing of these novels. Publishers promote cell phone novels as texts that do not go through the conventional review and editorial process. Kitano Hiroshi, an editor at Take Shobō, told me that this statement was not entirely true, but he was quick to admit that some cell phone novels were edited more invasively than others. He explained that novels had to be edited to attain maximum dramatic impact and to be checked for typos and grammatical errors. Interview with Kitano, Tokyo, June 21, 2010.

17 Interview with Chaco, September 20, 2010.

18 Interview with Mika, October 8, 2010. (In 2005, when Mika published *Love Sky*, she was twenty-one years old.)

19 Due to the spectacular growth rates in the early postwar years, a class structure had evolved within which over 90 percent of the population identified as middle class. Ezra Vogel described this social configuration as a "mass middle-class

200

society" (*chūkan taishū shakai*) (1965). William Kelly, however, noted that mass middle-class society was more of an aspirational ideal than a reality; only one third of the population had access to lifetime employment, which secured one's position in the middle class (1986).

20 Hani Yoko, "Cellphone Bards Hit Bestseller Lists," *The Japan Times*, September 23, 2007, http://search.japantimes.co.jp/cgi-bin/fl20070923x4.html, accessed May 16, 2018.

21 Patrick Galbraith, "Screen Dreams: A Digital-Age Literary Form Has Become a Publishing Powerhouse," *Metropolis Magazine*, January 22, 2009, http://metropolis.co.jp/features/feature/screen-dreams-2/, accessed October 6, 2017.

22 Patrick Galbraith, "Screen Dreams."

23 See Yuriko Nagano, "For Japan's Cellphone Novelists, Proof of Success Is in the Print," February 9, 2010, *Los Angeles Times*, http://articles.latimes.com/2010/feb /09/world/la-fg-japan-phone-novel9–2010feb09, accessed October 14, 2018.

24 Matsumura, "Mezasu wa Atarashii Karuchā." The theme of dreams continues to figure powerfully in the identity of Maho no i-rando. The site currently features a page called "Community of Dreams," based on the idea that one gets a step closer to realizing her dream by posting this dream on Maho no i-rando. This page encourages users to make dream-friends [*yume nakama*] by enabling them to connect with other users who have similar dreams. The page also generates statistics based on the themes of the dreams submitted to the site. The dreams that relate to work and occupation rank the highest among these dreams. Almost twice as many people articulate what their dream is in relation to work than in relation to romantic relationships, which is the second most popular dream. See "Dream Collection," http://ip.tosp.co.jp/p.asp?I=yumekore, accessed July 25, 2012, now defunct.

25 Indeed, this arrangement proved to be ingenious. The owners of Maho no i-rando continue developing applications to allow users to express themselves in more and more genres. In 2010, Maho no i-rando featured thirty genres, a wide range that included novels, photography books, and the satirical haiku [*senryū*].

26 No-ichigo, for example, encourages readers to evaluate novels. The function of "simple comment" [*kantan kansō*] allows readers to click on features—such as romantic, full of dreams, funny, educational, etc.—that characterize the novel. This data is used to improve search algorithms and hence to provide better search results.

27 In addition to a bulletin board where readers can communicate with each other, No-ichigo also offers an application called "comment notebook" (*kansō nōto*), which allows readers and authors to communicate. This application allows authors to respond to readers' comments, as well as to edit or delete these comments. Readers can also write reviews (*rebyū*) of novels. These reviews cannot be edited or revoked. As part of the review, readers can rate the novel on the scale of 1–5. The summary of these ratings appears along with the title of the novel.

28 Interview with Yusa Mari, Tokyo, September 28, 2010.

29 Kyounghwa Yonnie Kim notes that many readers use the "notice" function to be

immediately notified when a new chapter of a novel they are reading is posted (2012).

30 Matsumura, "Mezasu wa Atarashii Karuchā."

31 Matsushima Shigeru at Starts told me that not all novels that top the popularity rankings on cell phone novel platforms are published. He explained that many of the most highly ranked novels were "distasteful" stories of gang rape and other forms of excessive violence perpetrated on young women—stories whose publication would violate publishing standards. Interview with Matsushima, Tokyo, June 28, 2010.

32 The jury is composed of celebrities, acquisition editors, renowned writers, government officials, and other well-known media personalities.

33 "Keitai Shōsetsu Kontesuto Shōkin Sōgaku 1,000 Man Akai Ito no Tsugiwa?" *Oricon Career*, December 1, 2007, http://career.oricon.co.jp/news/50106/full/, accessed May 16, 2018.

34 Kyounghwa Yonnie Kim reports that the demographic group that predominantly reads and writes cell phone novels—young women in their late teens and early twenties—prefers to read these novels on cell phones. Kim finds that readers believed the cell phone "was the best platform in terms of the maximization of their enjoyment, and that other platforms would not allow them to savour the content to its full extent" (2012, 480). A college student reported to Kim that she read her favorite cell phone novel on her cell phone, personal computer, and in paperback, but only the experience of reading the novel on her cell phone moved her to tears. According to Kim's research, writers also report that not all cell phone models are appropriate for writing cell phone novels. Lastly, Kim observes that the portability of the cell phone does not significantly affect the reading of the novels. Many readers prefer not to read cell phone novels in public spaces but rather in intimate spaces and times, such as in bed before going to sleep (2012).

35 See Ohnishi, "Thumbs Race as Japan's Best Sellers Go Cellular."

36 Shōjo refers to young girls who are preoccupied with consumption-oriented and fun-loving lifestyles. In television dramas, shōjo stories refer to stories in which an "ugly duckling" heroine meets a handsome and capable hero; the heroine persists in pursuing the hero; and her perseverance earns her the hero's heart. In addition to television dramas, the shōjo genre was also extremely popular in graphic novels (manga) and in literature. Yoshimoto Banana's *Kitchen* is a typical shōjo novel, but I also include in the genre Kanehara Hitomi's *Snakes and Earrings*. Kanehara's novel is similar to graphic novels like the ones authored by Anno Moyoko or Okazaki Kyōko. They engage topics such as sex, homosexuality, prostitution, rape, and sadomasochism. In other words, it is not uncommon that the shōjo genre experiments with sexuality outside the realm of reproductive sexuality.

37 Cell phone novels are quintessential melodramas, which Peter Brooks defines as follows: "Melodrama starts from and expresses the anxiety brought by a frightening new world in which the traditional patterns of moral order no longer provide

the necessary glue. It plays out the force of that anxiety with the apparent triumph of villainy, and it dissipates it with the eventual victory of virtue. It demonstrates over and over that the signs of ethical forces can be discovered and can be made legible" (1995, 20). Brooks understands the melodramatic imagination as a response to the loss of the Sacred in the aftermath of the Enlightenment and the realization that resacralization can occur only in personal terms.

38 Edelman writes, "The Child, that is, marks the fetishistic fixation of heteronormativity: an erotically charged investment in the rigid sameness of identity that is central to the compulsory narrative of reproductive futurism" (2004, 21). Heather Love calls Edelman's future without the Child a backward future—"a future apart from the reproductive imperative, optimism, and the promise of redemption" (2009, 147).

39 Mōri Yoshitaka proposes that young people resort to artistic and cultural forms of expression to voice their political views, for they find conventional forms of party politics and political activism to be unappealing and inadequate (2005).

40 Interview with Mika, October 8, 2010.

41 Interview with Chaco, September 20, 2010.

42 See Starts Publishing, https://starts-pub.jp/business/novel, accessed May 16, 2018. See also 10th Japanese Cell Phone Novel Award, http://nkst.jp/pc/index.php, Maho no Airando, http://award.maho.jp/, accessed May 16, 2018.

43 As cell phone novel platforms and publishers commercialized the cell phone novel trend, the demographics of their writers and readers diversified. As the market expanded for cell phone novels, publishers divided the reading public among themselves and targeted different groups of readers with age-appropriate content. For instance, an editor told me that his company focused on preadolescent girls aged eight to twelve. He said that although his company refrained from publishing certain risqué novels, such as a story of a twelve-year-old single mother who was gang-raped by the mafia, they were still able to sell fairly turgid stories to elementary school students by wrapping the books in cute jacket covers that featured sweet young girls. He said that mothers *did* judge books by their cover and believed that their daughters were reading harmless Harlequin romance novels.

Epilogue: Digital Labor, Labor Precarity, and Basic Income

1 See Sam Gustin, "Unpaid Blogger Hits Slave Owner Huffington with $105 Million Class Action Lawsuit," *Wired*, April 12, 2011, https://www.wired.com/2011/04/tasini-sues-arianna/, accessed May 17, 2018. See also Fuchs (2014, 272).

2 See Jonathan Stempel, "Unpaid bloggers' lawsuit versus Huffington Post tossed," *Reuters*, March 30, 2012, http://www.reuters.com/article/us-aol-huffingtonpost-bloggers-idUSBRE82T17L20120330, accessed June 20, 2017.

3 See Associated Press, "Thai Police Raid 'Click Farm,' Find 347,200 SIM Cards," *Business Insider*, June 13, 2017, http://www.businessinsider.com/ap-thai-police

-raid-click-farm-find-347200-sim-cards-2017–6, and Associated Press, "Thai Police Raid WeChat 'Click farm,' Find 347,200 SIM Cards, Arrest Three Chinese Men," *South China Morning Post*, June 13, 2017, http://www.scmp.com/news/asia /southeast-asia/article/2098167/thai-police-raid-wechat-click-farm-find-347200 -sim-cards, both accessed May 17, 2018. Click farms are employed to ramp up popularity on social media. According to an article published in 2014, one million followers cost $600 on Facebook. Click farms are also able to inflate the valuation of social media platforms. See Tyler Durden, "It's A Click Farm World: 1 Million Followers Cost $600 and the State Department Buys 2 Million Facebook Likes," *ZeroHedge*, January 6, 2014, http://www.zerohedge.com/news/2014-01-06 /its-click-farm-world-1-million-followers-cost-600-and-state-department-buys -2-millio, and JP Buntinx, "Top 4 Large-scale Click Farm Projects around the World," *The Merkle*, June 15, 2017, https://themerkle.com/top-4-large-scale-click -farm-projects-around-the-world/, both accessed May 17, 2018.

4 See Wikipedia, https://en.wikipedia.org/wiki/Content_farm, accessed May 17, 2018.

5 Marx writes, "The only worker who is productive is one who produces surplus-value for the capitalist, or in other words contributes towards the self-valorization of capital" (Marx 1992, 644).

6 See Barnard College's web page, http://bcrw.barnard.edu/archive/workforce /Wages_for_Housework.pdf, accessed May 17, 2018.

7 Weeks adds that women's reproductive labor was not only confined to the reproduction of male labor power, but it was also extended to taking care of the "non-waged, underwaged, not-yet-waged, and no-longer waged" (Weeks 2011, 121).

8 McRobbie writes, "The women in the second—the so-called creative industries— enjoy full equality of access and unprecedented control over the scheduling of their lives at the same time as their gendered skills and aptitudes around networking, multitasking, and social finessing of a whole range of work-leisure overlaps have made them ideal workers for the most neoliberal forms of flexible accumulation" (2016, 30).

9 See Barnard College's web page, http://bcrw.barnard.edu/archive/workforce /Wages_for_Housework.pdf, accessed May 17, 2018.

10 See Wages for Facebook, http://wagesforfacebook.com, accessed May 17, 2018. Correspondingly, Hardt and Negri write the following: "The transformations of labor and labor-power have led to an era of biopolitical production, in which the production of subjectivity plays a significant role in the creation of economic value" (2017, 75).

11 See Wages for Facebook, http://wagesforfacebook.com, accessed May 17, 2018.

12 See WorkMarket, https://www.workmarket.com/about-us, accessed May 17, 2018.

13 Lilly Irani, who has written about the microwork platform, Amazon's MTurk, is also involved in designing, building, and maintaining Turkopticon, which offers a social support system for MTurk workers, and Dynamo, which allows workers to safely post and discuss ideas for actions (2015b).

14 In Japan, the developmental state, led by the MITI (Ministry of International

Trade and Industry), designed economic plans, coordinated the private sector via tax breaks and government loans, and protected the national economy from transnational capital. The developmental state directly intervened in the economy by designing and implementing industrial policies to secure long-term economic growth (Johnson 1982).

15 See Andreas Illmer, "Japanese Firm to Use Drone to Force Overtime Staff to Go Home," BBC News, December 8, 2017, https://www.bbc.com/news/world-asia -42275874 and Daniel Hurst, "First Step in Changing Japan's Workaholic Culture: Less Overtime, NBC News, January 8, 2018, https://www.nbcnews.com/news /world/first-step-changing-japan-s-workaholic-culture-less-overtime-n833051, both accessed November 10, 2018.

16 See "Stressed? Many Japanese Schools and Companies Are Encouraging People to Cry to Boost Mental Health," *The Japan Times*, October 13, 2018, https://www .japantimes.co.jp/news/2018/10/13/national/social-issues/crying-drawing -attention-japanese-schools-companies-mental-detox/#.XAwRLGRKjUo, accessed May 17, 2018.

17 Namba Tomoko, "Ninen no Kaigo de Kawatta Otto to Aiken no Sakura to Watashi no Kankei," *Blogos*, See http://blogos.com/article/111797/, accessed May 17, 2018.

18 See Mariko Sanchanta and Juro Osawa, "A Reluctant Icon Enters Private Life," *Wall Street Journal*, July 6, 2011, http://www.wsj.com/articles/SB100014240527023 04793504576429411182339874, accessed May 17, 2018.

References

Abegglen, James. 1958. *The Japanese Factory*. Glencoe, IL: Free Press.

Allison, Anne. 2013. *Precarious Japan*. Durham, NC: Duke University Press.

Allison, Anne. 2012. "Ordinary Refugees: Social Precarity and Soul in 21st Century Japan." *Theory, Culture, Society* 26 (2–3): 89–111.

Allison, Anne. 2000. *Permitted and Prohibited Desires: Mothers, Comics, and Censorship in Japan*. Berkeley: University of California Press.

Althusser, Louis. 2001. *Lenin and Philosophy and Other Essays*. New York: Monthly Review Press.

Andrejevic, Mark. 2013. "Estranged Free Labor." In *Digital Labor: The Internet as Playground and Factory*, edited by Trebor Scholz, 149–64. New York: Routledge.

Andrejevic, Mark. 2012. "Exploitation in the Data Mine." In *Internet and Surveillance: The Challenges of Web 2.0 and Social Media*, edited by Christian Fuchs, Kees Boersma, Anders Albrechtslund, and Marisol Sandoval, 71–88. New York: Routledge.

Aoki, Emi. 2005. *Daredemo Kantan! Tetori, Ashitori "Jibunryū" Burogu Nyūmon Konotōri Yareba Suguni Dekiru*. Tokyo: Gijutsu Hyōronsha.

Araki Nobuyoshi. 1992. *A Photomaniac's Journey*. Tokyo: Switch Shōseki Shuppanbu.

Araki Nobuyoshi. 1991. *Senchimentaruna Tabi/Fuyu no Tabi*. Tokyo: Shinchōsha.

Araki Nobuyoshi. 1990. *The First Years of Heisei*. Tokyo: IPC.

Araki Nobuyoshi. 1980. *Pseudo Diary*. Tokyo: Byakuya Shobō.

Aronowitz, Stanley, and William DiFazio. 1994. *The Jobless Future: Sci-Tech and the Dogma of Work*. Minneapolis: University of Minnesota Press.

Arvidsson, Adam. 2008. "The Ethical Economy of Customer Coproduction." *Journal of Macromarketing* 28 (4): 326–38.

Arvidsson, Adam. 2005. "Brands." *Journal of Consumer Culture* 5 (2): 235–58.

Arvidsson, Adam, and Elanor Colleoni. 2012. "Value in Informational Capitalism and on the Internet." *The Information Society* 28 (3): 135–50.

Aytes, Ayhan. 2012. "Return of the Crowds: Mechanical Turk and Neoliberal States of Exception." In *Digital Labor: The Internet as Playground and Factory*, edited by Trebor Scholz, 79–97. New York: Routledge.

Ayura. 2009. *Zettai Dekimasu! Muryō de Hajimeru Chōkantan Burogu*. Tokyo: Gijutsuhyōronsha.

BeaHime. 2006. *Teddy Bear*. Tokyo: Goma Books.

Becker, Gary. 1964. *Human Capital: A Theoretical and Empirical Analysis, with Special Reference to Education*. Chicago: University of Chicago Press.

Berlant, Lauren. 2011. *Cruel Optimism*. Durham, NC: Duke University Press.

Biao, Xiang. 2006. *Global Body Shopping: An Indian Labor System in the Information Technology Industry*. Princeton, NJ: Princeton University Press.

Biddulph, Ryan, and Matthew Capala. 2015. *Solopreneur Ronin: Break the Chains, Earn Your Freedom, and Engineer a Happy Life Blogging from Anywhere*. Scotts Valley, CA: CreateSpace.

Boellstorff, Thomas. 2008. *Coming of Age in Second Life: An Anthropologist Explores the Virtually Human*. Princeton, NJ: Princeton University Press.

Bohr, Marco. 2015. "Go Inside the Quirky World of a Tumblr Photo Star." *Time*, January 4. Accessed October 2, 2018. http://time.com/3628697/ go-inside-the-quirky-world-of-a-tumblr-photo-star/.

Boltanski, Luc, and Eve Chiapello. 2007. *The New Spirit of Capitalism*. Translated by Gregory Elliott. New York: Verso.

Boris, Eileen, and Rhacel Salazar Parreñas. 2010. "Introduction." In *Intimate Labors: Cultures, Technologies, and the Politics of Care*, edited by Eileen Boris and Rhacel Salazar Parreñas, 1–12. Palo Alto, CA: Stanford University Press.

boyd, danah. 2014. *It's Complicated: The Social Lives of Networked Teens*. New Haven, CT: Yale University Press.

Braidotti, Rosi. 2013. *The Posthuman*. New York: Polity.

Brinton, Mary C. 2010. *Lost in Transition: Youth, Work, and Instability in Postindustrial Japan*. Cambridge: Cambridge University Press.

Brinton, Mary C. 1993. *Women and the Economic Miracle: Gender and Work in Postwar Japan*. Berkeley: University of California Press.

Brooks, Peter. 1995. *The Melodramatic Imagination: Balzac, Henry James, Melodrama, and the Mode of Excess*. New Haven, CT: Yale University Press.

Brown, Wendy. 2015. *Undoing the Demos: Neoliberalism's Stealth Revolution*. New York: Zone Books.

Butler, Judith. 2015. *Notes toward a Performative Theory of Assembly*. Cambridge, MA: Harvard University Press.

Butler, Judith. 2004. *Precarious Life: The Powers of Mourning and Violence*. New York: Verso.

Butler, Judith. 1993. *Bodies That Matter: On the Discursive Limits of Sex*. London: Routledge.

Butler, Judith. 1990. *Gender Trouble: Feminism and the Subversion of Identity*. London: Routledge.

Caraway, Brett. 2011. "Audience Labor in the New Media Environment: A Marxian Revisiting of the Audience Commodity." *Media, Culture, and Society* 33 (5): 693–708.

Castel, Robert. 1996. "Work and Usefulness to the World." *International Labour Review* 135 (6): 615–22.

Castells, Manuel. 2001. *The Internet Galaxy: Reflections on the Internet, Business, and Society*. Oxford: Oxford University Press.

Chaco. 2005. *Tenshi ga Kureta Mono*. Tokyo: Starts Shuppan.

Chin, Bertha. 2014. "Sherlockology and Galactica.tv: Fan Sites as Gifts or Exploited

Labor?" *Transformative Works and Cultures*, 15. Accessed May 20, 2018. http://dx.doi.org/10.3983/twc.2014.0513.

Chun, Wendy Hui Kyong. 2013. *Programmed Visions: Software and Memory*. Cambridge, MA: MIT Press.

Chun, Wendy Hui Kyong. 2008. *Control and Freedom: Power and Paranoia in the Age of Fiber Optics*. Cambridge, MA: MIT Press.

Clough, Patricia. 2012. "The Digital, Labor, and Measure beyond Biopolitics," in *Digital Labor: The Internet as Playground and Factory*, edited by Trebor Scholz, 112–26. London: Routledge.

Cole, Robert E. 1972. "Permanent Employment in Japan: Facts and Fantasies." *Industrial and Labor Relations Review* 26 (1): 615–30.

Dalla Costa, Mariarosa. 2015. *Family, Welfare, and the State*. New York: Common Notions.

Dalla Costa, Mariarosa, and Giovanna Dalla Costa. 1999. *Women, Development, and Labor of Reproduction: Struggles and Movements*. Lawrence, NJ: Africa World Press.

Dalla Costa, Mariarosa, and Selma James. 1975. *The Power of Women and the Subversion of the Community*. Bishopston, Bristol, UK: Falling Wall Press Ltd.

Dean, Jodi. 2010. *Blog Theory: Feedback and Capture in the Circuits of Drive*. Oxford: Polity Press.

DeLanda, Manuel. 2006. *A New Philosophy of Society: Assemblage Theory and Social Complexity*. London: Continuum.

Deleuze, Gilles. 1995. *Cinema II: The Time-Image*. Minneapolis: University of Minnesota Press.

Deleuze, Gilles, and Félix Guattari. 1987. A *Thousand Plateaus: Capitalism and Schizophrenia*. Translated by Brian Massumi. Minneapolis: University of Minnesota Press.

Donzelot, Jacques. 1991. "Pleasure in Work." In *The Foucault Effect: Studies in Governmentality*, edited by Graham Burchell, Colin Gordon, and Peter Miller, 251–80. Chicago: University of Chicago Press.

Driscoll, Mark. 2007. "Debt and Denunciation in Post-Bubble Japan." *Cultural Critique* 65: 164–87.

Duffy, Brooke Erin, and Emily Hund. 2015. "'Having It All' on Social Media: Entrepreneurial Femininity and Self-Branding among Fashion Bloggers." *Social Media and Society* 1 (2): 1–11.

Dyer-Witheford, Nick. 2015. *Cyber-Proletariat: Global Labour in the Digital Vortex*. Toronto: Pluto Press.

Dyer-Witheford, Nick. 2005. "Cyber-Negri: General Intellect and Immaterial Labor." In *Resistance in Practice: The Philosophy of Antonio Negri*, edited by T. S. Murphy and A. K. Mustapha, 136–62. London: Pluto Press.

Dyer-Witheford, Nick. 1999. *Cyber-Marx: Cycles and Circuits of Struggle in High-Technology Capitalism*. Urbana-Champaign: University of Illinois Press.

Dyer-Witheford, Nick, and Greg de Peuter. 2009. *Games of Empire: Global Capitalism and Videogames*. Minneapolis: University of Minnesota Press.

Edelman, Lee. 2004. *No Future: Queer Theory and the Death Drive*. Durham, NC: Duke University Press.

Elyachar, Julia. 2010. "Phatic Labor, Infrastructure, and the Question of Empowerment in Cairo." *American Ethnologist* 37: 452–64.

Exley, Charles. 2013. "Dress-Up: Self-Fashioning and Performance in the Work of Yasumasa Morimura," *Yasumasa Morimura: Theater of the Self*. Pittsburgh: The Andy Warhol Museum.

Federici, Silvia. 2012. *Revolution at Point Zero: Housework, Reproduction, and Feminist Struggle*. Oakland, CA: PM Press.

Feher, Michel. 2009. "Self-Appreciation; or, The Aspirations of Human Capital." *Public Culture* 21 (1): 21–41.

Feigenbaum, Anna. 2007. "Remapping the Resonances of Riot Grrrl: Feminism, Postfeminism, and 'Processes of Punk.'" In *Interrogating Postfeminism*, edited by Lynn Spigel, 132–52. Durham, NC: Duke University Press.

Ferguson, James. 2015. *Give a Man a Fish: Reflections on the New Politics of Distribution*. Duham, NC: Duke University Press.

Ferguson, James. 1994. *The Anti-Politics Machine: "Development," Depoliticization, and Bureaucratic Power in Lesotho*. Cambridge: Cambridge University Press.

Field, Norma. 2009. "Commercial Appetite and Human Need: The Accidental and Fated Revival of Kobayashi Takiji's *Cannery Ship*." *Asia-Pacific Journal: Japan Focus* 7 (8): 1–11. Accessed May 20, 2018. http://apjjf.org/-Norma-Field/3058/article.pdf.

Fisher, Eran. 2010. *Media and New Capitalism in the Digital Age: The Spirit of Networks*. London: Palgrave Macmillan.

Fortunati, Leopoldina. 2007. "Immaterial Labor and Its Machinization." *ephemera* 7 (1): 139–57.

Fortunati, Leopoldina. 1995. *The Arcane of Reproduction*. New York: Autonomedia.

Foucault, Michel. 2010. *The Birth of Bio-politics: Lectures at the Collège de France, 1978–1979*. London: Picador.

Frosh, Paul. 2015. "The Gestural Image: The Selfie, Photography Theory, and Kinesthetic Sociability." *International Journal of Communication* 9: 1607–28.

Fuchs, Christian. 2014. *Digital Labor and Karl Marx*. New York: Routledge.

Fuchs, Christian. 2010. "Labor in Informational Capitalism and on the Internet." *The Information Society* 26 (3): 179–96.

Fuchs, Christian, and Eran Fisher. 2015. "Introduction: Value and Labour in the Digital Age." In *Reconsidering Value and Labour in the Digital Age*, edited by Eran Fisher and Christian Fuchs, 3–25. London: Palgrave Macmillan.

Fujiwara-Fanselow, Kumiko. 1995. "College Women Today: Options and Dilemmas." In *Japanese Women: New Feminist Perspectives on the Past, Present, and Future*, edited by Kumiko Fujiwara-Fanselow and Atsuko Kameda, 125–54. New York: Feminist Press.

Galbraith, Patrick. 2013. "Maid Cafés: The Affect of Fictional Characters in Akihabara, Japan." *Asian Anthropology* 12 (2): 104–25.

Galbraith, Patrick. 2009. "Screen Dreams: A Digital-Age Literary Form Has Become a Publishing Powerhouse," *Metropolis Magazine.* Accessed October 6, 2017. https://metropolisjapan.com/screen-dreams/,

Garon, Sheldon. 2006. "The Transnational Promotion of Savings in Asia: 'Asian Values' or the 'Japanese Model.'" In *The Ambivalent Consumer: Questioning Consumption in East Asia and the West,* edited by Sheldon Garon and Patricia L. MacLachlan, 163–88. Ithaca, NY: Cornell University Press.

Genda, Yūji. 2005. *A Nagging Sense of Job Insecurity: The New Reality Facing Japanese Youth.* Tokyo: International House of Japan.

Gill, Rosalind, and Andy Pratt. 2008. "In the Social Factory? Immaterial Labour, Precariousness, and Cultural Work." *Theory, Culture, and Society* 25 (7–8): 1–30.

Gillespie, Tarleton. 2014. "The Relevance of Algorithms." In *Media Technologies: Essays on Communication, Materiality, and Society,* edited by Tarleton Gillespie, Pablo Boczkowski, and Kirsten Foot, 167–93. Cambridge, MA: MIT Press.

Goodyear, Dana. 2008. "I ♥ Novels: Young Women Develop a Genre for the Cellular Age." Accessed May 20, 2018. http://www.newyorker.com/magazine /2008/12/22/i-%E2%99%A5-novels.

Gorz, Andre. 2009. *Reclaiming Work: Beyond the Wage-Based Society.* New York: Polity.

Gregg, Melissa. 2011. *Work's Intimacy.* Cambridge: Polity.

Hall, Stuart. 1996. *Stuart Hall: Critical Dialogues in Cultural Studies,* edited by David Morley and Kuan-Hsing Chen. London: Routledge.

Hamano, Satoshi. 2008. *Aakitekucha no Seitaikei: Jōhō Kankyō wa Ikani Sekkei Saretekitaka.* Tokyo: NTT Shuppan.

Hardt, Michael. 2000. "Guaranteed Income, or the Separation of Labor from Income." *Hybrid* 5: 21–31.

Hardt, Michael. 1999. "Affective Labor." *boundary 2* 26 (2): 89–100.

Hardt, Michael, and Antonio Negri. 2017. *Assembly.* Oxford: Oxford University Press.

Hardt, Michael, and Antonio Negri. 2004. *Multitude.* New York: Penguin Press.

Hardt, Michael, and Antonio Negri. 2000. *Empire.* Cambridge, MA: Harvard University Press.

Harvey, David. 2018. *Marx, Capital, and the Madness of Economic Reason.* New York: Oxford University Press.

Harvey, David. 2014. *Seventeen Contradictions and the End of Capitalism.* New York: Oxford University Press.

Harvey, David. 2011. "The Future of the Commons." *Radical History Review* 109 (winter): 101–7.

Harvey, David. 2005. *A Brief History of Neoliberalism.* Oxford: Oxford University Press.

Hayamizu, Kenro. 2008a. *Jibunsagashi ga Tomaranai.* Tokyo: SoftBank Shinsho.

Hayamizu, Kenro. 2008b. *Keitai Shōsetsuteki: Sai yankī-ka Jidai no Shōjotachi.* Tokyo: Hara Shōbo.

Hayashi, Fumio. 1986. "Why Is Japan's Saving Rate So Apparently High?" Accessed May 20, 2018. http://www.nber.org/chapters/c4247.

Hayashi, Natsuki. 2006. *Kyōi no Shūkyaku Teku! 90 Nichi de Oni no Yōni Mōkeru*

Burogu Jutsu: Kaseideru Burogā ga Zettai ni Kataranai Kyūkyoku no Hōhō. Tokyo: Chūkei Shuppan.

Hayles, Katherine. 1999. *How We Became Posthuman: Virtual Bodies in Cybernetics, Literature, and Informatics*. Chicago: University of Chicago Press.

Hesmondhalgh, David. 2010. "User-generated Content, Free Labour and the Cultural Industries." *ephemera* 10 (3–4): 267–84.

Hicks, Marie. 2018. *Programmed Inequality: How Britain Discarded Women Technologists and Lost Its Edge in Computing*. Cambridge, MA: MIT Press.

Higuchi, Yūichi. 2010. *Aipaddo Nomado Shigotojutsu*. Tokyo: Sanmākushuppan.

Higuchi, Yūichi. 2009. *Yomaseru Burogu: Kokoro wo Tsukamu Bunshōjutsu*. Tokyo: Besutoserāzu.

Hiromix. 2002. *Hiromix01*. Tokyo: Rockin'on.

Hiromix. 2001. *Hiromix-Paris 1997–1998*. Tokyo: Asahi Shuppansha.

Hiromix. 2000. *Hiromix Works*. Tokyo: Rockin'on.

Hiromix. 1998. *Hiromix*, edited by Patrick Remy. Göttingen, Germany: Steidl.

Hiromix. 1997a. *Hikari*. Tokyo: Rockin'on.

Hiromix. 1997b. *Japanese Beauty*. Tokyo: Magazine House.

Hiromix. 1996. *Girls Blue*. Tokyo: Rockin'on.

Ho, Karen. 2009. *Liquidated: An Ethnography of Wall Street*. Durham, NC: Duke University Press.

Hochschild, Arlie Russel. 1983. *The Managed Heart: Commercialization of Human Feeling*. Berkeley: University of California Press.

Honda, Tōru. 2008. *Naze Keitai Shōsetsu wa Ureru no Ka?* Tokyo: SoftBank Shinsho.

Horie, Takafumi. 2013. *Zero: Nani mo Nai Jibun ni Chīsana Ichi o Tashite Iku*. Tokyo: Daiyamondosha.

Horie, Takafumi. 2010a. *Jinseiron*. Tokyo: KK Ronguserāzu.

Horie, Takafumi. 2010b. *Kakusa no Kabe o Bukkowasu*. Tokyo: Takarajimasha.

Horie, Takafumi. 2010c. *Shūkan: Boku ga Kaetakatta Kinmirai*. Tokyo: Asahishinbunshuppan.

Horie, Takafumi. 2009a. *Kibōron: Isshun ni Mezamete Ikiru tameni*. Tokyo: Sanga.

Horie, Takafumi. 2009b. *Yume o Kanaeru Uchide no Kozuchi*. Tokyo: Seishisha.

Horie, Takafumi. 2005. *Mōkekata Nyūmon: 1000ku Kasegu Shikōhō*. Tokyo: PHP Kenkyūjo.

Horioka, Charles Yuji. 2006. "Are the Japanese Unique: An Analysis of Consumption and Saving Behavior in Japan." In *The Ambivalent Consumer: Questioning Consumption in East Asia and the West*, edited by Sheldon Geron and Patricia L. MacLachlan, 113–37. Ithaca, NY: Cornell University Press.

Hosono, Masahiro. 2005. *Hosono Masahiro no Sekai Ichi Wakariyasui Kabu no Hon*. Tokyo: Bungei Shunjū.

Howe, Jeff. 2008. *Crowdsourcing: Why the Power of the Crowd Is Driving the Future of Business*. New York: Three Rivers Press.

Huws, Ursula. 2014. *Labor in the Global Digital Economy*. New York: Monthly Review Press.

Huws, Ursula. 2003. *The Making of a Cybertariat: Virtual Work in the Real World*. New York: Monthly Review Press.

Iizawa, Kōtarō. 2012. *Fukayomi! Nihon Shashin no Chōmeisaku 100*. Tokyo: Pai Intānashonaru.

Iizawa, Kōtaro. 2010. *"Onna no Ko" Shashin no Jidai*. Tokyo: NTT Shuppan.

Iizawa, Kōtarō. 2005. *Japanīzu Fotogurafāzu: 14-nin no Shashinkatachi no "Ima."* Tokyo: Hakusuisha.

Iizawa, Kōtarō. 1996. *Shattā ando Rabu: Girls are Dancin' in Tokyo: Jūnin no Josei Shashinkatachi*. Tokyo: INFAS.

Ikebe, Yukiko. 2010. *Ano Yon'okuen Datsuzei Shufu ga Oshieru Efuekkusu Shōri no Shinzui*. Tokyo: Fusōsha.

Ikebe, Yukiko. 2009. *FX Futsū no Shufu demo Okuman Chōja ni Nareta Riyū: 10pun de Wakaru Mamotte Chakujitsu ni Fuyasu Hōhō*. Tokyo: Besutoserāzu.

Ikebe, Yukiko. 2008. *Ano 40okuen Datsuzei Shufu ga Oshieru FX no ōgi*. Tokyo: Fusōsha.

Inoue, Miyako. 2006. *Vicarious Language: Gender and Linguistic Modernity in Japan*. Berkeley: University of California Press.

Irani, Lilly. 2015a. "The Cultural Work of Microwork." *New Media and Society* 17 (5): 720–39.

Irani, Lilly. 2015b. "Difference and Dependence among Digital Workers: The Case of Amazon Mechanical Turk." *South Atlantic Quarterly* 114 (1): 225–34.

Ishida, Hiroshi. 1989. "Class Structure and Status Hierarchies in Contemporary Japan." *European Sociological Review* 5: 65–80.

Ishida, Hiroshi, and David H. Slater. 2010. *Social Class in Contemporary Japan: Structures, Sorting and Strategies*. New York: Routledge.

Ishihara, Chiaki. 2008. *Keitai Shōsetsu wa Bungaku Ka?* Tokyo: Chikuma Primer Shinsho.

Ito, Mizuko. 2005. "Introduction: Personal, Portable, Pedestrian." In *Personal, Portable, Pedestrian: Mobile Phones in Japanese Life*, edited by Mizuko Ito, Misa Matsuda and Daisuke Okabe, 1–16. Cambridge, MA: MIT Press.

Ito, Mizuko, Misa Matsuda, and Daisuke Okabe. 2005. *Personal, Portable, Pedestrian: Mobile Phones in Japanese Life*. Cambridge, MA: MIT Press.

Ivy, Marilyn. 2010. "The Art of Cute Little Things: Nara Yoshitomo's Parapolitics." *Mechademia* 5: 3–29.

Jarrett, Kylie. 2018. "Laundering Women's History: A Feminist Critique of the Social Factory." *First Monday* 23 (3–5), March. Accessed May 20, 2018. http://firstmonday.org/ojs/index.php/fm/article/view/8280/6647.

Jarrett, Kylie. 2017. *Feminism, Labour, and Digital Media: The Digital Housewife*. London: Routledge.

Jenkins, Henry, Sam Ford, and Joshua Green. 2013. *Spreadable Media: Creating Value and Meaning in a Networked Culture*. New York: New York University Press.

Johnson, Chalmers. 1999. "The Developmental State: Odyssey of a Concept." In *The

Developmental State, edited by M. Woo-Cumings, 32–60. Ithaca, NY: Cornell University Press.

Johnson, Chalmers. 1982. *MITI and the Japanese Miracle: The Growth of Industrial Policy, 1925–1975.* Palo Alto, CA: Stanford University Press.

Kalleberg, Arne. 2013. *Good Jobs, Bad Jobs: The Rise of Polarized and Precarious Employment Systems in the United States, 1970s to 2000s.* New York: Russel Sage Foundation.

Kambayashi, Takehiko. 2002. "Women Work Way Up in Japan; Entrepreneurial Spirit Helps Lift Ailing Economy." *Washington Times*, July 26, A17.

Kaneko, Yoshinori, ed. 1996. *Hiromix ga Suki, Studio Voice*, March.

Kanter, Rosabeth Moss. 1995. "Nice Work if You Can Get It: The Software Industry as a Model for Tomorrow's Jobs." *American Prospect* 6 (23): 52–58.

Kawauchi, Rinko. 2005. *Cui Cui.* Tokyo: Foil.

Kelly, William. 1986. "Romanticization and Nostalgia: Cultural Dynamics of New Middle-Class Japan." *American Ethnologist* 13 (4): 603–18.

Kelsky, Karen. 2001. *Women on the Verge: Japanese Women, Western Dreams.* Durham, NC: Duke University Press.

Kim, Kyounghwa Yonnie. 2012. "The Landscape of Keitai Shôsetsu: Mobile Phones as a Literary Medium among Japanese Youth." *Continuum* 26 (3): 475–85.

Kinsella, Sharon. 1995. "Cuties in Japan." In *Women, Media and Consumption in Japan*, edited by Brian Moeran and Lise Skov. Richmond, VA: Curzon Press.

Knorr Cetina, Karin, and Alex Preda. 2006. *The Sociology of Financial Markets.* New York: Oxford University Press.

Koga, Reiko. 2009. *Kawaii no Teikoku: Mōdo to Media to Onnanokotachi.* Tokyo: Seidosha.

Kondo, Dorinne. 1990. *Crafting Selves: Power, Gender, and Discourses of Identity in a Japanese Workplace.* Chicago: University of Chicago Press.

Kosugi, Reiko. 2008. *Escape from Work: Freelancing Youth and the Challenge to Corporate Japan.* Translated by Ross Mouer. Melbourne: Trans Pacific Press.

Krippner, Greta R. 2011. *Capitalizing on Crisis: The Political Origins of the Rise of Finance.* Cambridge, MA: Harvard University Press.

Kuehn, Kathleen, and Thomas F. Corrigan. 2013. "Hope Labor: The Role of Employment Prospects in Online Social Production." *The Political Economy of Communication* 1 (1): 9–25.

LaMarre, Thomas. 2009. *Anime Machine.* Minneapolis: University of Minnesota Press.

Lanier, Jaron. 2011. *You Are Not a Gadget: A Manifesto.* New York: Vintage Books.

Larkin, Brian. 2013. "The Politics and Poetics of Infrastructure." *Annual Review of Anthropology* 42: 327–43.

Latour, Bruno. 1996. *Aramis, or the Love of Technology.* Cambridge, MA: Harvard University Press.

Lazzarato, Maurizio. 1996. "Immaterial Labour." In *Radical Thought in Italy: A Potential Politics*, edited by Paolo Virno and Michael Hardt, 133–51. Minneapolis: University of Minnesota Press.

LiPuma, Edward, and Benjamin Lee. 2004. *Financial Derivatives and the Globalization of Risk*. Durham, NC: Duke University Press.

Lorey, Isabell. 2015. *State of Insecurity*. London: Verso.

Lotich, Bob. 2010. *How to Make Money Blogging: How I Replaced My Day Job with My Blog*. Lake Saint Louis, MO: Rendren Publishing.

Lotringer, Sylvere. 2004. "Foreword: We, the Multitude." In *Paolo Virno: A Grammar of the Multitude: For an Analysis of Contemporary Forms of Life*. Translated by Isabella Bertoletti, James Cascaito, and Andrea Casson, 7–12. Los Angeles: Semiotext(e).

Love, Heather. 2009. *Feeling Backward: Loss and the Politics of Queer History*. Cambridge, MA: Harvard University Press.

Lukacs, Gabriella. 2015a. "The Labor of Cute: Net Idols, Cute Culture, and the Digital Economy in Contemporary Japan." *Positions: Asia Critique* 23 (3): 487–513.

Lukacs, Gabriella. 2015b. "Labor Games: Youth, Work, and Politics in East Asia." *Positions: Asia Critique* 23 (3): 381–409.

Lukacs, Gabriella. 2015c. "Unraveling Visions: Women's Photography in Recessionary Japan." *boundary 2*, 42 (3): 171–84.

Lukacs, Gabriella. 2010a. *Scripted Affects, Branded Selves: Television, Subjectivity, and Capitalism in 1990s Japan*. Durham, NC: Duke University Press.

Lukacs, Gabriella. 2010b. "Iron Chef around the World: Japanese Food Television, Soft Power, and Cultural Globalization." *International Journal of Cultural Studies* 13 (4): 409–26.

MacKenzie, Adrian. 2006. *Cutting Code: Software and Sociality*. New York: Peter Lang.

MacLeod, Hugh. 2012. *Freedom Is Blogging in Your Underwear*. New York: Portfolio/Penguin.

Manovich, Lev. 2013. *Software Takes Command*. London: Bloomsbury Academic.

Marazzi, Christian. 2010. *The Violence of Financial Capitalism*. Los Angeles: Semiotext(e).

Martin, Lesley A. 2014. "Publishing the Body: Lesley A. Martin in Conversation with Miyako Ishiuchi and Yurie Nagashima." The Photobook Review. *Aperture* 6 (spring): 12–13.

Martin, Randy. 2002. *The Financialization of Daily Life*. Philadelphia: Temple University Press.

Marwick, Alice. 2013. *Status Update: Celebrity, Publicity, and Self-branding in Web 2.0*. New Haven, CT: Yale University Press.

Marx, Karl. 1993. *Grundrisse: Foundations of the Critique of Political Economy*. Translated by Martin Nicolaus. New York: Penguin Books.

Marx, Karl. 1992. *Capital, Volume I: A Critique of Political Economy*. New York: Penguin Books.

Mathias, Kraig. 2015. *Blogging to Freedom: 7 Steps to Creating Your Independence with Blogging*. Minneapolis: Mathias Media.

Matsuda, Misa. 2005. "Discourses of Keitai in Japan." In *Personal, Portable, Pedestrian: Mobile Phones in Japanese Life*, edited by Mizuko Ito, Daisuke Okabe, and Misa Matsuda, 19–39. Cambridge, MA: MIT Press.

Matsunaga, Hideaki. 2004. *Weblog Chōnyūmon!* Tokyo: Nihon Jitsugyō Shuppansha.

Mayuhime. 2010a. FX *Mama no Kosodate Shinagara Gesshū 100-man'en Maruhi Teku*. Tokyo: Fusōsha.

Mayuhime. 2010b. *Ichinichi Ichijikan de Ichiman'en Kasegu Efuekkusu Tōshi Nyūmon: Fukeiki demo Daijōbu Sukyarupingu de Tanjikan de Kotsukotsu Kasegu*. Tokyo: Kadokawa.

Mbembe, Achille. 2017. *Critique of Black Reason*. Durham, NC: Duke University Press.

McRobbie, Angela. 2016. *Be Creative: Making a Living in the New Culture Industries*. New York: Polity.

McRobbie, Angela. 2011. "Reflections on Feminism, Immaterial Labour, and the Post-Fordist Regime." *New Formations* 70 (winter): 60–76.

Mears, Ashley. 2011. *Pricing Beauty: The Making of a Fashion Model*. Berkeley: University of California Press.

Mika. 2006. *Koizora*. Tokyo: Starts Shuppan.

Mikitani, Hiroshi. 2018. *Business-Do: The Way to Successful Leadership*. Hoboken, NJ: Wiley.

Mills, C. Wright. 1951. *White Collar: The American Middle Classes*. Oxford: Oxford University Press.

Ministry of Finance Japan. 1999. *About the Financial System Reform, The Japanese Version of the Big Bang*. Accessed May 20, 2018. http://www.fsa.go.jp/p_mof /english/big-bang/ebb1.htm.

Miyazaki, Hirokazu. 2012. *Arbitraging Japan: Dreams of Capitalism at the End of Finance*. Berkeley: University of California Press.

Mizukawa, Jun. 2013. "The Crisis of Language in Contemporary Japan: Reading, Writing, and New Technology." PhD diss., Columbia University. Accessed May 29, 2018. http://academiccommons.columbia.edu/catalog/ac:188864.

Moeran, Brian, and Lise Skov. 1995. *Women, Media, and Consumption in Japan*. Honolulu: University of Hawaii Press.

Molony, Barbara. 1995. "Japan's 1986 Equal Employment Opportunity Law and the Changing Discourse on Gender." *Signs* 20 (2): 268–302.

Mone. 2007. *Eien no Negai*. Tokyo: Take Shobō.

Mōri, Yoshitaka. 2005. "Culture=Politics: The Emergence of New Cultural Forms of Protest in the Age of Freeter." *Inter-Asia Cultural Studies* 6 (1): 17–29.

Morini, Cristina. 2007. "The Feminization of Labour in Cognitive Capitalism." *Feminist Review* 87: 40–59.

Mosco, Vincent. 2004. *The Digital Sublime*. Cambridge, MA: MIT Press.

Muñoz, Jose Esteban. 1999. *Disidentifications: Queers of Color and the Performance of Politics*. Minneapolis: University of Minnesota Press.

Murai, Jun, Esaki Hiroshi, and Sunahara Hideki. 2008. *Broadband Internet Deployment in Japan*. Tokyo: Ohmsha Press.

Muramatsu, Takahide. 2001. *Netto Aidoru*. Tokyo: Hara Shobō.

Nagashima, Yurie. 2010. *Swiss*. Tokyo: Akaaka Publishing.

Nagashima, Yurie. 2004. *not six*. Tokyo: Switch.

Nagashima, Yurie. 2000. *Pastime Paradise?* Tokyo: Maora Shuppan.

Nagashima, Yurie. 1998. *Kazoku*. Tokyo: Kōrinsha Press.

Nagashima, Yurie. 1995a. *Nagashima Yurie Photo Book*. Tokyo: Fuga Shobō.

Nagashima, Yurie. 1995b. *Empty White Room*. Tokyo: Little More.

Nakamura, Lisa. n.d. "Workers without Bodies: Digital Labor, Race, and Gender." Accessed May 20, 2018. https: //www.youtube.com/watch?v=4-OkPRX2XVo.

Nakamura, Lisa. 2015. "The Unwanted Labour of Social Media: Women of Color Call Out Culture as Venture Community Management." *New Formations: A Journal of Culture, Theory, Politics*: 106–12.

Nakamura, Lisa. 2014. "'I Will Do Everything That Am Asked': Scambaiting, Digital Show-Space, and the Racial Violence of Social Media." *Journal of Visual Culture* 13 (3): 257–74.

Nakane, Chie. [1970] 1984. *Japanese Society*. Rutland, VT: Charles E. Tuttle Company.

Nana. 2009. *LoVe, LovE, LOve*. Tokyo: Take Shobō.

Nardi, Bonnie. 2010. *My Life as a Night Elf Priest: An Anthropological Account of World of Warcraft*. Ann Arbor: University of Michigan Press.

Neff, Gina. 2012. *Venture Labor: Work and the Burden of Risk in Innovative Industries*. Cambridge, MA: MIT Press.

Negri, Antonio. 1991. *Marx beyond Marx: Lessons on the Grundrisse*. London: Pluto Press.

Ngai, Sianne. 2015. *Our Aesthetic Categories: Zany, Cute, Interesting*. Cambridge, MA: Harvard University Press.

Ngai, Sianne. 2005. "The Cuteness of the Avant-Garde." *Critical Inquiry* 31 (4): 811–47.

Ninagawa, Mika. 2013. *Self-image*. Tokyo: Match and Company.

Ninagawa, Mika. 2012. *Oraora Onnaron*. Tokyo: Shōdensha.

Ninagawa, Mika. 2010. *Mika Ninagawa*. New York: Rizzoli.

Ninagawa, Mika. 2009. *Kanojo no Jinsei to Kanojo Jishin no Pōtoreito*. Tokyo: Kawade Shobō Shinsha.

Ninagawa, Mika. 2008a. *Ninagawa Mōsō Gekijo*. Tokyo: Shūeisha.

Ninagawa, Mika. 2008b. *Ninagawa Woman*. Tokyo: Kōdansha.

Ninagawa, Mika. 2004. *Over the Rainbow*. Tokyo: Kōdansha.

Ninagawa, Mika. 2003a. *Acid Bloom*. Edishon Toreviru/Nazraeli Press.

Ninagawa, Mika. 2003b. *Liquid Dreams*. Tokyo: EdishonToreviru.

Ninagawa, Mika. 2002a. *Like a Peach*. Tokyo: Kōdansha.

Ninagawa, Mika. 2002b. *A Piece of Heaven*. Tokyo: Edishon Toreviru.

Ninagawa, Mika. 2000. *Sugar and Spice*. Tokyo: Kawade Shobō Shinsha.

Noble, Safiya Umoja. 2018. *Algorithms of Oppression: How Search Engines Reinforce Racism*. New York: New York University Press.

Ogasawara, Yuko. 1998. *Office Ladies and Salaried Men: Power, Gender, and Work in Japanese Companies*. Berkeley: University of California Press.

Okazaki, Kyōko. 1992. *Happy House I–II*. Tokyo: Shufu to Seikatsusha.

Ōtsuka, Eiji. 2003. *Shōjotachi no Kawaii Tennō: Sabukaruchā Tennō Ron*. Tokyo: Kadokawa Shoten.

Parisi, Luciana. 2013. *Contagious Architecture: Computation, Aesthetics, and Space.* Cambridge, MA: MIT Press.

Parks, Lisa, and Nicole Starosielski. 2015. *Signal Traffic: Critical Studies of Media Infrastructures.* Champaign: University of Illinois Press.

Pasquale, Frank. 2015. *The Black Box Society: The Secret Algorithms That Control Money and Information.* Cambridge, MA: Harvard University Press.

Pham, Minh-Ha T. 2015. *Asians Wear Clothes on the Internet: Race, Gender, and the Work of Personal Style Blogging.* Durham, NC: Duke University Press.

Piketty, Thomas. 2014. *Capital in the Twenty-First Century.* Cambridge, MA: Belknap Press.

Rettberg, Jill Walker. 2013. *Blogging.* Cambridge: Polity.

Roberts, Glenda. 1994. *Staying on Line: Blue Collar Women in Contemporary Japan.* Honolulu: University of Hawaii Press.

Rohlen, Thomas P. 1974. *For Harmony and Strengths: Japanese White-Collar Organization in Anthropological Perspective.* Berkeley: University of California Press.

Roquet, Paul. 2016. *Ambient Media: Japanese Atmospheres of Self.* Minneapolis: University of Minnesota Press.

Ross, Andrew. 2012. "In Search of the Lost Paycheck." In *Digital Labor: The Internet as Playground and Factory*, edited by Trebor Scholz, 13–32. London: Routledge.

Rowse, Darren, and Chris Garrett. 2012. *ProBlogger: Secrets for Blogging Your Way to a Six-Figure Income.* Hoboken, NJ: Wiley.

Said, Edward. 1978. *Orientalism.* New York: Vintage Books.

Sakura Web Bunkakenkyūshitsu: Intaanetto no Rekishi (1984–1994). Accessed May 20, 2018. http://websitemap.sakura.ne.jp/history/junet.html.

Sano, Masahiro. 2007. *Otona ga Shiranai Keitai Saito no Sekai: PC towa Mattaku Chigau Mō Hitotsu no Netto Bunka.* Tokyo: Maikomi Shinsho.

Sas, Miryam. 2011. *Experimental Arts in Postwar Japan: Moments of Encounter, Engagement, and Imagined Return.* Cambridge, MA: Harvard University Press.

Sasaki, Toshinao. 2015. *Nijūisseiki no Jiyūron: Yasashī Riarizumu no Jidai e.* Tokyo: Enueichikeushuppan.

Sasaki, Toshinao. 2010a. *Denshi Shoseki no Shōgeki: Hon wa Ikani Hōkai Shi, Ikani Fukkatsu Uru ka.* Tokyo: Disukavau Toentiwan.

Sasaki, Toshinao. 2010b. *Netto ga Areba Rirekisho wa Iranai: Uebu Jidai no Serufu Burandingujutsu.* Tokyo: Takarajimasha.

Sasaki, Toshinao. [2009a] 2011. *Shigoto Surunoni Ofisu wa Iranai: Nomado Waakingu no Susume.* Tokyo: Kōbunsha.

Sasaki, Toshinao. 2009b. *Nikoniko Dōga ga Mirai wo Tsukuru: Dowango Monogatari.* Tokyo: Asukimediawaukusu.

Sasaki, Toshinao. 2008a. *Keitai Shōsetsuka: Akogare no Sakka 10-nin ga Hajimete Kataru "Jibun."* Tokyo: Shōgakkan.

Sasaki, Toshinao. 2008b. *Infokomonzu.* Tokyo: Kōdansha.

Sasaki, Toshinao. 2008c. *Burogu Rondan no Tanjō.* Tokyo: Bungei Shunjū.

Sasaki, Toshinao. 2007. *Sanjikan de Senmonka ni Naru Watakushi no Hōhō: Aitī Jaanarisuto no Chōjōhō Shūshū Seirijutsu.* Tokyo: PHP Fakutoriupaburisshingu.

Sasaki, Toshinao. 2006. *Netto vs. Riaru no Shōtotsu: Dare ga Uebu 2.0 o Seisuruka.* Tokyo: Bungei Shunjū.

Sasaki, Toshinao. 2005. *Raibudoa Shihonron.* Tokyo: Nihon Hyōronsha.

Sasaki, Toshinao. 2004. *Gūguru & Yafū de Shigoto ga 100bai Hayakunaru Hon.* Tokyo: Inpuresu Komyunikeushonzu.

Sassen, Saskia. 2006. "The Embeddedness of Electronic Markets: The Case of Global Capital Markets." In *The Sociology of Financial Markets*, edited by Karin Knorr Cetina and Alex Preda, 17–37. New York: Oxford University Press.

Scholz, Trebor. 2017. *Uberworked and Underpaid: How Workers Are Disrupting the Digital Economy.* New York: Polity.

Scholz, Trebor. 2016. "Think Outside the Boss: Cooperative Alternatives for the Post-Internet Age." In *Electronic Mediations: The Participatory Condition in the Digital Age*, edited by Jonathan Sterne, Gabriella Coleman, Christine Ross, Darin Barney, and Tamar Tembeck, 60–76. Minneapolis: University of Minnesota Press.

Schor, Juliet. 1993. *The Overworked American: The Unexpected Decline of Leisure.* New York: Basic Books.

Senft, Theresa. 2008. *Camgirls: Celebrity and Community in the Age of Social Networks.* New York: Peter Lang.

Senft, Theresa, and Nancy Baym. 2015. "What Does the Selfie Say? Investigating a Global Phenomenon." *International Journal of Communication* (9): 1588–606.

Shiokawa, Kanako. 1999. "Cute but Deadly: Women and Violence in Japanese Comics." In *Themes and Issues in Asian Cartooning: Cute, Cheap, Mad, and Sexy*, edited by John A. Lent, 93–125. Bowling Green, OH: Bowling Green State University Press.

Simondon, Gilbert. [1958] 2017. *On the Mode of Existence of Technical Objects.* Translated by Cecile Malaspina and John Rogove. Minneapolis: Univocal Publishing.

Simondon, Gilbert. 2012. "On Techno-Aesthetics." Translated by Arne de Boever. *Parrhesia* 4: 1–8.

Smythe, Dallas W. 1981. *Dependency Road: Communications, Capitalism, Consciousness, and Canada.* Norwood, NJ: Ablex Publishing.

Someya, Masatoshi. 2013. *Burogumeshi: Kosei wo Shunyu ni Kaeru Ikikata.* Tokyo: Impress Japan.

Song, Jesook. 2014. *Living on Your Own: Single Women, Rental Housing, and Post-Revolutionary Affect in Contemporary South Korea.* Albany: State University of New York Press.

Song, Jesook. 2007. "'Venture Companies,' 'Flexible Labor,' and the 'New Intellectual': The Neoliberal Construction of Underemployed Youth in South Korea." *Journal of Youth Studies* 10 (3): 331–51.

Standing, Guy. 2017. *Basic Income: A Guide for the Open-Minded.* New Haven, CT: Yale University Press.

Standing, Guy. 2011. *The Precariat: The New Dangerous Class.* New York: Bloomsbury.

Star, Susan Leigh, and Anselm Strauss. 1999. "Layers of Silence, Arenas of Voice: The Ecology of Visible and Invisible Work." *Computer Supported Cooperative Work* 8: 9–30.

Stiegler, Bernard. 2010. *For a New Critique of Political Economy.* Cambridge: Polity.

Stiegler, Bernard. 1998. *Technics and Time*. Volume 1. Translated by Richard Beardsworth and George Collins. Palo Alto, CA: Stanford University Press.

Stiglitz, Joseph. 2015. *The Great Divide: Unequal Societies and What We Can Do about Them*. New York: W. W. Norton.

Striphas, Ted. 2015. "Algorithmic Culture." *European Journal of Cultural Studies* 18 (August–October): 395–412.

Sugiura, Yumiko. 2008. *Keitai Shōsetsu no Riaru*. Tokyo: Chūōkōron-Shinsha.

Tabuchi, Takashige. 2013. *Mōkaru Ameburo: Shin Nettode Kasegu Hōteishiki*. Tokyo: Soshimu.

Tachibana, Takeshi. 2012a. *Nomado Wākā to Iu Ikikata: Basho wo Erabazu Yatowarenaide Hataraku Hito no Senryaku to Shūkan*. Tokyo: Tōyō Keizai Shinpōsha.

Tachibana, Takeshi. 2012b. *Aifōn Daietto: Yaseru Shikumi de Jinsei wo Gekiteki ni Kaeru*. Tokyo: Sanmākushuppan.

Tachibanaki, Toshiaki. 2010. *Muen Shakai no Shōtai: Ji-en, Chi-en, Sha-en wa Ikani Hōkaishita ka?* Tokyo: PHP Kenkyūjo.

Taguchi, Kazuhiro, and Matsunaga Hideaki. 2008. *Dekiru 100 Waza Burogu*. Kaiteihan (rev. ed.) Akusesu & Fukushunyū wo Gungun Fuyaseru Jissen Tekunikku. Tokyo: Impuresu Komyunikēshonzu.

Takahashi, Shigeko, and Yanagida Rumi. 2012. *Hajimete no FC2 Burogu: Saishin Kantan Burogu Sakusei Nyūmon*. Tokyo: Shūwashisutemu.

Takamori, Hideaki. 2006. *Ima Sugu Hajimeru Yafuoku de Hyakunijippāsento Mōkeru Hōhō Chōnyūmon*. Tokyo: Mainichi Komyunikēshonzu.

Takamori, Hideaki. 2005a. *Ima Sugu Hajimeru "Mōkaru Burogu Tsukuri" Chōnyūmon: Kihon no Zukai*. Tokyo: Mainichi Komyunikēshonzu.

Takamori, Hideaki. 2005b. *Ima Sugu Hajimeru Netto de Fukugyō ando Okozukai-kasegi Chōnyūmon: Kihon no Zukai*. Tokyo: Mainichi Komyunikēshonzu.

Takamori, Hideaki. 2005c. *Ima Sugu Hajimeru Netto de Kabu Tōshi Chōnyūmon*. Tokyo: Mainichi Komyunikēshonzu.

Takeuchi, Kayo, and Kawaharazuka Mizuho. 2011. "Keitai Shōsetsu ni okeru Onnadōshi no Kankei: 'Koizora' Būmu to wa Nan Datta no Ka?" *Ochanomizu Joshidaigaku Jinbunkagakukenkyū* 7: 25–40. Accessed September 30, 2016. http://teapot.lib.ocha.ac.jp/ocha/handle/10083/50688.

Takeyama, Akiko. 2016. *Staged Seduction: Selling Dreams in a Tokyo Host Club*. Palo Alto, CA: Stanford University Press.

Takeyama, Akiko. 2010. "Intimacy for Sale: Masculinity, Entrepreneurship, and Commodity Self in Japan's Neoliberal Situation." *Japanese Studies* 30 (2): 231–46.

Tanaka, Eris. 2004. *Kyururun Daikakumei*. Tokyo: Māburutoron.

Tanaka, Eris. 2003. *Kawaii Horokōsuto*. Tokyo: Middonaitopuresu.

Takita, Seiichiro. 2005. *Burogu Nyūmon: 50 dai ni mo Yoku Wakaru*. Tokyo: BestSellers.

Tanimoto, Mayumi. 2013a. *Nomado to Shachiku: Posuto Sanichiichi no Hatarakikata o Shinken ni Kangaeru*. Tokyo: Asahishuppansha.

Tanimoto, Mayumi. 2013b. *Kyaria Poruno was Jinsei no Muda Da*. Tokyo: Asahi Shinsho.

Terranova, Tiziana. 2004. *Network Culture: Politics for the Information Age*. London: Pluto Press.

Thompson, E. P. 1967. "Time, Work-Discipline and Industrial Capitalism." *Past and Present*, December 8, 56–97.

Toivonen, Tuukka. 2013. *Japan's Emerging Youth Policy: Getting Young Adults Back to Work*. London: Routledge.

Torii, Mayumi. 2013. *Efuekkusu de Tsuki Hyakuman'en Mōkeru Watakushi no Hōhō: Kosodate Mama Demo Gangan Kasegeru*. Tokyo: Daiyamondosha.

Torii, Mayumi. 2009. *Tsuki Hyakuman'en Mōkeru Watakushi no Efuekkusu Nōto*. Tokyo: Daiyamondosha.

Torii, Mayumi. 2007. *Efuekkusu de Tsuki Hyakuman'en Kasegu Watakushi no Hōhō: Kosodate Mama no FX Tōshihō*. Tokyo: Daiyamondosha.

Tronti, Mario. 2007. "Strategy of Refusal." In *Italy: Autonomia, Post-Political Politics*, edited by Sylvere Lotringer and Christian Marazzi, 28–35. Los Angeles: Semiotext(e).

Tronti, Mario. 1962. "Factory and Society." Translated by Guio Jacinto. Accessed May 20, 2018. https://operaismoinenglish.wordpress.com/2013/06/13/factory -and-society/.

Tronto, Joan. 2013. *Caring Democracy: Markets, Equality, and Justice*. New York: New York University Press.

Tsunemi, Yōhei. 2013. *Jiyūna Hatarakikata wo Tsukuru: Kueru Nomado no Shigoto-jutsu*. Tokyo: Nihonjitsugyōshuppansha.

Ume, Kayo. 1998. *Jīchansama*. Tokyo: Little More.

Ueno, Chizuko. 2010. *Onnakirai: Nippon no Mizoginī*. Tokyo: Kinokuniya Shoten.

Ueno, Chizuko. 1982. *Sekushii Gyaru no Dai Kenkyū: Onna no Yomi-kata, Yomare-kata, Yomase-kata*. Tokyo: Kobunsha.

Umemiya, Takako. 2001. *Jissen! Netto Aidoru no Narikata, Yarikata, Kasegikata: Hōmu Pe-ji Kaisetsu Kara Anzen Kanri Made*. Tokyo: Bug News Network.

Van Parijs, Philippe, and Yannick Vanderborght. 2017. *Basic Income: A Radical Proposal for a Free Society and a Sane Economy*. Cambridge, MA: Harvard University Press.

Virno, Paolo. 2007. "Post-Fordist Semblance." Translated by Max Henninger. *SubStance* 112, 36 (1): 42–46.

Virno, Paolo. 2004. *A Grammar of the Multitude: For an Analysis of Contemporary Forms of Life*. Translated by Isabella Bertoletti, James Cascaito, and Andrea Casson. Los Angeles: Semiotext(e).

Vogel, Ezra. 1965. *Japan's New Middle Class: The Salary Man and His Family in a Tokyo Suburb*. Berkeley: University of California Press.

Vogel, Steven. 2006. *Japan Remodeled: How Government and Industry Are Reforming Japanese Capitalism*. Ithaca, NY: Cornell University Press.

Wakabayashi, Fumie. 2006a. *Karisuma Toreedaa Wakabayashi Fumie no Hajimete no Kabuerabi*. Tokyo: Takarajimasha.

Wakabayashi, Fumie. 2006b. *Yappari Kabu ga Suki*. Tokyo: Asupekuto.

Wakabayashi, Fumie. 2004. *Kabu ga Suki!* Tokyo: Asupekuto.

Wakui, Kaito. 2012. *Ameba Burogu de Uriage wo 10bai ni Suru Gijutsu*. Tokyo: Shuwasisutemu.

Wallis, Cara. 2013. *Technomobility in China: Young Migrant Women and Cell Phones*. New York: New York University Press.

Warner, Michael. 2002. "Publics and Counterpublics." *Public Culture* 14 (1): 49–90.

Weeks, Kathi. 2011. *The Problem with Work: Feminism, Marxism, Antiwork Politics, and Postwork Imaginaries*. Durham, NC: Duke University Press.

Willis, Paul. 1977. *Learning to Labor: Why Working Class Kids Get Working Class Jobs*. New York: Columbia University Press.

Yamada, Masahiro. 2016. *Kekkon Kuraishisu: Chūryū Tenraku Fuan*. Tokyo: Tokyoshoseki.

Yamada, Masahiro. 2007. *Kibō Kakusa Shakai: Makegumi no Zetsubōkan ga Nihon o Hikisaku*. Tokyo: Chikuma Shobō.

Yamada, Masahiro. 1999. *Parasaito Shinguru no Jidai*. Tokyo: Chikuma Shobō.

Yamamoto, Isamu. 2015. "An Assessment of the Japanese Financial Services Sector." International Labour Office, Geneva. July 29. Accessed May 20, 2018. http://www.ilo.org/wcmsp5/groups/public/—asia/—ro-bangkok/—ilo-jakarta/documents/meetingdocument/wcms_396167.pdf.

Yamamoto, Yuka. 2018. *Kenja no ICO Tōshi: Sekai no Tōshika wa Koko wo Miteiru*. Tokyo: Amazon Services.

Yamamoto, Yuka. 2010. *Karisuma Shufu Toreudau ga Oshieru Yume o Kanaeru Hito no Sukima Jikanjutsu*. Tokyo: Nihon Keizai Shinbun Shuppansha.

Yamamoto, Yuka. 2009. *Efuekkusu Koredake wa Yattewa Ikenai Rokujū: Shōritsu Hachijippausentochō no Shufu ga Oshieru Ōzon Kaihi no Tessoku*. Tokyo: Nihon Keizai Shinbun Shuppansha.

Yamamoto, Yuka. 2007. *Yamamoto Yuka no Yasashī FX Tōshihō. Zenbu Oshiechaimasu. Yuka Yamamoto's Guide to Forex Trading: 10man'en Kara Hajimemashō*. Tokyo: Chūkei Shuppan.

Yamamoto, Yuka. 2004a. *Maitsuki 10man en wa Yume Janai: "Kabu" de 3000-man'en Mōketa Watakushi no Hōhō*. Tokyo: Daiyamondosha.

Yamamoto, Yuka. 2004b. *Karisuma Shufu Torēdā Yamamoto Yuka no Kabu no Ōtomēshon Torēdo de Mōkeru Hon*. Tokyo: Daiyamondosha.

Yamauchi, Hiroyasu. 2007. "Interview with Ume Kayo: Nichijōni Uzumaku 'Warai' no Shattā Chansu." *Bijutsu Techō*, July, 18–21.

Yanagi, Miwa. 2010. *Windswept Women: The Old Girl's Troupe*. Tokyo: Seigensha.

Yanagi, Miwa. 2009. *My Grandmothers*. Tokyo: Tankōsha.

Yanagi, Miwa. 2007a. *Elevator Girls (1994–1997)*. Kyoto: Seigensha.

Yanagi, Miwa. 2007b. *Yanagi Miwa*. Berlin: Sammlung, Deutsche Bank.

Yoda, Tomiko. 2006. "A Roadmap to Millennial Japan." In *Japan after Japan: Social and Cultural Life from the Recessionary 1990s to the Present*, edited by Tomiko Yoda and Harry Harootunian, 16–53. Durham, NC: Duke University Press.

Yomota, Inuhiko. 2006. *Kawaiiron*. Tokyo: Chikuma Shobō.

Yoshi. 2002. *Deep Love: Ayu's Love Story*. Tokyo: Starts Shuppan.

Yoshida, Satovi. 2008. *Keitai Shōsetsu ga Ukeru Wake*. Tokyo: Maikomi Shinsho.

Yoshihara, Tōru. 2004. *Yūmeini Narō! "Namae" de Shigoto ga Kuru Hito no Intānetto + PRJutsu*. Tokyo: Shoeisha.

Zaloom, Caitlin. 2006. *Out of the Pits: Traders and Technology from Chicago to London*. Chicago: University of Chicago Press.

Zelizer, Viviana. 2007. *The Social Meaning of Money: Pin Money, Paychecks, Poor Relief, and Other Currencies*. Princeton, NJ: Princeton University Press.

Blog Theory (Dean), 81–82

Boltanski, Luc, 171n30

boyd, danah, 171n32

Braidotti, Rosi, 172n43

brand value: blogging and building of, 83; building of, 5–6

Brinton, Mary, 9, 167n7

broadband infrastructure, 168n8

Brooks, Peter, 202n37

Brown, Wendy, 89, 105

bulletin board systems (BBS), 62, 84–85, 144, 185n8, 201n27

Butler, Judith, 44–46, 134, 151, 153, 176n31

Camera (journal), 33

Camera Mainichi (journal), 33

"camgirls" (United States), 73

Canon, 34

capitalism: blogging and, 83; digital economy and, 169n13; freedom and, 89; labor and, 13–14, 16–20, 24; social factory and, 8

care and healing *(iyashi)* practices, economic recession and, 74–77

Career Porn Is a Waste of Time (Tanimoto), 90–91, 150

Castells, Manuel, 4

Celebrities and Famous Bloggers, 85

Celebrity Blogs, 85, 87

celebrity culture: blogging and, 85–87, 95–96; microcelebrity and, 178n1

cell phone novelists: demographics for, 154, 202n34, 203n43; evolution of, 132–34; failure rate for, 26–27; feminized affective labor of, 18, 45–46, 132–54; financial success of, 146; precarity politics and, 132–34, 148–52; print sales by, 142; responsibility felt by, 152–53; as techno-social assemblage, 20–24

cell phones: internet access through, 4–5; young people's use of, 147–48

Chaco (cell phone novelist), 139, 145, 153–54

Charisma Housewife Will Tell You How

People Who Are Able to Fulfill Their Dreams Manage Their Time, The (Yamamoto), 116

Chiapello, Eve, 171n30

circulation: of assets, 195n25; of capital, 130; of money, 108

class structure: actual self and, 24–27; cell phone novelists and, 137–41; gender discrimination and, 25–27; middle class fragility and, 170n25, 200n19; online trading and, 107–9, 124–29; virtual self and, 24–27

click farms, 157, 203n3

cognitive labor, 17–18

Colleoni, Eleanor, 14

community involvement, online trading as, 117–18

compensation for online content, debate over, 156–65

content farms, 157–58

Corrigan, Thomas, 20, 156

Crab Cannery Ship (Kobayashi), 133–34

Creating the Freedom of Work (Tsunemi), 90

creative labor, 17–18, 140, 155–56, 204n8

Crimson Group, 6

crowd-sourced labor, 14, 158–59

cute culture, 30; invisible labor in, 78–80; Japanese *kawaii* and, 65–66; net idols and, 58–59, 64; production of, 65–73; women bloggers and, 98–104

Cute Holocaust (Tanaka Eris), 68–69

Cvetkovich, Ann, 175n23

CyberAgent Inc., 86–87, 189n29

Dalla Costa, Mariarosa, 8, 159–60

data commodities, 14

data mismanagement, racism and sexism and, 173n3

Dean, Jodi, 81–82, 86, 93

Deep Love (Yoshi), 135–36, 146

DeLanda, Manuel, 21–24

Deleuze, Gilles, 21, 66

155–56, 159–65; in digital economy, 7–8, 12–20, 159–61; gender divisions in financial sector, 109; media production costs and, 143–44; nonstandard forms of, 16–20; personality and impact of, 140–41; wage earners vs. salaried employees, 9, 167n3; workforce demographics, 188n22. *See also* digital labor, emotional labor; feminized affective labor; hope labor; immaterial labor; job security; lifetime employment; phatic labor
laborism, 9, 82–83, 163–65, 173n1
labor theory of value, 12–14, 22–23, 157, 159
Larkin, Brian, 167n4
Latour, Bruno, 21
Lazzarrato, Maurizio, 17
Licentious Notice Board (LNB), 84–85
Lifestyle of a Nomad Worker, The (Tachibana), 90
lifetime employment: blogging as alternative to, 88–94; decline in Japan of, 5–8; gender discrimination and, 10–12; human capital development and decline of, 75–77; meaning in work and, 170n22
Line Corporation, 169n16
Little More (publishing company), 34
Livedoor (social media platform), 5–6, 88
Lorey, Isabell, 153
Lotringer, Sylvere, 12
Love, Heather, 203n38
Lyft drivers, as digital labor, 14

Maho no i-rando (Magic Island) (cell phone novel platform), 132–33, 136, 141–48, 200n14, 201n24
Maho no i-rando Award, 146
Makihara, Susumu, 178n4
Marazzi, Christian, 130
Markiplier (Mark Fischbach), 155
marriage, class issues and, 26–27
Martin, Lesley, 44, 53

Martin, Randy, 108, 114
Marwick, Alice, 20, 92, 95, 178n1, 180n11
Marx, Karl, 12–13, 22–23, 159
Matsuko DeLuxe, 128
Matsumoto, Noriko, 34
Matsumoto, Oki, 111–12, 192n1, 194n16
Matsushima, Shigeru, 135, 202n31
Mbembe, Achille, 101
McRobbie, Angela, 78, 140, 155–56, 160, 204n8
meaningful work: blogging and, 82–83, 94; cell phone novels as, 139–41; definitions of, 11–12, 170n28, 171n30; digital economy and, 7–8, 12–20, 170n28; gender-stratified labor market and, 11, 29; lifetime employment and, 10–11, 170n22; romanticism about, 140–41
Mechanical Turk (MTurk), 16, 158, 204n13
media: blogging and, 86–88; net idols' coverage in, 60–64, 67, 79–80; women online traders in, 115–31
Media Net Japan, 63, 180n17
melodramas, cell phone novels as, 202n37
microcelebrity, 102, 178n1
microwork, 16, 158, 162
Mika (cell phone novelist), 136, 138–40, 146, 151–52
Mikitani, Hiroshi, 5–7, 64
Mills, C. Wright, 78
Minbe, Momo, 95–96
Ministry of Trade and Industry (MITI), 204n14
Minowa, Keiju, 179n10
mixi (social networking platform), 5
Miyasako, Chizuru, 174n12
Miyashita, Maki, 34
Miyazaki, Izumi, 37
Mizushima, Riko, 137–38, 152–54
Mobagē Shōsetsu Grand Prize, 146
Mobagē Taun (mobile gaming platform), 141–42, 146
Mogi, Ayako, 34

involvement in, 28; workforce reduction for, 5

online trading: as affective labor, 45–46, 121–23, 129–31; class structure and, 25–27; elite rejection of, 107; financialization of daily life and, 106–31; platforms for, 111–12; as techno-social assemblage, 20–24; transition from savings to, 107, 109–15; women's aspirations beyond, 123–29; women's involvement in, 8, 15, 18–20; women's paths to, 115–23

open source software movement, 93–94

Oricon (cell phone novel platform), 142

Ōtsuka, Eiji, 66

Otsuki, Nana, 195n30

Ozawa, Akiko, 34

OZPA (blogger), 102

Paltrow, Gwyneth, 95

parapolitics, 148–52

Parco Urban Art Prize, 39, 44, 175n19

Parks, Lisa, 172n41

paternalistic laborism, 82

patriarchy: in family albums, 40–42; "girly" photography and, 30–33; self-portraiture as critique of, 43–49

Pecheux, Michel, 37

personality, employment and, 78

Pham, Minh-ha T., 97–98, 104

phatic labor, 17–18, 94

photo books of net idols, 63, 178n4

photography contests, 34–35

photo-therapy, 59, 76–77

Photozou (photo hosting platform), 174n16

Piketty, Thomas, 169n13

Pinterest, 7

Play with Me (performance project) (Mori), 55

Ponytail Co. Ltd., 97

post-Fordism (lean production, just-in-time production, flexible accumulation), 17–20, 22–23, 159, 183n44. *See also* affective labor

poverty, in Japan, 162–63

precarity: cell phone novelists and, 132–34, 148–52; digital labor and, 158–59; labor and, 2, 26–27, 59, 104, 147; politics of, 132–34, 148–52

Preda, Alex, 111

promotion policy (*nenkō* system), 170n24

psychography (nensha), 62

publishing industry: cell phone novelists and, 145–48; photography boom and, 33–37

puro, Japanese concept of, 192n4

"Queens of Blogging, The" (television show), 84

Rakuten (retail platform), 5, 6–7

Rakuten Securities Inc., 111

Recruit (human resources company), 34, 90

rentier capitalism, digital economy and, 169n13

Rettberg, Jill, 85

Rin (cell phone novelist), 138

Riot Grrrl movement, 44–45

Rockin'on Japan magazine, 34

Roquet, Paul, 170n23

Ross, Andrew, 12, 20, 83, 160

RSS feeds, 89, 189n36

Saito, Tamaki, 51

Sakai, Mayumi (Mayuhime) (celebrity trader), 8, 15, 108, 114, 116–17, 197n51

Sakuran (film), 53

Sanai, Masafumi, 42, 54

Sarusaru Nikki (diary platform), 84

Sasai, Takashi, 62

Sasaki, Toshinao, 90, 136–37

Sassen, Saskia, 113–14, 193n13, 195n25

savings, transition to online trading from, 107, 109–15, 193nn7–8

Sawada, Tomoko, 34

Scholz, Trebor, 14, 16, 20, 158, 162, 187n16

Schor, Juliet, 171n35

science fiction, human-machine interface in, 2

Second Life, 25

second telecom deregulation, 61

second-wave feminism, 55–56

self-branding: bloggers and, 89–95, 104; employability security and, 19; net idols and, 60–64; online platforms' promotion of, 7, 157; by online traders, 125–26, 196n38; social media and, 20; virtual vs. actual self, 24–27

self-deprecation by online traders, 119–20

self-help movement: blogging and, 82–83, 91–94; popularity in Japan of, 6–7

selfie culture, 37, 101, 176n35

Self-Portraits (Nagashima), 39–40, 44–49

self-portraiture, disidentification and, 43–49

Senft, Theresa, 73, 176n35

service industries, 171n36; concentration of women in, 133–34; emotional labor in, 18–20, 78

Seventeen Girl Days (Hiromix), 46, 177n41

sex chat business, net idols and, 62–64

Shannon, Rachael, 175n23

Shinoyama, Kishin, 33–34

shōjo genres, 149–50, 202n36

Shutter and Love (*Studio Voice* special issue), 34–35

Simondon, Gilbert, 172n45

Sinka (cell phone novelist), 137, 200n13

sleep deprivation, of cell phone novelists, 137–38

Snakes and Earrings (Kanehara), 202n36

social citizenship, photography and, 38–43

social factory, 7–8, 159–60; blogging platforms and, 105; net idols and, 58–59; Tronti's theory of, 178n2

socially necessary labor, Marx's concept of, 13–14, 157

social media: blogging and, 86–88, 95–98; click farms and, 157, 203n3; connectivity imperative and, 172n42; entrepreneurship and, 95–96; media-generated fear culture and, 171n32; net idols and, 60–64, 67; selfie culture and, 37; self-performance on, 14, 20

social networks: cell phone novels and, 147–48; "girly" photography and, 38; online platforms for, 141–48

social reproduction: cute culture and, 65–73; labor and, 140–41; online trading and, 107–9

socioeconomic conditions: cell phone novels and, 150–52; digital technologies and, 2–3; "girly" photography as reflection of, 30–33

SoftBank, 161

Someya, Etsuko, 116

Someya, Masatoshi, 89

Song, Jesook, 198n56

Sony Corporation, 2

sovereignty, artistic reflections of, 175n23

Standing, Guy, 9, 82, 93, 167n3

Star, Susan Leigh, 3, 16–17

Starosielski, Nicole, 172n41

Star Trek series, 23

Starts Publishing, 135, 138, 142, 144–46

Stiegler, Bernard, 24, 156, 172n45

Stiglitz, Joseph, 167n6

Stoned and Dethroned (Sanai Masafumi), 54

Studio Voice magazine, 34

Success Networks Cooperation, 142

"Super Fashion Blogger Award," 96

surplus labor, Marx's concept of, 13–14

surplus value: brand names and, 5; digital economy and, 12–20; labor and, 140–41

Suzuki, Junko, 37, 96–102, 104, 174n15, 180n17

Suzuki, Masashi, 63

Sweet Netoa Jimusho Ōdishon, 179n10

Wages for Housework movement, 159–61

wagyu beef, branding of, 6

Wakabayashi Fumie, 11–12, 109, 117, 119, 122, 127–29, 170n27, 197n50, 198n58

Wallis, Cara, 200n13

Wall Street Daily, 115–16

Warner, Michael, 134

website development, net idols and, 61–64, 179nn7–8

WeChat, 157

Weeks, Kathi, 8, 140–41, 159–60, 165

We Love Hiromix (Kaneko), 34

Wiener, Norbert, 22–23

Willis, Paul, 163

Windswept Women: The Old Girl's Troupe (Yanagi), 55

women: aspirations beyond trading for, 123–29; as cell-phone novelists, 136–41; cute culture and, 65–73; dominance in online trading of, 106–9, 114–15; dominance of blogging by, 84–88, 94–104, 185n6; as financial analysts, 195n30; impact of economic recession on, 133–34; labor in digital economy by, 1–2, 13–20; labor precarity and, 151–52; misogyny in Japan and, 53–56; paths to online trading for, 115–23; phatic labor by, 94; pho-

tographers (*See* "girly" photography); in photography contests, 35

work. *See* labor; lifetime employment; meaningful work; microwork; nomad work

workaholism, 163–64

workforce reduction: digital economy and, 5–8; recession and, 167n6

WorkMarket.com, 161

World of Warcraft, 25

Yamada, Masahiro, 26–27

Yamamato, Kaori, 34

Yamamoto, Isamu, 109

Yamamoto, Yuka, 106–9, 111, 114–17, 119–29, 192n3, 195n33, 196n47, 197n51, 197nn48–49

Yamane, Akiko, 117

Yanagi, Miwa, 54–56

Yomota, Inuhiko, 65–66

Yoshi, 136, 146

Yoshida, Satovi, 142

Yoshimoto, Banana, 202n36

You Must Know "son!," 85–86

YouTube, digital economy and, 155–56

Zaloom, Caitlin, 195n29, 195n33

Zelizer, Viviana, 196n38

Zuckerberg, Mark, 7, 19